COMPUTER SYSTEMS APPLICATION

Viktor Borodin

TAP

Toronto Academic Press

Computer Systems Application

Viktor Borodin

Toronto Academic Press
224 Shoreacres Road
Burlington, ON L7L 2H2
Canada
www.tap-books.com
Email: orders@arclereducation.com

ISBN: 978-1-77469-708-5

ABOUT THE EDITOR

Viktor Borodin is Computer Science PhD at T.Shevchenko Kyiv National University, Kyiv, Ukraine. His interest areas are lying on the composite domains of AI and CS: medical image processing, machine learning, data analysis and Applied Mathematics: computational geometry, differential equations, number theory. Viktor Borodin is the author of several papers in the fields of Math and Computer Engineering and has 20+ years of teaching experience to engineering and math graduates and postgraduates, and 10+ years of practical SW programming.

Contents

7 Fundamentals of Database 191

8 IoT and Computer Science 221

List of Figures

List of Abbreviations

3-D	three-dimensional
AI	artificial intelligence
ALT	advanced learning technology
ALU	arithmetic logic unit
ANSI	American National Standards Institute
APs	access points
ASCII	American Standard Code for Information Interchange
ASI	artificial super intelligence
ASR	automatic speech recognition
ATM	asynchronous transfer mode
BCD	binary coded decimal
CC	cycle count
CISCs	complex instructions set computers
CPI	cycles per instruction
CPU	central processing unit
CRT	cathode ray tubes
CSS	cascading style sheet

CU	control unit
DARPA	Defense Advanced Research Projects Agency
DBMS	database management system
DCE	data communication equipment
DEC	digital equipment corporation
DRAM	dynamic random-access memory
DTE	data terminal equipment
DVHT	dynamic virtual human technology
EB	exabytes
EDVAC	electronic discrete variable automatic computer
EEPROM	electrically erasable programmable read-only memory
E-GAN	evolutionary generative adversarial networks
ENIAC	electronic numerical integrator and calculator
GHz	gigahertz
GPS	global positioning system
GUIs	graphical user interfaces
HD	hard drive
HDD	hard drive disc
HTML	hypertext markup language
HTTP	hypertext transfer protocol
Hz	hertz
I/O	input/output
IAS	Institute for Advanced Study
IIoT	industrial internet of things
IoT	internet of things
IP	instruction pointer
IRS	internal revenue service
ISO	International Organization for Standardization

ISR	interrupt service routine
iVRS	interactive VRS
JVM	java virtual machine
LAN	local area network
LCD	liquid crystal display
LHC	large Hedron collider
LPWA	low-power wide-area
LSL	linden scripting language
LSTM	long short-term memory
MAN	metropolitan area network
MB	megabytes
MMO	massively multi-player online
MRI	magnetic resonance imaging
NASA	National Aeronautics and Space Administration
OBD	on-board diagnostics
ODD	optical disc drive
OLIVE	online interactive virtual environment
OLTP	online transaction processing
OS	operating system
OSI	open systems interconnection
OSSL	open simulator scripting language
PC	personal computer
PDA	personal digital assistant
QD3D	quickdraw 3D
RAM	random access memory
RDBMS	relational database management systems
RFID	radio frequency identification
RGB	red, green, and blue

RISCs	reduced instructions set computers
ROM	read only memory
SAGE	semi-automatic ground environment
SGI	silicon graphics international
SID	speaker identification
TDP	thermal design power
UNIVAC	universal automatic computer
UOD	universe of discourse
USB	universal serial bus
UTP	unprotected twisted-pair
VDU	visual display unit
VHI	virtual heroes inc.
VLE	virtual learning environments
VR	virtual reality
VRML	virtual reality modeling reality language
VR-PAD	virtual reality point-and-direct
VSX	virtual space experiment
WAN	wide area network
WoW	window on the world
XML	extended markup language

PREFACE

This book introduces the readers to the basic concept of computer science. It sheds light on the background of computers, computer programs, languages, data communication, and computer network. In addition, this book also emphasizes the role of virtual reality, artificial intelligence, and IoT.

The first chapter explains the background of computers along with the components of computers. It also highlights psychology's connection to other areas of science. Different software and hardware components, microprocessors, and operating systems have also been discussed towards the end of this chapter.

The second chapter takes the readers through the concept of virtual reality as well as the history of virtual reality. It will provide knowledge about various components of virtual reality and its classification. Towards the end, this chapter talks about the impact of virtual reality technology on human lives.

After that, the third chapter explains about the basics of computer architecture. Also, it talks about architectural development and styles. Later, performance measures and the design of practical machines are also discussed to give a clear insight to the reader.

The fourth chapter provides insights into computer programs and languages. It also explains the nature and characteristics of basic programming. Fundamentals of C language and the Pros and cons of machine language have also been discussed later in the chapter.

Then the fifth chapter introduces the readers to the role of artificial intelligence in computer science and its various types. Also, the chapter deals with the pros and cons of artificial intelligence and the importance of artificial intelligence in future technology.

The sixth chapter sheds light on data communication and computer network. It talks about the data representation and mode of data flow. In addition, the chapter also discusses about the measuring capacity of communication media, wireless communication technology, etc.

The seventh chapter takes the readers through the fundamentals of the database. It will provide knowledge about the features of database strategy. Towards the end, this chapter talks about the brief history of a database application and the various advantages of using a DBMS.

In the last chapter of this book, the role of IoT in computers is discussed. Different advantages of IoT are also discussed. Towards the end of this chapter, applications and challenges in IoT have also been explained.

This book has been designed to suit the knowledge and pursuit of the researcher and scholars and to empower them with various aspects of computer science so that they are updated with the information. I hope that the readers find the book explanatory and insightful and that scholars across various fields refer to this book.

CHAPTER 1

INTRODUCTION TO COMPUTER

UNIT INTRODUCTION

Regardless of the perspective on the significance of computers, the phrase "computers are everywhere" is undeniable. In reality, one may discover computers in quite odd locations, such as the family vehicle, household appliances, and now even the alarm clock!

Over the past 20 years, computer systems have fundamentally transformed the way people live at home, at work, and at school. And over 50% of all households in the United States have at least one computer, and most of these are linked to the Web.

A majority of employers utilize technological devices in a certain capacity, and most corporations are linked either internally or internationally. Employees who formerly hardly ever used advanced technologies presently spend nearly every single minute of their working day using computer systems.

The different computer systems that are currently being used are examined throughout this learning segment. Readers would first gain knowledge about the numerous different types of computers which people use, as well as the purposes for which individuals employ them, whereas this lesson would then primarily examine personal computers (the same types that apparently rest on each and every desktop).

Even though one's understanding of computer systems advances, students will recognize that almost all computer systems, regardless of their configuration or intended use, share many fundamental characteristics. This means that all of them function in accordance with the same foundational concepts, are constructed by employing the same building blocks, and require commands in order to function.

Learning Objectives

After completing this chapter, you should be able to understand the following:

1. Understand the meaning and definition of computer
2. Identify the different nature, and subfields of computer components
3. Understand the key issues in computer
4. Educate about the relation of the central processing unit
5. Give advice about, classification of computer and its various kinds
6. Understand about data and information
7. Give advice about the storage structure in computer system

Key Terms

1. Computer
2. Data and Information
3. Digital Pen
4. Input/Output (I/O) Device
5. Microcomputer
6. Operating System
7. System View

1.1. THE COMPUTER DEFINED

The computer, in its simplest definition, is an electronic component that analyzes data and converts that into knowledge that is beneficial to individuals. Irrespective of the sort, all computers are operated by pre-programmed commands that provide the device with a task and guide it on how to accomplish it. These computers mentioned in this book, that are found all around people, are computers.

Digital computers are known as "by the numbers" devices since computers break down all types of information into small units and employ figures to describe these divisions, as students shall see in "Processing Data." Furthermore, digital computers obey very ordered commands in very rigid patterns, analyzing every piece of data separately.

KEYWORD

Digital computer is machine that stores data in a numerical format and performs operations on that data using mathematical manipulation.

The analog computer is a less popular product of the computer that operates quite differently from computer systems. Analog systems were employed in the first computers, resulting in a substantial influence on current electronic systems.

But even though analog or digital computer systems have several distinctions, the manner in which both types represent information remains the most significant one. Data is viewed by electronic systems as possessing one clear value or another, without any other alternatives.

Even so, information is displayed as changeable locations across a spectrum ranging from values in analog systems. As an outcome, analog computers are slightly more capable of adapting than electronic versions, though they aren't generally more accurate or dependable. Initial analog computers were big and clunky, with mechanical equipment energized by motor drives and gears that weighed a few tons. Aged slide rules serve as a more controllable sort of Analog computer.

There are numerous subcategories of computers. A few systems, for instance, are built to be operated by a single individual, others by a group of individuals, and still a few are not utilized in any way. Computers could also be classified according to their performance, which refers to both the speed and the sort of activities that computer systems are able to perform. A computer could be divided into categories based on its price, the technology that it includes, what applications it could execute, and other factors (Figure 1.1).

Figure 1.1. My computer and desk.

Source: Image by Flickr.

1.2. BACKGROUND OF COMPUTERS

Up until the formation of the initial suction tube-based desktops, there have been a number of breakthroughs in computer technologies, especially with regard to mechanical computing devices. In the following subsections, the most important advancements that occurred prior to the invention of the initial desktop are discussed.

1.2.1. Evaluating Machines

For adding up large numbers, ABACUS was the initial mechanical calculator (Figure 1.2). Abacus is an abbreviation for calculation devices. On top of horizontal bars, sets of beads are placed to form the structure. Ten beads are connected on each of the horizontal bars to depict tens, dozens, hundreds, and so on.

Figure 1.2. Abacus.

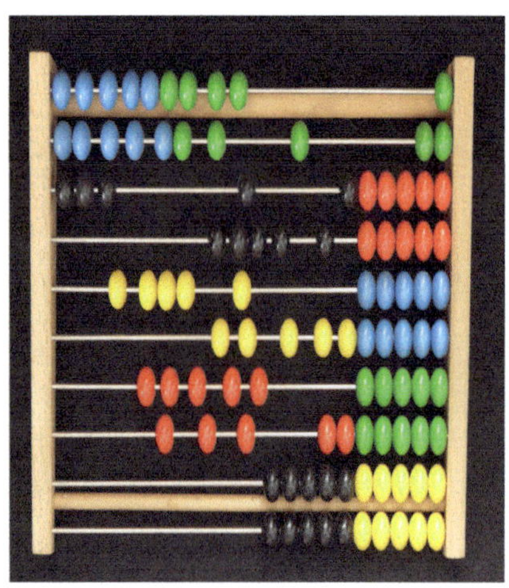

Source: Image by Raw pixel.

1.2.2. Napier's Bones

An addition made in 1617 by an English mathematician named John Napier was termed "Napier's bones," a piece of electrical equipment for multiplying.

1.2.3. Slide Rule

The 16th century saw the discovery of the slide rule by English mathematician Edmund Gunter. Tasks such as addition, subtraction, multiplication, and division can be carried out by employing the slide rule. Up until the late 1970s, it was broadly utilized.

KEYWORD

Punch cards are paper cards where holes may be punched by hand or machine to represent computer data and instructions.

1.2.4. The Adding and Subtracting Machine of Pascal

Pascal is believed to have invented Pascal's Additions and Subtraction Device. This might increase and decrease. The device was made up of mechanical multiplications and divisors, which included wheels, gears, and cylinders. It was created about 1673 by the German mathematician and philosopher Gottfried Leibniz.

1.2.5. Punch Card System

In order to operate the power loom, Jacquard created the Punch Card System in 1801. Jacquard created the punched card reader, which can distinguish between binary ones and zeroes depending on whether there is a hole in the card. Today's electronic computers are built on a foundation of 0s and 1s.

1.2.6. Analytical Engine by Babbage

In 1823, an Englishman named Charles Babbage formed Babbage's Analytical Engine, a mechanical device which could undertake complicated math equations. The device went by the name "different engine." The analytical engine, a general-purpose calculator created later by Charles Babbage and Lady Ada Lovelace, was presented. Another name for Charles Babbage is the "father of the computer."

1.2.7. Punched Card Tabulating Machine by Hollerith

Herman Hollerith is the inventor of Hollerith's Punched Card Tabulating Machine. The device was designed to read and digitally process data from punched cards.

1.3. COMPONENTS OF COMPUTERS

Hardware and software are the two components of every computer type.

1.3.1. Hardware

The various physical parts that make up a computer system are referred to as the hardware. The term "computer hardware" explains the tangible, physical elements that comprise a computer, for example, the screen, cursor, keypad, hard drive disc (HDD), system unit (graphics cards, sound cards, memory, motherboard, and chips), and so on.

KEYWORD

Hard disk drive (HDD) is composed of a platter that contains compartments to hold data.

1.3.2. Input Device

An input device is any peripheral (a piece of computer hardware used to supply input and output signals to a computer or other data device) that converts data from a format that humans can understand into one that a computer can use. The most popular options are the keyboard and cursor.

1.4. CENTRAL PROCESSING UNIT (CPU)

A CPU is brain of a computer. It is responsible for all functions and processes. Regarding computing power, the CPU is the most important element of a computer system (Figure 1.3). The CPU is comprised of three main parts:

- Arithmetic Logic Unit (ALU): Executes all arithmetic and logical operations. Arithmetic calculations like as addition, subtraction, multiplication and division. Logical operation like compare numbers, letters, or special characters
- Control Unit (CU): controls and co-ordinates computer components.

1. Read the code for the next instruction to be executed.
2. Increment the program counter so it points to the next instruction.
3. Read whatever data the instruction requires from cells in memory.
4. Provide the necessary data to an ALU or register.
5. If the instruction requires an ALU or specialized hardware to complete, instruct the hardware to perform the requested operation.

- Registers: Stores the data that is to be executed next, "very fast storage area."

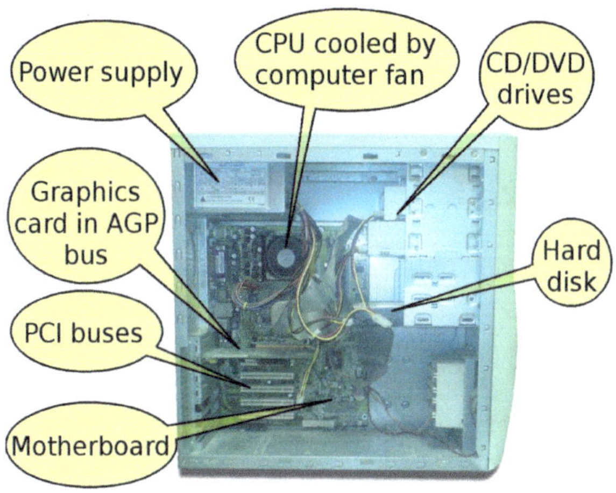

Figure 1.3. Quick overview of PC hardware.

Source: Image by Wikimedia Commons.

1.5. PRIMARY MEMORY

1.5.1. RAM

Random Access Memory (RAM) is a memory scheme within the computer system responsible for storing data on a temporary basis, so that it can be promptly accessed by the processor as and when needed. It is volatile in nature, which means that data will be erased once supply to the storage device is turned off. RAM stores data randomly and the processor accesses these data randomly from the RAM storage. RAM is considered "random access" because you can access any memory cell directly if you know the row and column that intersect at that cell.

1.5.2. ROM

(Read Only Memory): ROM is a permanent form of storage. ROM stays active regardless of whether power supply to it is turned on or off. ROM devices do not allow data stored on them to be modified.

1.6. SECONDARY MEMORY

1.6.1. Hard drive (HD)

A hard disk is part of a unit, often called a "disk drive," "hard drive," or "hard disk drive," that store and provides relatively quick access to large amounts of data on an electromagnetically charged surface or set of surfaces.

KEYWORD

Blu-ray Disc (BD) is an optical disc storage medium designed to supersede the DVD format.

1.6.2. Optical Disk

An optical disc drive (ODD) is a disk drive that uses laser light as part of the process of reading or writing data to or from optical discs. Some drives can only read from discs, but recent drives are commonly both readers and recorders, also called burners or writers. Compact discs, DVDs, and Blu-ray discs are common types of optical media which can be read and recorded by such drives.

Optical drive is the generic name; drives are usually described as "CD" "DVD," or "Bluray," followed by "drive," "writer," etc. There are three main types of optical media: CD, DVD, and Blu-ray disc. CDs can store up to 700 megabytes (MB) of data and DVDs can store up to 8.4 GB of data.

Blu-ray discs, which are the newest type of optical media, can store up to 50 GB of data. This storage capacity is a clear advantage over the floppy disk storage media (a magnetic media), which only has a capacity of 1.44 MB.

1.6.3. Flash Disk

A storage module made of flash memory chips. A Flash disk have no mechanical platters or access arms, but the term "disk" is used because the data are accessed as if they were on a hard drive. The disk storage structure is emulated.

1.7. OUTPUT DEVICES

An output device is any piece of computer hardware equipment used to communicate the results of data processing carried out by an information processing system (such as a computer) which converts the electronically generated information into human-readable form.

1.8. SOFTWARE

Software is a broad term for organized sets of computer information and instructions. It is usually divided into two primary classifications: system software and application software. The software system serves as the fundamental, non-task-specific capabilities of the computer, and software applications are employed by users to accomplish specific jobs.

1.8.1. System Software

System software is in charge of maintaining, integrating, and regulating the several hardware elements of a computer system so that additional software and the system's users could focus on higher-level functions like text translation and data transmission from RAM to DISC rather than low-level features like these. The majority of the time, system software comprises an operating system as well as some basic utilities, including disc formats, file managers, display managers, text editors, user authentication (login) and administration tools, networking, and device control software.

KEYWORD

Data transmission refers to the process of transferring data between two or more digital devices.

1.8.2. Application Software

Furthermore, having to run the computer system, software applications are employed to complete particular tasks. Software applications can be a single program, like an image viewer, or a small group of related systems that work tightly with one another to finish a task, such as a word processor, spreadsheet, database, etc.; a larger collection (frequently named a software suite) of linked and yet independent programs and packs that have a common user interface or shared data format; or a software system, like a database management system, that includes a collection of fundamental programs that could include some service to a wide range of other independent programs.

1.9. STORAGE MEASUREMENTS

A bit is a term for the fundamental unit used to store data on computers (binary digit). Such tiny bits, which are made up of ones and zeros, are employed by computer systems to carry out operations and communicate with other computer systems. All of the files, for example, are saved on the computer as binary files that the software converts into text and images (which are also ones and zeros). As there are only two numbers in this two-number system, it is referred to as a "binary number system." In comparison, the decimal number system uses ten distinct digits, from 0 to 9.

KEYWORD

Decimal number system is the number system that we use on a daily basis based on the 10 digits.

An example of the size:

- 1 bit-a yes/no response to a question
- 1 byte, a number between 0 and 255.
- 90 bytes, which is sufficient to store a typical book line of text.
- An average page of text is 4 KB.
- Text for a typical pocketbook is 120 KB.
- 3 MB, a song lasting three minutes
- A CD-ROM with 650–900 MB.
- 114 mins of unencrypted CD-quality audio in 1 GB at a bit rate of 1.4
- 8 to 16 GB, which is the size of a typical flash drive.

1.9.1. Speed Measurement

Hertz (Hz), which also stands for a CPU cycle, is a unit of measurement for Central Processing Unit (CPU) speed. Computer pace is the term used to describe CPU speed.

1.10. COMPUTER CLASSIFICATION

Today's electronic computer systems come in a wide range of sizes and configurations. Based on their dimensions and category, computer systems are broadly classified into four types:

1. Microcomputers
2. Minicomputers
3. Mainframe computers

4. Supercomputer.

1.10.1. Microcomputers

Small, inexpensive, single-user digital computers are known as microcomputers. A CPU, an input unit, an output unit, a storage unit, and software make up these components. Microcomputers are independent devices; however, Microcomputers can be joined to form a network of computers which can accommodate multiple users.

Microcomputers include the Apple Macintosh and IBM PC, both of which are based on Pentium processors. Microcomputers are devices like desktops, laptops, netbooks, tablets, handheld devices, smartphones, and laptops.

KEYWORD

Microcomputers are small computers designed for tinkering instead of user friendliness and aesthetics.

1.10.2. Personal Computer (PC) or Desktop Computer

Microcomputers are most commonly available in the form of desktops or personal computers (PCs). It is an independent device that could even be set up on a desk. It is composed of three components on the outside: a keyboard, a monitor, and a system unit that contains the CPU, memory, hard drive, and other components.

It is fairly priced and appropriate for small businesses, organizations, and lone users at home. PC makers include Apple, Microsoft, HP, Dell, and Lenovo.

1.10.3. Notebook or Laptop Computers

Notebook Notebooks look similar to computers or laptops. All of the features of a desktop computer are available but are compact. The benefit of a laptop is that it can be carried anyplace, is portable (this can fit inside a backpack), does have a battery backup, and includes all of the features of a desktop computer. It is possible to work while using a laptop on a lap (hence the name). Laptop computers are more expensive than desktop computers.

1.10.4. Netbook

Netbooks are more compact laptops that are made to access web-based applications and thus are intended for low weight and an affordable price. But since the launch of the first netbook in late 2007, netbooks have rapidly increased in demand. Music streaming or videos, e-mailing, surfing the internet, and online chatting are just a few of the regular tasks that netbooks make possible. The Internet and notebook were combined to get the term "netbook."

1.10.5. Tablet Computer

The characteristics of a tablet computer are comparable to those of a portable computer, but rather than a keyboard and mouse, this model accepts a touchscreen or a pen. It is a laptop or tablet. The latest new type of PC is the touch screen computer.

1.10.6. Personal Digital Assistant (PDA) or Handheld Device

A portable computer, also known as a handheld computer or personal digital assistant (PDA), could be kept on the top of the palm. This is a small object. PDAs don't have keyboards; input is done with a pen or a stylus. Disk drives are absent from PDAs.

Their memory is constrained, and their strength is diminished. WiFi connections allow PDAs to access the Web. PDAs are made by a number of companies, including Apple and Casio. Smartphones were created in recent years as a consequence of the combination of PDAs and mobile phones.

TIPS

computers store these things as data, not as information, but you'll learn the difference between the two later in the book. So, when you consider the importance of computers in our society, think instead about the importance of information.

1.10.7. Smartphones

Mobile phones, known as "smart phones," have dual-purpose processing capabilities. A small keyboard or a stylus, as well as a pen, can be used. They have wireless Internet connectivity choices. They are often used to play games, download music, and access electronic mail, among several other things. Makers of smartphones include Blackberry, Apple, HTC, Nokia, and LG.

1.11. DATA TRANSFER BETWEEN MEMORY AND CPU

Data need to be transferred between the CPU and primary memory as well as between the primary and secondary memory. Data are transferred between different components of a computer system using physical wires called bus.

For example, bus is used for data transfer between a USB port and hard disk or between a hard disk and main memory. Bus is of three types:

i. Data bus to transfer data between different components,
ii. Address bus to transfer addresses between CPU and main memory. The address of the memory location that the CPU wants to read or write from is specified in the address bus,
iii. Control bus to communicate control signals between different components of a computer. All these three busses collectively make the system bus.

As the CPU interacts directly with main memory, any data entered from input device or the data to be accessed from hard disk needs to be placed in the main memory for further processing. The data is then transferred between CPU and main memory using bus.

The CPU places on the address bus, the address of the main memory location from which it wants to read data or to write data. While executing the instructions, the CPU specifies the read or write control signal through the control bus. As the CPU may require reading data from main memory or writing data to main memory, a data bus is bidirectional. But the control bus and address bus are unidirectional. To write data into memory, the CPU places the data on the data bus, which is then written to the specific address provided through the address bus.

In case of read operation, the CPU specifies the address, and the data is placed on the data bus by a dedicated hardware, called memory controller. The memory controller manages the flow of data into and out of the computer's main memory.

KEYWORD

Main memory is the central storage unit. It is an essential component of a digital computer since it stores data and programs.

1.12. MICROPROCESSORS

The central processing unit (CPU) of a computer once required a sizable space or several cabinets. But thanks to technological advancements, the CPU's physical size has shrunk, which makes it possible to fit one CPU onto a single microchip. A microprocessor is a processor (CPU) that is put in place on a single microchip.

The majority of CPUs presently are microprocessors. Consequently, the terms are interchangeable in everyday speech. A microprocessor is a diminutive electrical device found inside computers that perform a variety of arithmetic, logical, and data analysis tasks. A modern microprocessor is formed on an integrated circuit that contains millions of small parts, including resistors, transistors, and diodes.

In aspects of their enhanced processing capacity, decreasing physical dimensions, and drop in price, microprocessors have progressed over time. Millions of commands can be processed per millisecond on the microprocessors that are available at the moment. This includes a listing of the various varieties of microprocessors, their generations, eras, and underlying hardware as of their invention in the early 1970s (Figure 1.4).

Figure 1.4. An illustration of a microprocessor.

Source: Image by Wikimedia Commons.

1.12.1. Specifications for Microprocessors

The various aspects of microprocessors, like chip type, word size, memory size, clock speed, and so on, are employed to classify them. Such aspects are succinctly defined below.

1.12.1.1. Word Size

The most bits a microprocessor can process in one go is called a word size. Words used to be 8 bits long back then due to the highest possible bit length. Presently, the minimum and the maximum word sizes are 16 bits and 64 bits, respectively.

1.12.1.2. Memory Size

RAM capacity depends greatly on word size. Since 4/8 bits was the default word size, RAM was at first quite small (4MB). It is now possible to use RAM with capabilities of up to 16 Exabytes (EB) because of the change in word size to 64 bits.

1.12.1.3. Clock Speed

A clock within computers makes pulses (signals) at regular intervals in time. The amount of pulses made by a computer's internal clock each second is identified as clock speed. The clock speed represents the pace at which the computer could carry out instructions. In the past, it was determined in Hertz (Hz) and Kilohertz (kHz). But due to improvements in chip density and technology, it is currently assessed in Gigahertz (GHz), or billions of pulses per second.

KEYWORD

Computation unit is a block of code (which is used to perform a task or calculate some value and so on).

1.12.1.4. Cores

The CPU's core is its fundamental computational component. Early CPUs could only manage each task at the same time since they only had one computation unit. The ability to carry out several tasks at once on the computer has been made possible through the creation of multi-core processors that have improved system performance. Dual-core, quad-core, and octa-core processors are terms that refer to CPUs that have two, four, and eight cores, respectively.

1.12.2. Microcontrollers

Unlike a microprocessor, which also only contains a CPU on the chip, a microcontroller is a small computing device with a CPU, a fixed amount of RAM, ROM, as well as other peripheral devices all integrated on a single chip. Microcontrollers are made of key technologies with microcontrollers, including the keyboard, cursor, microwave, washing machine, digital camera, pen drive, and USB. These are smaller and less expensive since they are only meant to accomplish particular tasks.

Due to the microcontroller's diminutive size, it is integrated into another gadget or system to carry out a particular task. For instance, a fully automatic laundry machine uses its microcontroller to automatically manage the washing cycle.

The process begins with the water being filled; the clothes are then drenched and cleaned up; the water is then drained; and finally, the clothes are spun dry. Microcontrollers' straightforward application has made it feasible for routine tasks to be carried out automatically without human involvement, and save valuable time.

1.13. INFORMATION AND DATA

Data processing is the primary objective of a computer. All that a computer system processes are viewed as data, which includes programs, images, music, videos, documents, and more. Data could also consist of unstructured, uncooked factual information which is processed to generate crucial data.

Therefore, it is important to realize the idea of data as well as the various types of data in order to fully comprehend how a computer functions as a whole. Data, information, and knowledge are frequently used synonymously, which is inaccurate.

KEYWORD

Factual information is information that solely deals with facts. It is short, non-explanatory, and rarely gives in-depth background on a topic.

1.13.1. Data and Its Types

There are numerous input devices that offer computers access to initial data in the form of factual information, ideas, instructions, and so on. However, a computer needs to store everything internally in binary form (0 and 1), data may also be entered from external sources using the English alphabet (A-Z, a-z), numbers 0 through 9, and special symbols such as @, #, and so on.

Data may be read from a file system or input in other languages as well. The input data could be derived from various sources, and as an outcome, it could be in multiple formats. As an illustration, a fee invoice is comprised of characters that are both numeric and non-numeric and is composed of Red, Green, and Blue (RGB) pixels. A video is composed of frames. The three main categories of data are as described in the following:

- **Structured Data**

Structured data is data that abides by a restrictive record structure and is simple to grasp. A data file that includes such information in a tabulated form that has been decided in advance may well be kept and used later. This is the formally organized information that the school needs to keep on the students' monthly participation.

This type of data is obviously arranged in a row-by-column layout and is simple to comprehend. You can arrange structured data either ascending or descending. In this illustration, the column "month" in the attendance records is arranged in ascending order. The purchase of goods, ordering train tickets online, using an ATM, and other activities are additional examples of structured data.

- **Unstructured Data**

Unstructured data are those that are not set up in a predetermined specific layout. One might think of graphics, text documents, social media posts, audio and video files satellite data, and much more.

Parents receive a scorecard that includes information about the monthly attendance records. The above types of data are unstructured since they contain both text and graphics that don't comply with a set layout.

- **Semi-structured Data**

Semi-structured data refers to data that has no clear structure but nevertheless contains internal tags or markings to differentiate its multiple aspects. Electronic mail documents, HTML pages, CSV files, and other formats are explanations.

An illustration of semi-structured data that depicts attendance information for students divided by month. There isn't a set format for every attendance register in this illustration. In this, a tag (Name, Month, Class, and Attendance) is placed before every data value to assist readers in comprehending what that value means.

KEYWORD

Database is an organized collection of structured information, or data, typically stored electronically in a computer system.

1.13.2. Data Retrieval, Storage, and Capturing

Data must first be input or captured before it can be processed. The next step is to store it in a file or database in order to be used later. Each time data is required to be processed, it is first taken out of the file or database in order to proceed with the processing.

1.13.2.1. Data Collection

It entails the procedure of collecting digital data gathered from various sources. Simple tools such as keyboards, barcode readers used by major retailers, remarks or posts made on social media, remote sensors on an earth-orbiting satellite, and so on, could be employed for this capturing. Data capture can occasionally be a challenging task due to the diversity of the data sources.

1.13.2.2. Data Storage

It includes saving the captured data in order to be processed afterwards. Because of the rapid pace at which data is generated currently, data storage has become a hard process. Even so, the above process has been made much easier by the drop in the price of digital storage systems. Market vendors offer a wide variety of digital storage devices.

KEYWORD

Data server (DS) is a software program/platform used to provide database services like storing, processing and securing data.

Data is growing rapidly over time. As a consequence, it is necessary to frequently upgrade the storage devices as well. To store huge amounts of data, larger companies utilize data servers, which are computer systems with faster processors and more storage. Such highly specialized computers facilitate effective data processing. Even so, establishing and maintaining a data server is costly, particularly for small and new businesses (both in terms of hardware and software).

1.13.2.3. Data Retrieval

Data from storage devices should be fetched in for it to be processed in full compliance with customer requirements. The complications associated with locating and retrieving data in an appropriate amount of time grow as databases expand. For quicker data processing, lowering data access time is vital.

1.13.3. Data Deletion and Recovery

Digital data's ability to be deleted is one of its major risks. The stored data could be lost if the storage devices fail or collapse. Data on storage devices could be accidentally deleted by users, hackers, malware, or malicious attackers. Electronically stored information must be altered at the bit level in order to be removed, which can be a lengthy process. This means that if certain data is merely deleted, its address entry is defined as free and the remaining space is visible to the user as empty, without genuinely erasing the data.

This becomes essential to retrieve the data when it is unknowingly removed or corrupted. Data recovery would only be possible if the components of storage space labeled as removed have not been overwritten by additional data.

Data recovery is a process of retrieving deleted, corrupted and lost data from secondary storage devices. There are usually two security concerns associated with data. One is its deletion by some unauthorized person or software. These concerns can be avoided by limiting access to the computer system and using passwords for user accounts and files, wherever possible.

There is also an option of encrypting files to protect them from unwanted modification. The other concern is related to unwanted recovery of data by un authorized user or software. Many a times, we discard our old, broken or malfunctioning storage devices without taking care to delete data.

We assume that the contents of deleted files are permanently removed. However, if these storage devices fall into the hands of mischief-mongers, they can easily recover data from such devices; this poses a threat to data confidentiality. This concern can be mitigated by using proper tools to delete or shred data before disposing off any old or faulty storage device.

KEYWORD

Data confidentiality is about protecting data against unintentional, unlawful, or unauthorized access, disclosure, or theft.

1.14. OPERATING SYSTEM

An operating system (OS) can be considered to be a resource manager which manages all the resources of a computer, i.e., its hardware including CPU, RAM, Disk, Network and other input-output devices. It also controls various application software and device drivers, manages system security and handles access by different users. It is the most important system software.

Examples of popular OS are Windows, Linux, Android, and Macintosh and so on. The primary objectives of an operating system are two-fold. The first is to provide services for building and running application programs. When an application program needs to be run, it is the operating system which loads that program into memory and allocates it to the CPU for execution.

When multiple application programs need to be run, the operating system decides the order of the execution. The second objective of an operating system is to provide an interface to the user through which the user can interact with the computer. A user interface is a software component which is a part of the operating system and whose job is to take commands or inputs from a user for the operating system to process.

1.15. USER VIEW

The user's view of the computer varies according to the interface being used. Most computer users sit in front of a PC, consisting of a monitor, keyboard, mouse, and system unit. Such a system is designed for one user to monopolize its resources.

The goal is to maximize the work (or play) that the user is performing. In this case, the operating system is designed mostly for ease of use, with some attention paid to performance and none paid to resource utilization—how various hardware and software resources are shared. Performance is, of course, important to the user; but such systems are optimized for the single-user experience rather than the requirements of multiple users.

In other cases, a user sits at a terminal connected to a mainframe or a minicomputer. Other users are accessing the same computer through other terminals. These users share resources and may exchange information. The operating system in such cases is designed to maximize resource utilization—to assure that all available CPU time, memory, and I/O are used efficiently and that no individual user takes more than her fair share.

Did you Know?

In other cases, users sit at workstations connected to networks of other workstations and servers. These users have dedicated resources at their disposal, but they also share resources such as networking and servers, including file, compute, and print servers. Therefore, their operating system is designed to compromise between individual usability and resource utilization.

Recently, many varieties of mobile computers, such as smart phones and tablets, have come into fashion. Most mobile computers are standalone units for individual users. Quite often, they are connected to networks through cellular or other wireless technologies. Increasingly, these mobile devices are replacing desktop and laptop computers for people who are primarily interested in using computers for e-mail and web browsing.

The user interface for mobile computers generally features a touch screen, where the user interacts with the system by pressing and swiping fingers across the screen rather than using a physical keyboard and mouse.

Some computers have little or no user view. For example, embedded computers in home devices and automobiles may have numeric keypads and may turn indicator lights on or off to show status, but they and their operating systems are designed primarily to run without user intervention.

1.16. SYSTEM VIEW

From the computer's point of view, the operating system is the program most intimately involved with the hardware. In this context, we can view an operating system as a resource allocator. A computer system has many resources that may be required to solve a problem: CPU time, memory space, file-storage space, I/O devices, and so on. The operating system acts as the manager of these resources. Facing numerous and possibly conflicting requests for resources, the operating system must decide how to allocate them to specific programs and users so that it can operate the computer system efficiently and fairly. As we have seen, resource allocation is especially important where many users access the same mainframe or minicomputer.

KEYWORD

Memory space is a concept related to collective memory, stating that certain places, objects or events can have special significance related to group's remembrance.

A slightly different view of an operating system emphasizes the need to control the various I/O devices and user programs. An operating system is a control program. A control program manages the execution of user programs to prevent errors and improper use of the computer. It is especially concerned with the operation and control of I/O devices.

By now, you can probably see that the term operating system covers many roles and functions. That is the case, at least in part, because of the myriad designs and uses of computers. Computers are present within toasters, cars, ships, spacecraft, homes, and businesses.

They are the basis for game machines, music players, cable TV tuners, and industrial control systems. Although computers have a relatively short history, they have evolved rapidly. Computing started as an experiment to determine what could be done and quickly moved to fixed-purpose systems for military uses, such as code breaking and trajectory plotting, and governmental uses, such as census calculation.

Those early computers evolved into general-purpose, multifunction mainframes, and that's when operating systems were born. In the 1960s, Moore's Law predicted that the number of transistors on an integrated circuit would double every 18 months, and that prediction has held true. Computers gained in functionality and shrunk in size, leading to a vast number of uses and a vast number and variety of operating systems.

Remember

In 1998, the United States Department of Justice filed suit against Microsoft, in essence claiming that Microsoft included too much functionality in its operating systems and thus prevented application vendors from competing. (For example, a Web browser was an integral part of the operating systems.) As a result, Microsoft was found guilty of using its operating-system monopoly to limit competition.

How, then, can we define what an operating system is? In general, we have no completely adequate definition of an operating system. Operating systems exist because they offer a reasonable way to solve the problem of creating a usable computing system. The fundamental goal of computer systems is to execute user programs and to make solving user problems easier.

Computer hardware is constructed toward this goal. Since bare hardware alone is not particularly easy to use, application programs are developed. These programs require certain common operations, such as those controlling the I/O devices.

The common functions of controlling and allocating resources are then brought together into one piece of software: the operating system. In addition, we have no universally accepted definition of what is part of the operating system. A simple viewpoint is that it includes everything a vendor ships when you order “the operating system.” The features included, however, vary greatly across systems.

TIPS

The largest organizational computers support thousands of individual users at the same time, from thousands of miles away. W hale some of these large-scale systems are devoted to a special purpose, enabling users to perform only a few specific tasks, many organizational computers are general.

Some systems take up less than a megabyte of space and lack even a full-screen editor, whereas others require gigabytes of space and are based entirely on graphical windowing systems. A more common definition, and the one that we usually follow, is that the operating system is the one program running at all times on the computer—usually called the kernel.

Along with the kernel, there are two other types of programs: system programs, which are associated with the operating system but are not necessarily part of the kernel, and application programs, which include all programs not associated with the operation of the system. The matter of what constitutes an operating system became increasingly important as personal computers became more widespread and operating systems grew increasingly sophisticated.

Today, however, if we look at operating systems for mobile devices, we see that once again the number of features constituting the operating system is increasing. Mobile operating systems often include not only a core kernel but also middleware—a set of software frameworks that provide additional services to application developers.

For example, each of the two most prominent mobile operating systems—Apple's iOS and Google's Android—features a core kernel along with middleware that supports databases, multimedia, and graphics (to name a only few).

1.17. COMPUTER-SYSTEM ORGANIZATION

Before we can explore the details of how computer systems operate, we need general knowledge of the structure of a computer system. In this section, we look at several parts of this structure. The section is mostly concerned with computer-system organization, so you can skim or skip it if you already understand the concepts.

1.17.1. Computer-System Operation

A modern general-purpose computer system consists of one or more CPUs and a number of device controllers connected through a common bus that provides access to shared memory. Each device controller is in charge of a specific type of device (for example, disk drives, audio devices, or video displays).

The CPU and the device controllers can execute in parallel, competing for memory cycles. To ensure orderly access to the shared memory, a memory controller synchronizes access to the memory. For a computer to start running—for instance, when it is powered up or rebooted—it needs to have an initial program to run. This initial program, or bootstrap program, tends to be simple.

Typically, it is stored within the computer hardware in read-only memory (ROM) or electrically erasable programmable read-only memory (EEPROM), known by the general term firmware. It initializes all aspects of the system, from CPU registers to device controllers to memory contents. The bootstrap program must know how to load the operating system and how to start executing that system. To accomplish this goal, the bootstrap program must locate the operating-system kernel and load it into memory. Once the kernel is loaded and executing, it can start providing services to the system and its users.

Some services are provided outside of the kernel, by system programs that are loaded into memory at boot time to become system processes, or system daemons that run the entire time the kernel is running. On UNIX, the first system process is "in it," and it starts many other daemons. Once this phase is complete,

KEYWORD

Shared memory is memory that may be simultaneously accessed by multiple programs with an intent to provide communication among them or avoid redundant copies.

the system is fully booted, and the system waits for some event to occur.

ACTIVITY 1.1.

Fill in the blanks

1. A ________ is a machine for manipulating data according to a list of instructions known as ________.
2. ________ and _______ are the most commonly used output device.
3. ________ is used to display videos, images or computer data on a largest screen.
4. The storage device of a computer system is referred as _______.

The occurrence of an event is usually signaled by an interrupt from either the hardware or the software. Hardware may trigger an interrupt at any time by sending a signal to the CPU, usually by way of the system bus. Software may trigger an interrupt by executing a special operation called a system call (also called a monitor call).

When the CPU is interrupted, it stops what it is doing and immediately transfers execution to a fixed location. The fixed location usually contains the starting address where the service routine for the interrupt is located.

KEYWORD

Interrupt mechanism provides a link between external asynchronous events and software routines that provide service.

The interrupt service routine executes; on completion, the CPU resumes the interrupted computation. A timeline of this operation. Interrupts are an important part of a computer architecture. Each computer design has its own interrupt mechanism, but several functions are common. The interrupt must transfer control to the appropriate interrupt service routine.

The straightforward method for handling this transfer would be to invoke a generic routine to examine the interrupt information. The routine, in turn, would call the interrupt-specific handler. However, interrupts must be handled quickly. Since only a predefined number of interrupts is possible, a table of pointers to interrupt routines can be used instead to provide the necessary speed.

The interrupt routine is called indirectly through the table, with no intermediate routine needed. Generally, the table of pointers is stored in low memory (the first hundred or so locations). These locations hold the addresses of the interrupt service routines for the various devices. This array, or interrupt vector, of addresses is then indexed by a unique device number, given with the interrupt request, to provide the address of the interrupt service routine for the interrupting device.

Operating systems as different as Windows and UNIX dispatch interrupts in this manner. The interrupt architecture must also save the address of the interrupted instruction. Many old designs simply stored the interrupt address in a fixed location or in a location indexed by the device number. More recent architectures store the return address on the system stack.

If the interrupt routine needs to modify the processor state—for instance, by modifying register values—it must explicitly save the current state and then restore that state before returning. After the interrupt is serviced, the saved return address is loaded into the program counter, and the interrupted computation resumes as though the interrupt had not occurred.

1.17.2. Storage Structure

The CPU can load instructions only from memory, so any programs to run must be stored there. General-purpose computers run most of their programs from rewritable memory, called main memory (also called random-access memory, or RAM). Main memory commonly is implemented in a semiconductor technology called dynamic random-access memory (DRAM).

Computers use other forms of memory as well. We have already mentioned read-only memory, ROM) and electrically erasable programmable read-only memory, EEPROM). Because ROM cannot be changed, only static programs, such as the bootstrap program described earlier, are stored there. The immutability of ROM is of use in game cartridges.

EEPROM can be changed but cannot be changed frequently and so contains mostly static programs. For example, Smartphone's have EEPROM to store their factory-installed programs. Each byte has its own address. Interaction is achieved through a sequence of load or store instructions to specific memory addresses.

The load instruction moves a byte or word from main memory to an internal register within the CPU, whereas the store instruction moves the content of a register to main memory. Aside from explicit loads and stores, the CPU automatically loads instructions from main memory for execution.

KEYWORD

Dynamic random-access memory is a type of random-access semiconductor memory that stores each bit of data in a memory cell, usually consisting of a tiny capacitor and a transistor, both typically based on metal–oxide–semiconductor technology.

A typical instruction–execution cycle, as executed on a system with a von Neumann architecture, first fetches an instruction from memory and stores that instruction in the instruction register. The instruction is then decoded and may cause operands to be fetched from memory and stored in some internal register.

After the instruction on the operands has been executed, the result may be stored back in memory. Notice that the memory unit sees only a stream of memory addresses. It does not know how they are generated (by the instruction counter, indexing, indirection, literal addresses, or some other means) or what they are for (instructions or data). Accordingly, we can ignore how a memory address is generated by a program.

We are interested only in the sequence of memory addresses generated by the running program. Ideally, we want the programs and data to reside in main memory permanently. This arrangement usually is not possible for the following two reasons:

TIPS

When the CPU is interrupted, it stops what it is doing and immediately transfers execution to a fixed location.

1. Main memory is usually too small to store all needed programs and data permanently.
2. Main memory is a volatile storage device that loses its contents when power is turned off or otherwise lost. Thus, most computer systems provide secondary storage as an extension of main memory.

The main requirement for secondary storage is that it be able to hold large quantities of data permanently. The most common secondary-storage device is a magnetic disk, which provides storage for both programs and data.

Most programs (system and application) are stored on a disk until they are loaded into memory. Many programs then use the disk as both the source and the destination of their processing. Hence, the proper management of disk storage is of central importance to a computer system.

In a larger sense, however, the storage structure that we have described—consisting of registers, main memory, and magnetic disks—is only one of many possible storage systems. Others include cache memory, CD-ROM, magnetic tapes, and so on. Each storage system provides the basic functions of storing a datum and holding that datum until it is retrieved at a later time.

The main differences among the various storage systems lie in speed, cost, size, and volatility. The wide variety of storage systems can be organized in a hierarchy according to speed and cost. The higher levels are expensive, but they are fast. As we move down the hierarchy, the cost per bit generally decreases, whereas the access time generally increases.

This trade-off is reasonable; if a given storage system were both faster and less expensive than another—other properties being the same—then there would be no reason to use the slower, more expensive memory. In fact, many early storage devices, including paper tape and core memories, are relegated to museums now that magnetic tape and semiconductor memory have become faster and cheaper.

The top four levels of memory may be constructed using semiconductor memory. In addition to differing in speed and cost, the various storage systems are either volatile or nonvolatile. As mentioned earlier, volatile storage loses its contents when the power to the device is removed. In the absence of expensive battery and generator backup systems, data must be written to nonvolatile storage for safekeeping.

In the hierarchy shown in the storage systems above the solid-state disk are volatile, whereas those including the solid-state disk and below are nonvolatile. Solid-state disks have several variants but in general are faster than magnetic disks and are nonvolatile.

One type of solid-state disk stores data in a large DRAM array during normal operation but also contains a hidden magnetic hard disk and a battery for backup power. If external power is interrupted, this solid-state disk's controller copies the data from RAM to the magnetic disk. When external power is restored, the controller copies the data back into RAM.

Another form of solid-state disk is flash memory, which is popular in cameras and personal digital assistants (PDAs), in robots, and increasingly for storage on general-purpose computers. Flash memory is slower than DRAM but needs no power to retain its contents. Another form of nonvolatile storage is NVRAM, which is DRAM with battery backup power.

This memory can be as fast as DRAM and (as long as the battery lasts) is nonvolatile. The design of a complete memory system must balance all the factors just discussed: it must use only as much expensive memory as necessary while providing as much inexpensive, nonvolatile memory as possible. Caches can be installed to improve performance where a large disparity in access time or transfer rate exists between two components.

Remember

In the hierarchy shown in the storage systems above the solid-state disk are volatile, whereas those including the solid-state disk and below are nonvolatile. Solid-state disks have several variants but in general are faster than magnetic disks and are nonvolatile.

1.17.3. I/O Structure

Storage is only one of many types of I/O devices within a computer. A large portion of operating system code is dedicated to managing I/O, both because of its importance to the reliability and performance of a system and because of the varying nature of the devices. Next, we provide an overview of I/O. A general-purpose computer system consists of CPUs and multiple device controllers that are connected through a common bus. Each device controller is in charge of a specific type of device. Depending on the controller, more than one device may be attached.

1.18. SUMMARY

1. Definition of Computer and its Components

In this chapter, definitions of computer and its various components have been explained. It also provides various components of the computer such as hardware, software, input devices, output devices, CPU, and so on.

2. Classification of Computer

In this chapter, Classification of Computer and its various kinds according to purpose, data handling and functionality. According to purpose, computers are either general purpose or specific purpose. General purpose computers are designed to perform a range of tasks. They have the ability to store numerous programs, but lack in speed and efficiency.

3. Storage Structure and OS

Towards the end of the chapter, it addresses about the concept of computer – system organization which includes, computer – system operation, storage structure, and input or output structure.

1.19. REVIEW QUESTIONS

1. What do you understand by the term computer?
2. Name the two types of memory.
3. What is the relationship between the computer hardware and software?
4. Explain computer memory and its types.
5. What do you do when your computer is hung?
6. What do you understand by an Operating System?
7. What is the different in Data and Information?
8. Explain the key issues in Computer.

1.20. MULTIPLE CHOICE QUESTIONS

1. DRAM stands for.

a. Dynamic Random-Access Memory
b. Data Random-Access Memory
c. Dynamic Read-Access Memory
d. Direct Read-Access Memory

2. **An ___________ can be considered to be a resource manager which manages all the resources of a computer**
   a. operating system
   b. input system
   c. optical disk
   d. interrupt
3. **The _____________ of a computer once required a sizable space or several cabinets.**
   a. Information
   b. central processing unit (CPU)
   c. microcontroller
   d. memory
4. **The CPU specifies the address, and the data is placed on the data bus by a dedicated hardware, called _________.**
   a. microcontroller
   b. interface
   c. optical disk
   d. memory controller
5. **Which device is an abbreviation for calculation devices?**
   a. Abacus
   b. Computer
   c. Laptop
   d. Mobile

Answers to Multiple Choice Questions

1. (a) 2. (a) 3. (b) 4. (d) 5. (a)

REFERENCES

1. (n.d). *Introduction to Computer* (pp. 1–628). [e-Book] gpnanakpur. Available at: https://gpnanakpur.ac.in/wp-content/uploads/2019/04/computerfundamentals-e-notes.pdf (accessed on 03 March 2023).
2. Peter Norton, (2008). *Introduction to Computers* (6th edn., pp. 2–476). Tata McGraw-Hill.
3. Silberschatz, A., Galvin, P., & Gagne, G., (n.d). *Operating System Concepts* (9th edn., pp. 4–904). Wiley.

4. (n.d). *Introduction to Computing* (pp. 1–15). [e-Book] cs.calvin.edu. Available at: https://cs.calvin.edu/activities/books/processing/text/01computing.pdf (accessed on 03 March 2023).
5. (n.d). *Computer Science* (pp. 1–26). [e-Book] NCERT. Available at: https://ncert.nic.in/textbook/pdf/kecs101.pdf (accessed on 03 March 2023).
6. (n.d). *Introduction to Computer* (pp. 1–10). [e-Book] Available at: https://www.just.edu.jo/~mqais/CIS99/PDF/Ch.01_Introduction_%20to_computers.pdf (accessed on 03 March 2023).

CHAPTER 2

UNDERSTANDING VIRTUAL REALITY TECHNOLOGY: ADVANCES AND APPLICATIONS

UNIT INTRODUCTION

Virtual reality (VR) entails the use of computer modeling and simulation to authorize an individual to communicate with an illusionary three-dimensional (3-D) visual or some other visual input. VR applications immerse the user in a computer-generated environment that replicates real-world situations with the aid of fun, wearable devices that transmit and receive data and can therefore take the form of eyewear, headphones, gloves, or body suits.

A user viewing animated images of a virtual environment while wearing headgear with a stereo vision screen is a pretty standard VR format. Motion detectors pick up the user's moves and modify the view on the display correspondingly, generally in actual time at the moment the user's action occurs. The above gives the appearance of "being in it" (telepresence).

As a consequence, a user could discover a virtual suite of rooms whilst also beginning to experience evolving viewpoints and perspectives which persuasively correspond to one's own head motion and steps. The user could even grab and control things that can be seen in the simulated space while wearing data gloves, which are fitted with force-feedback gadgets that give the sensation of touching.

Jaron Lanier, whose studies and engineering have generated a range of products for the developing VR sector, invented the term "virtual reality" in 1987. Initial VR studies and advancement in the US were connected by the federal government's involvement, especially that of the Department of Defense, the National Science Foundation, and the National Aeronautics and Space Administration (NASA).

Programs are funded through these organizations and managed to be carried out at university-based research facilities, resulting in a large pool of skilled staff in fields like computer graphics, modeling, and networked environments, as well as connections among academic, military, and commercial work.

An idea which has emerged in different forms ever since the late 1960s, virtual reality (VR) is not a brand-new idea. When VR was broadly used, this was meant to refer to titles like synthetic environment, cyberspace, artificial reality, simulator technology, and more. Desktop VR is the most recent VR implementation. Desktop VR too is referred to as Window on the World (WoW) or non-immersive VR (Onyesolu, 2006).

The emergence of desktop VR has resulted in the creation of application areas which are less interactive than total immersion. The price and technical issues of such non-immersive VR applications are substantially lower, while they have already made progress in the development and training of the sector. More noticeably in education, in which computer-based virtual learning environments (VLE) are bundled as desktop VR, VR may finally become within the range of possibilities for its overall formation and use.

This in turn implies that it should be incorporated into educational initiatives (Ausburn & Ausburn, 2004). Medical education, the study of the physical sciences, and engineering are just a handful of the disciplines that have benefited greatly from the emergence of these computer-based virtual learning environments (VLEs). Students have the advantage of being able to accomplish educational targets thanks to VLEs. Therefore, VLE-based applications are becoming widely used in schools and universities as efficient techniques to complement traditional learning approaches.

It has been noticed that these learning environments are more instructional and impactful for learners. Perspectives into the structures and operations of any system can be obtained through virtual learning environments in three dimensions (3D). Thus, by engaging with and navigating through the environment designed for this type of system, learners could understand the precepts of such a system in a quick, efficient, and exciting manner (Onyesolu, 2009a; Onyesolu, 2009b). It's widely understood that virtual reality (VR) can make artificial objects as realistic as, or even more believable than, the actual ones (Negroponte, 1995).

Learning Objectives

After completing this chapter, you should be able to understand the following:

1. Understand the concept of virtual reality technology
2. Understand the history of the virtual reality technology
3. Educate about the VR development tools and resources

4. Give advice about application of VR technology
5. Understand about virtual rendering system
6. Give advice about impact of virtual reality technology on human lives

Key Terms

1. 3D Modeling Software
2. Computer Workstation
3. Low-Cost VR
4. Virtual Reality Technology
5. Visual Display Unit (VDU)
6. VR Simulation Software

2.1. THE TECHNOLOGY: VIRTUAL REALITY

A few people regard virtual reality (VR) as a particular category of technology, including headphones, gloves, and walkers (Haag et al., 1998; Williams & Sawyer, 2001; Isdale, 1993). Virtual reality (VR) is described as a highly engaging, computer-based multimedia environment in which the user gets involved in a virtual world (Kim et al., 2000; Onyesolu, 2009a; Onyesolu&Akpado, 2009).

It is a representation of a genuine or made-up environment that is able to be perceived visually in the three dimensions of width, height, and depth and that also provides the option of an engaging cinematic experience in full real-time movement with audio as well as haptic and other kinds of feedback. Virtual reality (VR) empowers individuals to interact, envision, and deceive highly complicated data stored on computers (Isdale, 1998).

KEYWORD

Virtual reality (VR) is a simulated experience that employs pose tracking and 3D near-eye displays to give the user an immersive feel of a virtual world.

It is an artificial environment created with computer hardware and software and provided to the user in a manner that makes this seem and believe like a real-world situation (Baieier, 1993). Virtual reality (VR) is a computer-generated, three-dimensional environment where a large number of human people involved, when properly hooked up, can communicate with and deceive simulated physical components in the environment as well as, in certain cases, connect and interact with depictions of actual or imagined living beings or fictional characters.

It is a computer-based technique for simulating the sensory elements of complicated environments, such as sight, sound, and touch (Onyesolu, 2009b). Virtual reality uses 3D technologies to create a false impression of reality. Virtual reality generates a simulation of actual events (Haag et al., 1998).And hence, the term "VR" alludes to a 3D computer-generated environment that is fun, engaging, sensorimotor, and viewer-centered as well as the set of technologies necessary to create quite an environment (Aukstakalnis & Blatner, 1992; Cruz-Niera, 1993).

VR technology decreases obstacles for both people and computers by drenching audiences in a stereoscopic environment created by a computer. By simulating the natural stereoscopic viewing procedures, the VR technique enables computers to create right-eye and left-eye visuals of an assigned 3D object or scenario.

To generate the impression of three-dimensional space, the user's central nervous system combines the data from such two points of view. In this way, VR technology gives the perception that things on display have detail and existence, which are clearly different from the plain image that is projected onto a display. Rather than employing typical visualization tools, audiences could more precisely and realistically interpret the range and spatial connections between various object elements when using virtual reality technology (such as traditional CAD tools).

Technology and creative thinking are much like fuel and fire, respectively. Technology is fueled by intent and creativity working together. These are among the explanations why technology is currently developing at an accelerating rate. Virtual reality, on the other hand, submerges the viewer in a particular time or location. This is facilitated by visual and auditory innovations that trap the brain into thinking that it is in another place. It is the perception of an imagined universe. Sounds interesting, doesn't it?

KEYWORD

Input monitoring is when you listen to your live signal after it travels through and is processed by the computer.

With the help of computers and virtual reality, a 3D world could be experienced and, more curiously, conversed with. Having to wear a helmet showcase that transmits input monitoring facilitates this. In order to provide the user with a graphic experience, the screen is divided between the eyes, creating a realistic three-dimensional effect.

The technology uses the imagery of the objects that were taken from different angles to give the impression of being strong and having detail. The LCD or OLED panels within it are reflected back by lenses, which must fill the entire field of vision with the data that is intended to be seen and experienced. A realistic, thrilling, and interactive world is produced by the computer thanks to technology and input monitoring.Many years ago, there was what we nowadays refer to as virtual reality. returning to a time when 360° works of art shocked the world by introducing a virtual component. Virtual reality is simply "The Wise Guy" of the internet. It creates a world where nothing happens because of users and nothing happens because of what users do. It enables users to participate in and connect with the world made, as well as obtain first-hand experience, including the aftereffects of an occasion.

This technology offers great possibilities for knowing how the human brain functions. The potential of VRs to diagnose health issues ranging from severe pain to social phobia is claimed by scientists and medical professionals. Even so, the use of VR to alter the nervous system remains in its infant stages.

While the majority of people were preoccupied with its innovations and leaps in video games and industry exploration, many were unaware of its achievements in the medical field. Since the 1990s, VRs have effectively treated post-traumatic stress disorder; consequently, the new initiatives cope with a significantly wider range of ailments.

The VR material reveals the sick people to a governed, safe virtual world that allows them to discover and soon understand that now the risks people are concerned about are attentively dealt with, such as time, thought, and analysis.

There are different kinds of VR display systems. From the more expensive options that rely on the VR method and software on smartphones to the cheaper options that split the feed for each eye using a connector to transmit the feed to the device. Some head-mounts that make use of this configuration are the Sony PlayStation VR, the HTC Vive, and the Oculus Rift.

Users can build their own Virtual Reality Box at home, along with a mobile phone that supports the VR mode. No matter the purpose, virtual reality generates a collection of data that can be employed to build models, communication, training techniques, but also interaction. The options are endless, to put it simply.

Remember

This technology offers great possibilities for knowing how the human brain functions. The potential of VRs to diagnose health issues ranging from severe pain to social phobia is claimed by scientists and medical professionals. Even so, the use of VR to alter the nervous system remains in its infant stages.

2.2. VIRTUAL REALITY HISTORY

The first idea that comes to mind when users think of virtual reality is typically an advanced VR headset, in addition to all of the different PC programs that have begun to support it. With such an idea, which can be traced back to the 1930s, virtual reality actually has quite a long history. In this article, the author will talk about the origins of virtual reality and how it developed into the spectacular simulation experience that users can now enjoy in their own homes.

2.2.1. VR Development in 1930s

In Pygmalion's Spectacles, Stanley G. Weinbaum explains a goggle-based game in which individuals can watch a holographic recording of virtual stories including touch and smell. This amazing vision of the future would actually turn into what we think of as virtual-reality today. While it's difficult to introduce touch and smell elements into the average virtual-reality experience, these are visions that creators have in mind for the very near future of virtual-reality experiences.

It's amazing to think that 85+ years ago, people was already thinking about creating simulation experiences using technology. We still think of these types of plans as we look towards the future of VR. With rapidly changing technology however, these improvements to the VR simulation experience may be far closer than decades away.

2.2.2. VR Development in 1960s

VR headsets actually started development in the 1960s. Just 30 years from the original thought of a VR headset, Ivann Sutherland created the very first VR headset for use with military applications. Using specialized military software as well as a motion control platform, the first VR headsets were designed for use in training exercises.

These VR training tools have now become the standard in the military for training for flight exercises, combat situations and more. An immersive experience is definitely required to push military personnel and prepare them in a safe training environment before they enter into the field. Many air forces around the world require an extensive amount of VR training simulations before they will even let a pilot into one of their aircraft.

With the initial development using specialized software and motion controls, VR research would continue to pave the way for training in the military and beyond. Today's military VR headsets are far more advanced, compact and immersive and these training programs as well as the technology will continue to develop a little bit faster than some of the products that we might find as regular consumers.

KEYWORD

Average consumer means the consumer who is reasonably observant and circumspect, who belongs, as appropriate, to the population group targeted by the claim.

2.2.3. VR Development in 1990s

VR headsets begin to make their way into a few arcade games for simulations and Nintendo announced the first home VR system. Virtual Boy was one of the first home systems available for use with a widespread appeal. Sega also introduced a Sega VR headset for the Sega Genesis console in the year 1993. These wraparound prototypes had stereo sound, LCD screens and head tracking.

Technical development in this VR headset dooms the project and the cost of the headset was extensive making it a massive flop for Sega. The Virtual Boy however was a 3-D game console that experienced a little more success. Virtual Boy was released in North America at a price of $180. The games were entirely made in red and black and there were only a few pieces of software available with the device.

Users would wear a VR headset and control the action on a regular Nintendo controller. Unfortunately, the console was very uncomfortable to use and because of the lack of games as well as the lack of color, it didn't present the same strong sales as the other Nintendo consoles out at the time.

2.2.4. VR Development in 2014

KEYWORD

Virtual environment is a networked application that allows a user to interact with both the computing environment and the work of other users.

Oculus VR represents the latest revolution in VR technology. When Facebook officially acquired the Oculus VR system, this showed that virtual-reality was becoming a huge concern for many of the world's top developers. Although the Oculus Rift was formed out of a kick-starter campaign in 2012, the deal in 2014 represented a huge boost in their funding and confidence. Later in 2015, Oculus began to acquire other companies like Surreal Vision and built partnerships with Samsung to develop the Samsung gear VR. As one of the leading companies in VR development, Oculus has fully functioning VR systems for consumers to purchase and use at home. With support for a wide range of applications and further applications being developed for specific use with their VR systems, this was a huge leap forward for VR. After gaining international attention with the demand after the Facebook deal, this would propel many other developers into creating their own VR development firms. Oculus in a way started a brand-new VR renaissance with a call to create immersive and simulated experiences for the average consumer. Previous VR headsets were very technical and inaccessible for the average computer user, but with plug-and-play compatibility and a wide host of supported applications, Oculus gave the average consumer hope that they can enjoy VR again.

2.2.5. VR Development in 2016 and Beyond

With the initial surge after Oculus Rift, companies all over the world began building their own VR headsets and producing some fantastic new tech (Figure 2.1). With so many new devices coming out from many of the world's top manufacturers, we are seeing huge developments when it comes to apps, 360° cameras, inexpensive headsets, VR glass experiences and more. As 3-D graphics continue to get better and is processing power lines at an exponential rate, VR is becoming a focus for many developers in the future. There are many consumer products coming out to compete with Oculus based off its demand as well as generic products for use with smart phone technology.

As many smart phones have the accelerometer data, advanced soundcards and graphic sets for 3D rendering users are opting to watch 360 videos and try virtual-reality apps with their smartphone and home devices like Google Cardboard. Other users however are holding out for products like the Oculus Rift, Play station VR and more. With all of these devices set to drop in mass circulation by the end of 2016 or the start of 2017 we are truly going to start seeing at home VR experiences which are widespread.

Figure 2.1. History of virtual reality.

2.3. VIRTUAL REALITY COMPONENTS

The hardware parts and the software parts are the two major categories of components required to create and use virtual reality.

2.3.1. Components of Hardware

Input devices, process acceleration cards, tracking systems, sensory displays, and computer desktops are the five sub-components that end up making up the hardware.

a. **Computer Workstation:** A high-end microcomputer formed for scientific or technological applications is a desktop computer. Desktops operate multi-user operating systems and thus are typically connected to a local area network. Those are mainly designed for the use of one individual at a time.

Furthermore, a mainframe computer port or a PC that's also networked have been referred to as desktops. Especially in comparison to personal computers, desktops performed better, notably in terms of CPU and graphics, memory capacity, and multitasking capabilities.

They are especially suitable for controlling and displaying a wide range of complex types of data, such as arithmetic plots, 3D mechanical designs, animations produced by engineering simulations, and animations of moving gifs. Desktops are the initial area of the computer market to offer cutting-edge accessories and teamwork tools.

The desktop computer marketplace is currently very commercialized and ruled by big computer manufacturers like Dell and HP, who sell Microsoft Windows and Linux powered by Intel Xeon and AMD Opteron processors. Additional UNIX-based platform suppliers are Sun Microsystems, Silicon Graphics International (SGI), and Apple Inc. (http://en.wikipedia.org/wiki/Workstation). Many sensory screen devices are operated by a computer workstation to fully plunge users into a 3D virtual environment.

b. **Sensory Display:** One of the most fundamental aims of a virtual reality system is to feed data from the computer-generated reality to one's senses in a manner comparable to how users encounter the real world. Because most individuals possess two eyes, viewing the world normally requires not one, but two computer displays. Placing a small computer screen in front of every eye is a typical method of creating a believable 3-d image of a virtual environment. Every screen reproduces the viewpoint that the correlating eye will indeed experience in a real-world setting. The term "binocular head-mounted display" refers to such a device (HMD).

c. **Head-mounted displays:** A monitor is constantly in front of every user's eyes with head-mounted display. Orientation sensors are mounted on the "helmet" to regulate the view and the area of the generated and showcased simulated reality. A new viewpoint of the incident is produced when the computer detects head motion. In most instances, a collection of optical lenses and mirrors is employed to expand the vision, fill the field of vision, and guide the scene to the eyes (Lane, 1993).

The BOOM, or binocular Omni-orientation monitor, is a mechanical arm with joints that have monitoring detectors. The monitor is matched using a counterpoint in order for it to stay in place after the user leaves it. The user must hold the screen and look at it directly in order to perceive the digital world.

As a consequence, choosing to leave a virtual world and attempting to enter the real world only demands turning one head away from the BOOM.

The visual display unit (VDU) or monitors: VDU, which stands for visual display unit, is an outdated British term for just about any computer-related gadget that shows both text and images. VDUs include things like projectors and flat-panel displays, for instance. Even though flat-panel screen technologies like LED have supplanted the CRT monitor, which is an outdated benchmark, the term "VDU" is most frequently used when referring to it.

The initial VDUs had a 13 "display size." 15" and 17" VDU screen sizes were more widespread by the mid-1990s, and some 20" commencing to appear in the marketplace are display dimensions. CRT monitors were being overtaken by flat-panel displays with bigger screens of 15" and 17" by the early 2000s.

d. **Process acceleration cards:** The number of companies making 3D computer graphics accelerator cards for personal computers has shot through the roof. The efficiency of such cards (as of September 1996) varies from 500,000 to 2,000,000 polygons per second, and their price varies broadly from $300 to $20,000 (and performance does not always fit price!).

It was acknowledged to avoid purchasing 3D graphics accelerator cards too soon. In an attempt to get personal computers to conduct "perfectly," NASA VR research teams are cooperating with numerous 3D accelerator businesses. With more affordable hardware, Silicon Graphics' "new" desktop variants of its graphics powerhouses may expedite the advancement of virtual reality.

Furthermore, there seem to be countless makers of 3D sound cards. Such sound cards let users consider giving a few (1–4) independent sound sources a mildly accurate idea of location, but even the ultimate is yet to come. The introduction of VRML 2.0 on the Internet has made 3D sounds a necessity.

Remember

In accordance with the place and orientation of the mechanical arm's joints, the computer would then create a suitable situation (Aukstakalnis & Blatner, 1992). A BOOM screen could indeed help to resolve a few of those issues that come with HMDs. Unlike with an HMD, the user is not obligated to wear a BOOM screen.

2.3.2. Components of Software

The four sub-components of the software are 3D modeling software, 2D graphics software, digital sound editing software, and VR simulation software.

a. **3D modeling software**

3D modeling software is applied to build the geometric features of virtual world objects and stipulates their visual features.

b. **2D graphics software**

To apply texture to objects and improve their visual elements, 2D graphics software is being used.

c. **Software for editing digital sound**

To combine and modify the sounds that virtual world objects create, digital sound editing software is often used.

d. **VR simulation software**

The elements are combined using simulation software. It is utilized to establish the guidelines that the digital world strictly adheres to and program how all these objects act.

TIPS

By the mid-1990s, 15" and 17" VDU screen sizes became more common, with some 20" screen sizes starting to emerge on the market

2.4. VIRTUAL REALITY SYSTEM CLASSIFICATION

VR can be separated into three categories:

1. non-immersive virtual reality systems;
2. semi-immersive virtual reality systems; and
3. VR systems that are fully immersive (immersive).

Levels of VR and VR methodology are two additional classified categories. The development of VR technology is discussed in terms of levels. Users have entry level, basic level, advanced level, immersive systems, as well as big-time systems under such a categorization. The techniques used to create VR systems are covered in the categorization of VR systems. This category includes systems that rely on simulation, projectors, avatars, and desktops.

2.4.1. Non-Immersive VR Systems

The least immersive application of VR technology is called a non-immersive system, as the title suggests. By utilizing a regular high-resolution screen on the desktop computer, the virtual environment is accessed through a portal or window. Traditional input devices like keyboards, mouse, and trackball mouse can be employed to communicate with the virtual world, but 3D interaction tools like a SpaceBall or DataGlove are also advantageous.

The non-immersive system has economic benefits in that it is compatible with high-end PC clones and does not need the most advanced graphic fidelity hardware or efficiency. The above suggests that such processes could be considered to be the most flexible and cheapest available VR solution. Even so, due to their minimal price, such processes will constantly be surpassed by much more powerful systems, provide a minimal to no experience of immersion, and are rather constricted by the abilities of 2D interaction devices right now. Moreover, such processes are not very beneficial in situations in which the perspective of level is essential. But in the coming years, some may predict a rise in the prominence of these VR devices. This is because it is anticipated that perhaps the Virtual Reality Modeling Reality Language (VRML) will emerge as the de-facto norm for the online transfer of 3D model data and virtual worlds. As compared to several patented technologies for VR authoring tools, VRML continues to run comparatively efficiently on a personal computer, which is beneficial for desktop computer users. Moreover, a number of manufacturers of professional VR applications are now adding VRML support to their products and investigating the potential revenue streams from desktop VR in general.

KEYWORD

VRML is a standard file format for representing 3-dimensional interactive vector graphics, designed particularly with the World Wide Web in mind. It has been superseded by X3D.

2.4.2. Semi-Immersive VR Systems

As a comparatively recent application of virtual reality technology, semi-immersive systems strongly sketch inventions created within the field of flight simulation.

A semi-immersive system will consist of a fairly strong graphics processor that may be paired with any one of the following:

1. a large-screen television;
2. a projector system with a large screen; and
3. a number of projection televisions.

All such projection technologies have many similarities with IMAX cinemas. The above systems boost the user's sense of being present or involved by utilizing a large field of vision. Even so, the projected picture's quality plays a crucial role.

To avoid distortions, it is essential to line up the geometric features of the projected picture with the curves of the display. Likewise, the resolution will impact the appearance of the textures, colors, the capability of defining shapes, as well as the user's capability of reading text on-screen. The resolutions of projection systems vary from 1000 to 3000 lines, and yet various, more costly projection systems might well be needed to ensure the highest level.

And hence, particularly in comparison to non-systems, semi-immersive systems create a wider sense of awareness and a deeper understanding of level. Furthermore, photos that have a substantially higher resolution than some of those generated by HMDs could be supplied, and so this application enables information exchange of the virtual experience. Even though head-mounted immersive systems would not make it possible for simultaneous VE experiences, this could be incredibly advantageous in an educational setting. Besides this, three-dimensional imagery could be accomplished, utilizing some form of shuttered glasses in synchronism with the image processing system.

KEYWORD

BOOM is "a small box containing two CRT monitors that can be viewed through the eye holes."

2.4.3. Immersive (Fully Immersive) VR Systems

The most direct experience of virtual environments is provided by fully immersive VR systems. These systems are probably the most widely known VR implementation where the user either wears an HMD or uses some form of head-coupled display such as a Binocular Omni-Orientation Monitor or BOOM (Bolas, 1994).

An HMD uses small monitors placed in front of each eye which can provide stereo, bi-ocular or monocular images. Stereo images are provided in a similar way to shutter glasses, in that a slightly different image is presented to each eye.

The major difference is that the two screens are placed very close (50–70mm) to the eye, although the image, which the wearer focuses on, will be much further away because of the HMD optical system. Bi-ocular images can be provided by displaying identical images on each screen and monocular images by using only one display screen.

The most commonly used displays are small Liquid Crystal Display (LCD) panels but more expensive HMDs use Cathode Ray Tubes (CRT) which increase the resolution of the image. The HMD design may partially or fully exclude the user's view of the real world and enhances the field of view of the computer-generated world. The advantage of this method is that the user is provided with a 360°; field of regard meaning that the user will receive a visual image if they turn their head to look in ANY direction.

All fully immersive systems will give a sense of presence that cannot be equaled by the other approaches discussed earlier, but the sense of immersion depends of several parameters including the field of view of the HMD, the resolution, the update rate, and contrast and illumination of the display.

Fully immersive VR systems tend to be the most demanding in terms of the computing power and level of technology (and consequently cost!) required achieving a satisfactory level of realism and development is constantly underway to improve the technologies. Major areas of research and development include field of view vs. resolution trade-offs, reducing the size and weight of HMDs and reducing system lag times (Figure 2.2).

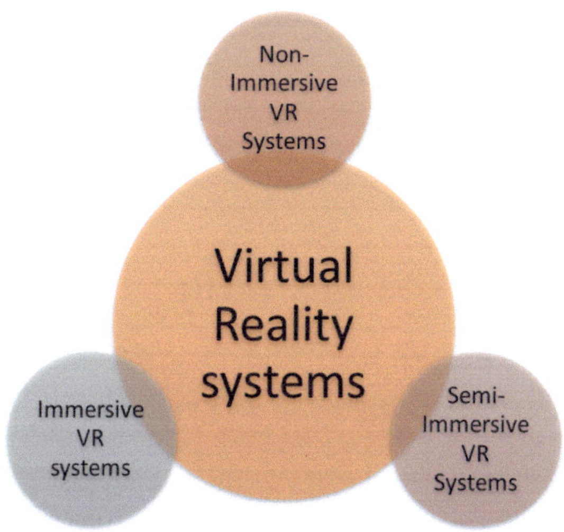

Figure 2.2. Virtual reality system.

2.5. LOW-COST VR TECHNOLOGY

Low-cost VR, also called personal computer (PC)-based VR, uses inexpensive devices such as PC workstations and VR glasses, combined with VR-enabled software applications or play stations and projectors, to partially immerse viewers in a virtual scene (Fang et al., n.d.). A low-cost VR system developed with three play stations, a network switch and two projectors.

The benefits of low-cost virtual reality hardware are obvious; high performance systems which were previously exclusive to research institutions with well-funded budget can now be constructed relatively cheaper. The reduced price/performance ratio has positive implications for hospitals, educational institutions, museums and other organizations where funding of new technologies is often limited.

Previously disadvantaged communities can also benefit from this new technology. In education, cheap VR can provide massive quality education through the interactive learning environment; in medicine, cheap virtual environment has been shown to provide promising results in the field of exposure therapy (Fang et al., n.d.).

KEYWORD

Self paced learning is a style of instruction in which learners progress through the material at their own speed and on their own schedule.

2.6. VR DEVELOPMENT TOOLS AND RESOURCES

There are many VR development tools and resources. Some of these tools and resources are free (open source to use), some are proprietary (closed source) (Wang & Canon, 1996). VR related development is in progress regarding the availability, usability and capability of customization for existing development tools and resources. VR development tools and resources are quite numerous; some examples are presented.

2.6.1. Virtual Heroes Inc. (VHI)

This is an "Advanced Learning Technology Company" that creates collaborative interactive learning solutions for Federal Systems, Healthcare and Corporate Training markets. VHI applications facilitate highly interactive, self-paced learning and instructor-led, distributed team training on its Advanced Learning Technology (ALT) platform. Major components of this platform include the Unreal by Epic Games, and Dynamic Virtual Human Technology (DVHT).

ALT leverages simulation learning and digital game-based learning paradigms to accelerate learning, increase proficiency and reduce costs. DVHT combines best-in-class electronic computer game technology with a digital human physiology engine, digital pharmacokinetic drug models, accurate biomechanical parameters and artificial intelligence subroutines for the most realistic virtual humans available anywhere.

2.6.2. Online Interactive Virtual Environment (OLIVE)

This is a product of Forterra Systems Inc., which builds and distributes virtual world technology and turnkey applications for defense, homeland security, medical, corporate training, and entertainment industries. Using the Online Interactive Virtual Environment (OLIVE) technology platform, customers can rapidly generate realistic three-dimensional virtual environments that easily scale from single user applications to large scale simulated environments supporting many thousands of concurrent users.

Fonterra's technology and services enable organizations to train, plan, rehearse, and collaborate in ways previously considered impossible or impractical. OLIVE combines multimedia, scalable computing and network enabled connectivity to provide a complete IT-ready platform for developing and supporting truly collaborative, multiplayer interactive virtual environments. It is a 3D client-server virtual world platform using PC clients connected to a central server via a network.

The architecture scales from a Windows based development environment to large scale Linux clusters. This architecture supports many thousands of concurrent, geographically distributed users.

KEYWORD

Corporate training is a set of educational activities provided to employees, typically free of cost.

2.6.3. Icarus Studios Inc.

The company offers tools and products for creating massively multi-player online (MMO) environments, virtual worlds, and serious games for major entertainment, corporate, and government clients. Icarus provides next generation technology, tools and production services enabling publishers and marketers to develop immersive environments to create new revenue streams and branding opportunities. Icarus Studios products include compatibility with industry standard tools such as 3D Max, Collada, and other 3D applications with simple editors.

2.6.4. Open Simulator (Open Sim)

Open Simulator is a 3D application server. It can be used to create a virtual environment (world) which can be accessed through a variety of clients, on multiple protocols. Open Simulator allows you to develop your environment using technologies you feel work best. Open Simulator has numerous advantages which among other things are:

- Open Simulator is released under BSD license, making it both open source, and commercially friendly to embed in products.
- It has many tools for developers to build various applications (chat application, buildings, and avatars among others).
- Open Simulator can be extended via modules to build completely custom configuration.
- It is a world building tools for creating content real time in the environment.
- Supports many programming languages for application development such as Linden Scripting Language/Open Simulator Scripting Language (LSL/OSSL), C#, and/or Jscript and VB.NET
- It incorporates rich and handy documentations and tutorials.

KEYWORD

HyperText Markup Language or HTML is the standard markup language for documents designed to be displayed in a web browser.

2.6.5. Croquet

Croquet is an open-source 3D graphical platform that is used by experienced software developers to create and deploy deeply collaborative multi-user online virtual world applications on and across multiple operating systems and devices. Croquet is a next generation virtual operating system (OS) written in Squeak. Squeak is a modern variant of Smalltalk.

Squeak runs mathematically identical on all machines. Croquet system features a peer-based messaging protocol that dramatically reduces the need for server infrastructures to support virtual world deployment and makes it easy for software developers to create deeply collaborative applications. Croquet provides rich tutorials, resources and videos as educational materials for developers.

2.6.6. Ogoglio

Ogoglio is an open-source 3D graphical platform like Croquet. The main goal of the Ogoglio is to build an online urban style space for creative collaboration. Ogoglio platform is built from the languages and protocols of the web. Therefore, its scripting language is java script; its main data transfer protocol is hypertext transfer protocol (HTTP), its 2D layout is hypertext markup language (HTML) and cascading style sheet (CSS), and it has light wave object geometry format for its 3D. Ogoglio is very different from the other virtual reality world development platforms because it uses Windows, Linux, Solaris operating system platforms and runs on web browsers such as Internet Explorer, Firefox, and Safari.

2.6.7. QuickDraw 3D (QD3D)

QuickDraw 3D is a 3D graphics API developed by Apple Inc. in 1995. It was delivered as a cross-platform system, though originally developed for their Macintosh computers. QD3D provides a high-level API with a rich set of 3D primitives that is generally much fuller featured and easier to develop than low-level APIs such as OpenGL or Direct3D.

2.6.8. Autodesk 3d Max (3D Studio MAX)

Autodesk 3d Max (formerly known as 3D Studio MAX) is a modeling, animation and rendering package developed by Autodesk Media and entertainment. 3d Max is the third most widely-used off the shelf 3D animation program by content creation professionals.

It has strong modeling capabilities, a flexible plug-in architecture and a long heritage on the Microsoft Windows platform. It is mostly used by video game developers, television commercial studios and architectural visualization studios. It is also used for movie effects and movie pre-visualization.

TIPS

The most direct experience of virtual environments is provided by fully immersive VR systems. These systems are probably the most widely known VR implementation

2.7. APPLICATIONS AND DEVELOPMENTS IN VR TECHNOLOGY

Virtual reality technology has many uses and recent developments. Virtual reality (VR) is being employed in all aspects of human endeavor, and numerous applications have now been created for production, education, simulation, layout assessment (virtual prototyping), architecture and design overviews, intuitive research, simulating building and maintenance procedures, assisting the disabled, investigating and treating irrational fears (such as a fear of heights), enjoyment, and rapid prototyping (Onyesolu, 2006).

Because of VR's ability to move users to imaginary worlds and offer people the assumption that they too are actually there, it's now entirely feasible (Wittenberg, 1993). VR has been demonstrated to be a valuable tool in the workplace for employees to analyzes new products. BMW researched VR's potential for validating design concepts in 1999 (Gomes de Sa & Zachmann, 1999).

They reached the conclusion that VR does have the ability to minimize the range of physical illustration opportunities to enable overall product performance and to quickly and accurately get responses during the concept stage of the product. Furthermore, Motorola built an electronic reality training program for employees to function as a walkie-talkie production line (Wittenberg, 1995). They observed that virtual reality (VR) can also be used to efficiently coach production staff and that attendees who undertake VR training outperform all who undertake the same training in real-world environments.

KEYWORD

Merchandise is products that are bought, sold, or traded. Several stores have reported running out of merchandise.

Merchandise Vision and Galileo, two VR software programs created by GE Corporate Research in 1998, authorized technologists to communicate with a simulated jet engine (Abs hire, & Barron, 1998). The two applications were effectively utilized, as per their study, to improve layout interaction and find servicing issues beforehand with minimal price, delays and effort.

Additionally, they mentioned that wanting to make upkeep a crucial aspect of their product design process was made possible due to the VR applications. Accomplishments from the field prove the requirement for VR-savvy experts in the current and future. Even so, the majority of learners presently are not given access to virtual reality technology when they are at school.

Consequently, it is crucial to incorporate VR into the layout and visual curriculum content in order to keep up with the evolving requirements of the industry. Boeing, the world's biggest aerospace company, created the Virtual Space Experiment (VSX). VSX serves as an illustration of how virtual world devices can be employed to create complex systems involving human interactions, like aircraft (Kalawsky, 1993).

It is an interactive three-dimensional virtual prototype of a fully adjustable aero plane's exterior and interior which lets users interact with different parts, like the freight ramp and upkeep hatch. A Requirement 100 VPX system is being used by McDonnell Douglas to investigate the efficacy of a simulated space in the creation of brand-new types of engines.

The system is being used to examine how electric motors are added to and removed from systems,—in particular to search for possible interfaces with some other hardware. Beginning with car creation and construction, the auto sector is utilizing Virtual reality technology. A unique type of automobile could undergo a number of development phases before its final production model is prepared to leave the production plant, which might take two years or more.

To enhance the adaptability of passive robot checking, the point-and-direct (VR-PAD) system was designed (Wang & Cannon, 1996). A controller in a remote-control room utilizes the simulated clamp to signify ideal picking and putting places whilst also keeping an eye on the actual work environment through live stream views that are visible on the monitor. To allow the software to detect faults, the machine in the inspection program accomplishes material management as required.

CERN, the European Research Facility for Particle Physics, conducted a pilot program to analyze and encourage the application of virtual world technology to support the design, construction, and maintenance of the Large Hedron Collider (LHC) equipment and facilities (Balaguer & Gennaro, 1996).

In order to address the requirements of LHC engineers, the project includes a variety of application areas, which include network design and integration, territory impact research, and assembly control and management.

Considering that individuals understand pictures far more rapidly than they understand text lines or articles of figures, VR technology is a beneficial educational tool. Virtual reality creates immersive, multiple-sensory environments that involve learners and assist them in visualizing data (Eslinger, 1993). VR has been applied by math and science educators to specify abstract spatial information.

VR was adopted by Winn and Bricken (1992) to assist learners in learning basic algebra. To communicate algebraic ideas and engage with spatial depictions in a virtual world, they used three-dimensional space. Based on the analyzes of their studies, VR has the power to drastically increase students' understanding of math.

VR was implemented in the algebra and geometrical curricula by Haufmann et al. (2000), notably in the teaching of vector analysis and descriptive geometry. All ten respondents to the research study (students) classed virtual reality as a very great research facility for experiments and expressed a wish to use it once more, based on the results of their study.

KEYWORD

Descriptive geometry is the branch of geometry which allows the representation of three-dimensional objects in two dimensions by using a specific set of procedures.

Additionally, learners felt that viewing a 3D world in VR instead of on a flat screen was relatively simple. Bell (1996) and Bell & Fogler (1998) used virtual reality to illustrate molecular mechanisms in chemical engineering disciplines.

Although no statistical analysis was presented, a few proofs of improved education in certain instances have been mentioned. To educate children about catalyst decay, non-isothermal impacts in kinetics, reactor design, and chemical factory security at the University of Michigan, the Synthetic Engineering Team created Vicher (Virtual Chemical Reactors) (Bell & Fogler, 1996a, 1996b).

KEYWORD

Educational Technology is the field of study that investigates the process of analyzing, designing, developing, implementing, and evaluating the instructional environment, learning materials, learners, and the learning process in order to improve teaching and learning.

The founders assumed that when individuals fully engage in teaching methods, close to 90% of it is managed to retain. The use of VR in the learning of the disabled provides some of the most intriguing possible applications for this educational technology.

In order to further investigate the effectiveness of VR in engineering degrees, Sulbaran and Baker (2000) developed an online teaching method. Participants were instructed about how to operate a lock and recognize heavy machinery utilizing VR technology.

In contrast to reading literature and listening to presentations that used overheads with visuals or images, they discovered that 82% of students found training with VR to be significantly captivating. In addition, they observed that 69% of students learn through observation that they had managed to learn how a lock tends to work and 57% continued to believe they had learnt how and where to recognize heavy machinery after conducting their initial survey. 92% of the trainees were still allowed to use a lock and recognize construction equipment 7 to 21 days later). Last but not least, 91% of respondents in their second report were of the opinion that using VR enhances the learning process.

By omitting the requirement for physical renders, virtual reality software guarantees to drastically shorten the duration of the product development process (Vince, 1995). A VR system for determining the viability of method setup in automobiles was created by Ford's Alpha concurrent engineering group.

Consumers insert the architectural design of their home kitchen at the Matsushita shop in Japan to build a virtual replica of it (Newquist III, 1993). Consumers can set up kitchen cupboards and equipment, modify the color schemes and dimensions, and view how their entire kitchen would look prior to putting a single thing into place. Mike Rosen and Affiliates have been aiding its construction industry customers with layout, visualization, advertising, and sales that use interactive and simulated virtual reality technology (Neil, 1996).

Consumers can participate fully in the interpretation stage using the applications by instantaneously modifying the color schemes, textures, materials, lighting, and furniture. A virtual physics research lab that facilitates students to examine suggestions like gravity, friction, and dragging in an engaging virtual world has been created by scientists at NASA Johnson Space Center in Texas for high school learners.

Students can experiment with a pendulum as well as several balls. Furthermore, they get a number of research equipment, including an electronic countdown clock and distance measurement equipment. The computer also offers a variety of fascinating characteristics, like the capability to see dynamic events in slow motion or to display trails on things to more simply demonstrating their movement patterns (Dedula, 1997).

2.8. VIRTUAL RENDERING SYSTEM

VRS is an object-oriented, scene graph-based 3D computer graphics system written in C++, which provides numerous building blocks for composing 3D scenes, animated 3D objects, and 3D interaction. VRS concentrates on OpenGL for real-time rendering and supports advanced rendering techniques such as multi pass algorithms for global illumination.

In addition, VRS wraps and supports various other 3D rendering libraries, e.g., the Render Man, the global illumination system Radiance and also ray tracing renderers such as POVRay. Since VRS completely encapsulates low-level 3D rendering systems through a uniform interface, applications can switch between different rendering systems at runtime without any need for reimplementing the application.

Low-level code specific to a rendering system can be integrated into VRS source code; but this low-level code causes loss of flexibility of the rendering system. In interior design prototyping, for instance, a modeled scene can be rendered for interactive exploration and sound propagation using OpenGL and an arbitrary spatial sound library.

Did you Know?

It is an interactive three-dimensional virtual prototype of a fully adjustable aero plane's exterior and interior which lets users interact with different parts, like the freight ramp and upkeep hatch.

Rendering the scene with Radiance can simulate interior light dispersion, while an additional photorealistic impression of this room can be achieved using the POVRay interface. Applications based on other graphics systems need a reimplementation to switch to another rendering system.

VRS is available for most common platforms such as Windows, Linux, UNIX, and Mac OS. All major user interface systems such as Qt, X11, wxWidgets, Tcl/Tk, and GTK+ are incorporated.

KEYWORD

Runtime debugging involves inspecting the state of a running application, potentially pausing execution at certain points so that the contents of variables in memory can be inspected.

VRS is designed to support rapid development of interactive 3D applications. Furthermore, it also serves as a framework and test bed for application-specific and experimental rendering, and design of innovative interaction techniques. For run-time debugging, developers can use the Tcl/Tk package interactive VRS (iVRS), which is intended as a rapid prototyping graphics environment. IVRS provides access to almost all features of VRS through the scripting language without the need of compiling the source code of the application.

2.9. THE IMPACT OF VIRTUAL REALITY TECHNOLOGY ON HUMAN LIVES

Virtual reality seems to be the next big thing after the advent of internet. This is because it has virtually changed the way business is done with its numerous applications. It is like every top app development companies keeps thinking of new ways to apply the VR technology with their apps. Here are some important applications of virtual reality.

2.9.1. Pilot Training

The oldest application of virtual reality is on pilot training. Before any new pilot is allowed to fly a real plane, he has to be tested on simulation first. He can only fly a real plane if he passes the simulation test. This is why every aviation school has its VR app development company.

The simulation is designed in such a way that it looks so real and a student will feel like he is flying a real plane. As mentioned earlier, it is one of the oldest applications of virtual application.

2.9.2. Medical Application

Nowadays surgeons, make use of virtual artificial to check through a patient's body so that he can determine exactly where tumors are located and he can also determine how best to reach all of them. Every big healthcare provider now works with a VR app development company to develop different medical VR apps.

For example, an experienced VR app development company developed an app for virtual reality therapy. This app has been very useful in the medical field. It can be used for people that have certain phobias. These people are made to face their phobias head-on so that they can get over it and begin to live a normal life.

Virtual reality therapy can also be used to treat people with mental issues by creating soothing environments and simulations. A lot of marines and soldiers have to cope with PTSD when they get back from battlefields. Virtual reality therapy can be used to treat them. They will be exposed to different battlefield scenarios to help them get over the stress and begin to lead a normal live.

There are several medical VR apps that are used to teach student surgeons on how to carry out operations. In fact, every medical VR app development company knows how to design apps that will simulate an operation. So, a student can only be allowed to handle a real operation if he performs well in the simulation (Figure 2.3).

Source: Image by Flickr.

KEYWORD

Virtual reality therapy is not the same as teletherapy, or talking to a therapist over video instead of commuting to their office.

2.9.3. Watching of Movies

A lot of cinemas now distribute VR headsets to viewers before watching a movie. Movies are so real and engaging when viewed through VR headsets. To make the whole movie immersive, some cinemas install hefty speakers in different parts of the cinema hall. So, with the speakers and the view offered by the headsets collectively give a very immersive experience.

In fact, it makes you feel like you are part of the movie. This is the main reason scary movies are 5 times scarier when viewed on a VR platform. Apart from fear, the anxiety and suspense will also double on VR platforms.

One little challenge with watching a movie via VR headsets is addiction. Once you get used to watching movies through the VR headsets, you will have problems watching movies on conventional TV sets as they will seem boring. Remember, with VR, you will "participate" in the movie. This is why there are two major kinds of cinemas now: the ones that have adopted virtual reality and the ones that are being run out of business (Figure 2.4).

TIPS

In 1998, GE Corporate Research developed two VR software applications, Product Vision and Galileo, which allowed engineers to interactively fly through a virtual jet engine

Figure 2.4. Boy wearing a black and white virtual reality goggles.

Source: Image by Pexels.

2.9.4. In the Automobile World

Virtually every automobile manufacturing company now has its own VR app development company. With the virtual reality technology, 3-D images of the prototype of a proposed car can be viewed and assessed by all concerned automobile engineers before the physical car is manufactured.

This technology allows them to assess the engine, the exterior and even the interior so they can make their recommendations before the car is manufactured. This is more convenient and cheaper than having to manufacture a prototype before corrections are made.

Ford is said to be the first automobile manufacturing company to apply the technology. Toyota followed suit and several other manufacturing companies have joined the bandwagon.

2.9.5. In Military Training

Virtual reality is now being applied to military training. This is cheaper, more convenient, and it also makes learning more entertaining. Several battlefield scenarios can be simulated on virtual reality platforms and soldiers are trained on how to handle each situation.

The training has become more effective because every battlefield scenario can be simulated. Over the years, soldiers that were trained with virtual reality applications have been compared with their counterparts that received physical training. And it was found out that both categories of soldiers have been performing equally (Figure 2.5).

Figure 2.5. Soldier in VR headset touching virtual screen for simulation training military technology.

Source: Image by Flickr.

2.9.6. In Video Games

Video games are much more interesting when played via a virtual reality platform. It is more engaging and much more immersive and most of all, it is more compelling and addictive. The games you have on your device can never give you as much fun as you will encounter on VR games. This is why a lot of people still prefer to go to game houses when they have more than five games on their device.

Apart from video games, there are several ways virtual reality can be used for entertainment. Universal Studios provides unlimited fun with their virtual tour rides. Some scenes in the ride require VR headsets while many others do not.

KEYWORD

Uploading refers to transmitting data from one computer system to another through means of a network.

2.9.7. In Museums

Some museums have uploaded their collection of items on different virtual reality platforms. All you need is to have both VR headset and access to any of the platforms. You will be able to access the museums from the comfort of your home at any time of the day. This is nothing but real convenience.

Even if you are in another continent, you can still access the museum. Imagine how much time and cost you will save by accessing a museum from your VR headset. Right now, only a few museums have uploaded their collections on VR platforms, but several others are working on uploading theirs too. For instance, British Museum in London recently uploaded its collections and it also launched a virtual tour of the museum. American Museum of Natural History has also uploaded its collections too.

2.10. THE FUTURE OF VIRTUAL REALITY

Virtual Reality is one of the technologies with the highest projected potential for growth. According to the latest forecasts from IDC Research (2018), investment in VR and AR will multiply 21-fold over the next four years, reaching 15.5 billion Euros by 2022. In addition, both technologies will be key to companies' digital transformation plans and their spending in this area will exceed that of the consumer sector by 2019. It is, therefore expected that by 2020 over half of the larger European companies will have a VR and RA strategy.

Nowadays, the market is demanding applications that go beyond leisure, tourism or marketing and are more affordable for users. Virtual interfaces also need to be improved to avoid defects such as clipping, which makes certain solid objects appear as though they can be passed through. Or to minimize the effects that VR produces in people, among them motion sickness, which consists of a dizziness induced by the mismatch between the movement of our body and what is being seen in the virtual world.

The big technology companies are already working to develop headsets that do not need cables and that allow images to be seen in HD. They are developing Virtual Reality headsets in 8K and with much more powerful processors. There is even talk that in the next few years they could integrate Artificial Intelligence. The latest 5G standard can also provide very interesting scenarios for the evolution of VR. This standard will allow more devices and large user communities to be connected. In addition, it's almost imperceptible latency will make it possible for consumers to receive images in real time, almost as if they were seeing them with their own eyes.

This entire means that Virtual Reality is no longer science fiction. It is integrated into our present and, in the coming years; it will lead to advances that will shape the future.

ACTIVITY 2.1.

Google Expeditions is a free app that enables your students to go on an array of adventures outside the classroom. How far outside the classroom is up to you.

2.11. SUMMARY

1. Definition and nature of virtual reality

In this chapter, the concept of Virtual Reality (VR) has been discussed. It also discussed about the history of virtual reality which includes VR development in various timeframes such as VR development in 1930s, VR development in 1960s, VR development in 1990s, VR development in 2014s,

2. Virtual reality system classification and its components

This chapter provide highlights on the components of virtual reality such as component of hardware, and components of software. It also explains about the different virtual reality system classification which consists non – immersive VR systems, semi – immersive VR systems, and immersive VR systems.

3. Relation of VR development tools and resources

In this chapter, different virtual reality development tools and resources such as virtual heroes Inc. (VHI), Icarus Studio Inc., Open simulator, Croquet, Ogoglio, Quick Draw 3D, and Autodesk 3D Max (3D studio MAX) have been discussed.

4. Impact of VR on human lives

Towards the end of the chapter, it discusses about the applications of the virtual reality technology on the life of humans such as pilot training, medical application, military training, video games, travel and hospitality, museums, and so on.

2.12. REVIEW QUESTIONS

1. What do you understand by virtual reality?
2. Explain the history of virtual reality.
3. What is the main purpose of virtual reality?
4. What are three types of virtual reality?
5. Explain the Pros and Cons of virtual reality.
6. What are the different components of virtual reality?
7. What are the advantages of virtual reality?
8. What are examples of virtual reality in everyday life?

2.13. MULTIPLE CHOICE QUESTIONS

1. VR stands for.

a. Video Recorder

b. Video Read

c. Virtual Reality

d. Virtual Record

2. **BOOM stands for**

a. Binocular Omni-Operating Monitor

b. Binocular Omni-Orientation Monitor

c. Binocular Optical-Orientation Monitor Disk

d. Binocular Optical-Orientation Memory Disk

3. **Open Simulator is a ________ application server**

a. Information

b. Central Processing Unit (CPU)

c. Microcontroller

d. 3D

4. **Whose studies and engineering have generated a range of products for the developing VR sector**

a. Williams

b. Oculus

c. Wang

d. Jaron Lanier

5. **Low-cost VR, also called________?**

a. Abacus

b. Personal Computer

c. Laptop

d. Mobile

Answers to Multiple Choice Questions

1. (c) 2. (b) 3. (d) 4. (d) 5. (b)

REFERENCES

1. Agocg.ac.uk (n.d). *Types of VR System*. [online] Available at: http://www.agocg.ac.uk/reports/virtual/37/chapter2.htm (accessed on 03 March 2023).

2. Benjamin, A., (2022). *A Brief History of Virtual Reality [2021]*. [online] Filmora.wondershare.com. Available at: https://filmora.wondershare.com/virtual-reality/history-of-vr.html (accessed on 03 March 2023).

3. Finextra Research, (2017). *The Impact of Virtual Reality Technology on Human Lives*. [online] Available at: https://www.finextra.com/blogposting/14870/the-impact-of-virtual-reality-technology-on-human-lives (accessed on 03 March 2023).
4. GeeksforGeeks, (n.d). *Virtual Reality – Introduction* – GeeksforGeeks. [online] Available at: https://www.geeksforgeeks.org/virtual-reality-introduction/ (accessed on 03 March 2023).
5. Henry, E. L., (2022). *Virtual Reality | Definition, Development, Technology, Examples, & Facts*. [online] Encyclopedia Britannica. Available at: https://www.britannica.com/technology/virtual-reality (accessed on 03 March 2023).
6. Iberdrola, (n.d). *Virtual Reality, the Technology of the Future* – Iberdrola. [online] Available at: https://www.iberdrola.com/innovation/virtual-reality (accessed on 03 March 2023).
7. Okechukwu, M., & Udoka, F., (2011). Understanding virtual reality technology: Advances and applications. *Advances in Computer Science and Engineering*, [online] Available at: https://www.intechopen.com/chapters/14397 (accessed on 03 March 2023).

CHAPTER 3

BASICS OF COMPUTER ARCHITECTURE

UNIT INTRODUCTION

The technological advancements in the computer sector are also the outcome of a prolonged sequence of massive and efficient attempts undertaken by two powerful factors. These include the academic community, defined by academic research facilities, as well as the business community, defined by computer businesses.

Although it's true to claim that university research facilities were responsible for today's technological developments in the computer field. One must reflect back on the evolution of computers in order to comprehend the latest new technologies in the computing industry. Knowing the determinants influencing computer technology as people recognize it nowadays and attempting to predict its future are the objectives of such a historical overview. Most of the computer systems people use on a regular basis are categorized as general-purpose devices.

These would be computers which can undertake the calculation required by a broad range of applications despite not being designed with any one particular software application in mind. Such devices must be differentiated from all those created to accomplish (be tailored to) particular purposes.

The second group is referred to as special purpose machines. Historically, computer systems have been categorized by their integrations at various tiered abstraction levels, for each level to provide functional assistance for the preceding one.

The application programs, high-level languages, and set of machine instructions are all levels. Different computer structures could be classified depending on how the system's various levels interact with one another. The correlation between such a high-level language and implementation programs is referred to it as language architecture.

The basic machine operating system interacts with the runtime and I/O control as per the guidance set architecture. Four fundamental tenets form the foundation of an alternative meaning of computer architecture. These four factors are performance, organization, structure, and implementation.

In this description, the framework identifies how different hardware parts are joined, the setup procedures how different components interact and are handled proactively, the application recognizes the precise design of hardware devices, and the effectiveness helps to identify how the computer system behaves. Several advanced technologies are debated, such as architectural development as well as designs. A full debate of CPU performance indicators finishes up this chapter's debate.

Learning Objectives

After completing this chapter, you should be able to understand the following:

- Understand the concept of computer architecture
- Educate about the architectural development and styles
- Understand the concept of instructional language
- Educate about the significance of the power and energy trends in integrated circuits
- Understand the performance measures in computer architecture
- Give advice about the importance of computer architecture

Key Terms

- Computer Architecture
- Dumb Machines
- Harvard Architecture
- Instruction Cycle
- Microprocessor
- Translator
- Trends in Power
- Von Neumann

3.1. HISTORICAL CONTEXT

In this segment, the authors want to share a few historical insights into the development of important concepts in the computer sector. Researchers have every reason to believe that the first computer was built in a number of distinct locations.

Researchers also strongly believe that cooperation is essential when generating a computer. As a result, when someone attributes a computer to the name of a specific research scientist, what they really mean is that this research scientist may have carried the league that invented the computer.

KEYWORD

Configuration is an arrangement of a group of things.

And hence, researchers believe it is more correct to refer to the device without directly mentioning it while bringing up the location where it is being used first. One such tactic, in viewpoint, is just and must put an end to every issue involving researchers and their identities. It is correct to conclude that the Z1 was the very first program-controlled (mechanical) computer ever made (1938).

The Z2, the first operations and maintenance program-controlled computer with fixed-point mathematics, arrived after this in 1939. But in the 1940s, Iowa State University's campus was the site of the first recognized university-based effort to build a desktop. A small-scale, special-purpose electronic computer was created by researchers on that campus.

That computer, regrettably, was never fully functional. An entire design for a fully functioning, configurable special device, the Z3, was declared in Germany around the same time in 1941. An application of this configuration seems to have been affected by insufficient funding. According to history, whereas these 2 different endeavors were ongoing, researchers from numerous nations seemed to have the opportunity to acquire first-hand familiarity by visiting the research facilities and organizations where the job was being accomplished.

It is claimed that these first-hand encounters as well as the shared knowledge grant the attendees the ability to begin similar tasks within their own laboratory facilities back home. In regards to general-purpose computers, it is understood that the Electronic Numerical Integrator and Calculator (ENIAC) device was built at the University of Pennsylvania in 1944.

It was the first functional general-purpose vacuum tube device. Throughout World War II, the device was usually fabricated to aid in calculating artillery firing tables. It can be programmed by manually adjusting switches and plugging in cables. The device had limited capacity, restricted programmability, and was slow by today's standards.

Within the same location, an upgraded ENIAC was brought forward. In an endeavor to enhance software entrance and investigate the idea of saved programs, the Electronic Discrete Variable Automatic Computer (EDVAC), an upgraded version of the ENIAC, was created. The EDVAC project did not get finished till 1952.

KEYWORD

Programmability implies that something is capable of following instructions — a capacity that sets the computer apart from other electronic devices.

The IAS machine, which was designed and created in 1946 by research teams at Princeton's Institute for Advanced Study (IAS), was around ten times more efficient than that of the ENIAC. Whereas the EDVAC program was underway in 1946, a comparable initiative was launched at Cambridge University. Construction of the Electronic Delay Storage Automatic Calculator, a stored-program computer, was the project's goal (EDSAC).

The first fully formed, stored-program, perfectly functioning computer was the EDSAC, which made its debut in 1949. A variety of devices were presented at Harvard as an outcome of an EDSAC turn. The MARK I, II, III, and IV series were the components. The latter two devices were the first to use specific memories for both data and instructions.

To signify the usage of distinct memories, these computers were referred to as Harvard Architecture. It must be mentioned that modern computers with independent caches for data and instruction have been alluded to as having Harvard architecture. Nearly halfway through 1951, the Universal Automatic Computer (UNIVAC I), the first general-purpose commercial computer, went on sale.

Especially in comparison to the 1949-built BINAC, it depicted progress. In 1952, IBM launched the IBM 701, which was the company's first computer. The advancement of computers started to slow down beginning in the 1950s. IBM made its debut production line in 1964 under the title "IBM 360 series. A wide range of models in the series was available, with each having a specific price and level of functionality."

This compelled Digital Equipment Corporation (DEC) to start releasing the PDP-8, the very first minicomputer. This one was assumed to be an unbelievably inexpensive device. In 1971, Intel released the Intel 4004, their first microprocessor. In 1977, when the initial Apple computer series was launched, the globe could see the beginning of the initial desktop PC (PC). Likewise, in 1977, DEC uncovered the VAX-11/780 to the world. Following the same path, Intel revealed the 8086 series, the very first of the most well-known microprocessors. The emergence of personal computers in 1977 by manufacturers like Altair, Processor Technology, North Star, Tandy, Commodore, Apple, and several more increased end-user productive capacities in a broad range of fields.

KEYWORD

local area network (LAN) is a group of computers and peripheral devices that share a common communications line or wireless link to a server within a distinct geographic area.

The widespread use of personal computers, including all those made by Compaq, Apple, IBM, Dell, and various other businesses, has quickly modified the computing terrain. Supercomputers were all being developed alongside small-scale devices. Control Data Corporation uncovered the very first supercomputer, the CDC 6600, in 1961. The greatest supercomputer in terms of price/performance was released in 1976 by the Cray Research Centre and is known as the Cray-1. A large number of advertisements for concurrent computers with multiprocessors were presented in the 1980s and 1990s.

They are divided into two categories, broadly speaking:

(1) Distributed memory systems; and
(2) Shared memory systems.

From a few on a shared memory computer to tens of millions in a hugely concurrent system, a single machine could contain any number of processing units. Case studies from such a period of time involve Sequent Symmetry, Intel I PSC, n CUBE, Intel Paragon, Thinking Machines (CM-2, CM-5), MsPar (MP), Fujitsu (VPP500), and a few other parallel computer networks.

The transformation from centralized servers to networked computers is among the most apparent developments in computer technology. Such channels link reasonably priced, powerful and effective desktops and laptops to create unprecedented processing power. By 1990, mainframe computers and minis had been initiated to be supplanted by local-area networks (LAN) of powerful and effective workstations and personal computer systems. In short, large-area networks would tie such personal desktops and laptops to bigger computer science structures (WAN).

The Internet's prevalent usage sparked an interest in network servers and, quite lately, grid computing. The computing platforms known as "grids" are diffused geologically. Exposure to enhanced computer capabilities must be reliable, stable, freely accessible, and fairly priced. This has been adjusted from a table laid out by Lawrence Tesler (1995). Beginning with the 1960s, each decade of computer science is depicted in this table alongside some of the important features of the multiple computational frameworks (Figure 3.1).

Figure 3.1. Computer architecture block diagram.

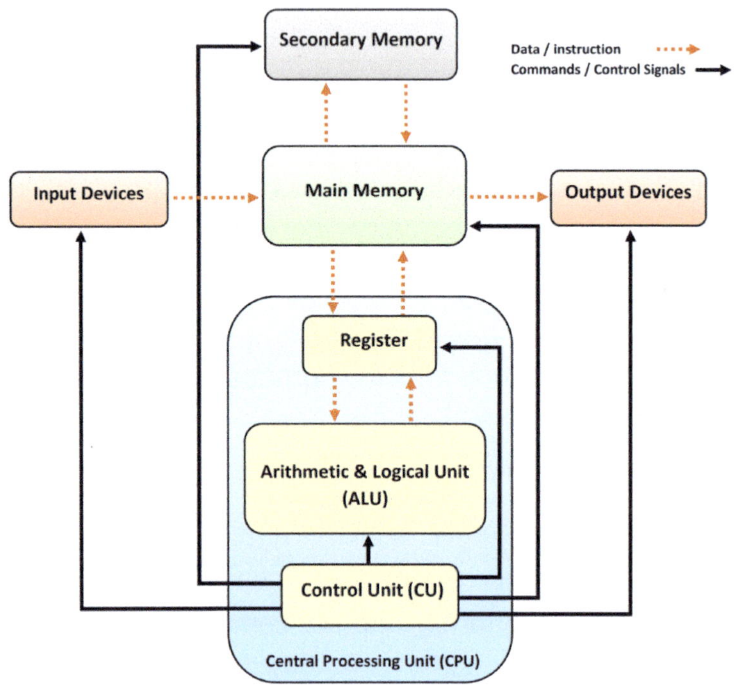

Source: Image by Wikimedia Commons.

TIPS

It was in 1949 that the EDSAC became the world's first full-scale, stored-program, fully operational computer. A spin-off of the EDSAC resulted in a series of machines introduced at Harvard.

3.2. ARCHITECTURAL DEVELOPMENT AND STYLES

Computer architects have always been striving to increase the performance of their architectures. This has taken a number of forms. Among these is the philosophy that by doing more in a single instruction, one can use a smaller number of instructions to perform the same job.

The immediate consequence of this is the need for fewer memory read/write operations and an eventual speedup of operations. It was also argued that increasing the complexity of instructions and the number of addressing modes has the theoretical advantage of reducing the "semantic gap" between the instructions in a high-level language and those in the low-level (machine) language.

A single (machine) instruction to convert several binary coded decimal (BCD) numbers to binary is an example for how complex some instructions were intended to be. The huge number of addressing modes considered (more than 20 in the VAX machine) further adds to the complexity of instructions. Machines following this philosophy have been referred to as complex instructions set computers (CISCs).

Examples of CISC machines include the Intel Pentium TM, the Motorola MC68000TM, and the IBM & Macintosh Power PCTM. It should be noted that as more capabilities were added to their processors, manufacturers realized that it was increasingly difficult to support higher clock rates that would have been possible otherwise.

This is because of the increased complexity of computations within a single clock period. It was also surprising to find out that simple assignment statements constitute almost 50% of those operations.

These findings caused a different philosophy to emerge. This philosophy promotes the optimization of architectures by speeding up those operations that are most frequently used while reducing the instruction complexities and the number of addressing modes. Machines following this philosophy have been referred to as reduced instructions set computers (RISCs). Examples of RISCs include the Sun SPARCTM and MIPSTM machines.

The above two philosophies in architecture design have led to the unresolved controversy as to which architecture style is "best." It should, however, be mentioned that studies have indicated that RISC architectures would indeed lead to faster execution of programs. The majority of contemporary microprocessor chips seems to follow the RISC paradigm. In this book we will present the salient features and examples for both CISC and RISC machines.

Did you Know?

A number of studies from the mid-1970s and early-1980s also identified that in typical programs more than 80% of the instructions executed are those using assignment statements, conditional branching and procedure calls.

3.3. COMPUTERS ARE DUMB MACHINES

Irrespective of the underlying technology, a fundamental concept that we need to understand is that a computer is fundamentally a dumb machine. Unlike our brains, it is not endowed with abstract thought, reason, and conscience. At least at the moment, computers cannot take very sophisticated decisions on their own.

All they can do is execute a program. Nonetheless, the reason computers are so powerful is because they are extremely good at executing programs. They can execute billions of basic instructions per second. This makes them dumb yet very fast.

If we combine the processing power of computers, with intelligent programs written by the human brain, we have the exquisite variety of software available today. Everything from operating systems to word processors to computer games is written this way.

KEYWORD

Monotonicity is an important part of application of derivatives.

Computers are these tireless machines that can keep on doing calculations very quickly without ever complaining about the monotonicity of the work. As compared to computers, our brains are creative, tire easily, and do not like to do the same thing over and over again.

To combine the best of both worlds, our brains need to produce computer programs that specify the set of tasks that need to be performed in great detail. A computer can then process the program, and produce the desired output by following each instruction in the program.

Hence, we can conclude that we should use the creative genius of our brains to write programs. Each program needs to contain a set of basic instructions that a computer can process. Henceforth, a computer can produce the desired output. An instruction is defined as a basic command that can be given to a computer.

3.4. THE INSTRUCTIONAL LANGUAGE

Researchers notice that communicating a computer's language is essential for interaction. A collection of fundamental commands that the computer could indeed fully comprehend make up this language. Calculating the average distance between New Delhi and the North Pole is indeed a command that the computer cannot comprehend as it is not intelligent sufficiently. Nevertheless, it is capable of performing straightforward processes such as adding the two figures.

The very same is applicable to individuals. For instance, it does not make sense to talk to an individual in Russian if the individual only comprehends Spanish. Making arrangements for an interpreter is the obligation of the group that wishes to converse. Correspondingly, it is required to translate conceptual ideas and concepts into simple, machine-understandable commands.

The majority of the time, coders use a high-level language such as C or Java™ to generate their initiatives. The above languages have advanced structures like courses, unions, switch-case remarks, structures, and inheritance. Such ideas are just too challenging for a computer to perceive.

It is therefore essential to run a C or C++ program through a special program named a processor, which can turn it into a series of fundamental commands. The task of writing machine-readable code is essentially taken away from the coder by a developer. Only high-level logic allows the coder to concentrate on the movement of events. The ability to write a program in a high-level language, including C or C++, is the first step. The next step is to assemble it. A program usually contains machine language generated by the developer by using a high-level program as input. Generally, this program is meant to be referred to as a compiled code or binary. Take into account that perhaps the coder is a program created out of simple machine commands.

KEYWORD

Machine language is a low-level language made up of binary numbers or bits that a computer can understand.

Let's continue moving on to the semantic information of commands themselves. The number of foundational and elementary commands which a CPU could assist must be restricted, merely as there are a finite number of words in any language. Usually referred to as the instruction set, the above collection of commands.

In addition, simple arithmetic, multiplication, rational or, and logic not are just a few illustrations of basic instructions. Each instruction must operate on a particular collection of variables and constants prior to actually saving the outcome in a parameter, it should be noted. Such factors are internal aspects of the computer; they are not factors characterized by the coder.

The definition of instruction set architecture that researchers use is The way software comprehends hardware by using the command set architecture.

It may be regarded as the set of basic operations that the hardware reveals to the outside world. It is referred to as the "computer language."

As an illustration, x86 is the instruction set used by Intel and AMD CPUs, PowerPC R is the instruction set used by IBM processors, PA-RISC is the instruction set used by HP processors, and ARM is the instruction set used by ARM processors (or variants of it such as Thumb-1 and Thumb-2). Consequently, it is impossible to execute a binary that was generated for an Intel system on an ARM-based device.

Due to incompatibility, the instruction sets of The C program could, even so, usually be reprocessed. A code generator for that architecture must be bought to properly compile a C program on that architecture.

KEYWORD

Microarchitecture, also called computer organization and sometimes abbreviated as µarch or uarch, is the way a given instruction set architecture is implemented in a particular processor.

3.5. GENUINE COMPUTER ARCHITECTURE: DESIGNING THE ORGANIZATION AND HARDWARE TO MEET GOALS AND FUNCTIONAL REQUIREMENTS

The implementation of a computer has two components: organization and hardware. The term organization includes the high-level aspects of a computer's design, such as the memory system, the memory interconnect, and the design of the internal processor or CPU (central processing unit—where arithmetic, logic, branching, and data transfer are implemented).

The term micro architecture is also used instead of organization. For example, two processors with the same instruction set architectures but different organizations are the AMD Opteron and the Intel Core i7. Both processors implement the x86 instruction set, but they have very different pipeline and cache organizations.

The switch to multiple processors per microprocessor led to the term core to also be used for processor. Instead of saying multiprocessor microprocessor, the term multicore has caught on. Given that virtually all chips have multiple processors, the term central processing unit, or CPU, is fading in popularity.

Hardware refers to the specifics of a computer, including the detailed logic design and the packaging technology of the computer. Often a line of computers contains computers with identical instruction set architectures and nearly identical organizations, but they differ in the detailed hardware implementation.

For example, the Intel Core i7 and the Intel Xeon 7560 are nearly identical but offer different clock rates and different memory systems, making the Xeon 7560 more effective for server computers. In this book, the word architecture covers all three aspects of computer design—instruction set architecture, organization or micro architecture, and hardware.

Computer architects must design a computer to meet functional requirements as well as price, power, performance, and availability goals. Summarizes requirements to consider in designing a new computer. Often, architects also must determine what the functional requirements are, which can be a major task. The requirements may be specific features inspired by the market.

KEYWORD

Software is a set of computer programs and associated documentation and data.

Application software often drives the choice of certain functional requirements by determining how the computer will be used. If a large body of software exists for a certain instruction set architecture, the architect may decide that a new computer should implement an existing instruction set.

The presence of a large market for a particular class of applications might encourage the designers to incorporate requirements that would make the computer competitive in that market. Later chapters examine many of these requirements and features in depth. Architects must also be aware of important trends in both the technology and the use of computers, as such trends affect not only the future cost but also the longevity of an architecture.

3.6. POWER AND ENERGY TRENDS IN INTEGRATED CIRCUITS

Power is currently the most significant problem affecting computer developers in almost all computer science classes. Modern microprocessors use large numbers of connectors and numerous interconnect layers only for power and ground, which is the primary thing that needs to be introduced into and distributed around the chip. Second, the heat produced by power must always be eliminated.

3.6.1. A Systems Perspective on Power and Energy

What are the most appropriate methods for a system architect as well as an operator to consider efficiency, power, and energy? Three major concerns must be considered from the perspective of a system developer. Dynamics in Integrated Circuits Power and energy What is the highest amount of power a CPU has ever required? For effective functioning, it might be crucial to fulfill this requirement. As an illustrative example, if a central processing unit tries to consume more power than what a power supply system could deliver (by consuming more current than even the system could handle), the likeliest scenario is a power loss, which might also lead to the failure of the machine.

Modern computers possess sustained high current flow and a broad range of energy usage; as an outcome, they provide wattage searchable approaches that enable the central processing unit to slow down as well as restrict voltage within a significant margin. There is no question that it reduces efficiency. Secondly, How much sustained power usage is there? Because of its function in evaluating the cooling demand, the above stat is commonly known as the "thermal design power" (TDP).

KEYWORD

Energy consumption is the total amount of energy required for a given process and is measured in kilowatt hours (kWh).

TDP does not represent the average percentage of power consumed during a given calculation, which is likely to be relatively low, nor the maximum power, which is frequently 1.5% higher. An ordinary cooling system is commonly built to meet or surpass the TDP, and a standard power supply is typically customized to surpass the TDP.

Unless appropriate cooling is provided, the heat dissipation in the processing unit would then increase above its highest possible value, breaking down the system and potentially causing lasting damage. Because the peak voltage (and consequently heat and temperature increase) could surpass the long-term average stated by the TDP, modern computers suggest two features that assist in handling heat.

At the start, the circuit board decreases the clock speed to cut off power as the heat temperature comes nears the junction temperature limit value. In the circumstance that such an approach is ineffective, a second heating heavy load trip is stimulated to completely cut the processor off. Energy consumption and energy effectiveness are the third elements that users and developers must take into consideration.

Don't forget that power is just energy conveyed as a measure of time: 1 watt equals 1 joule per second. Is that also a metric—power or energy—suitable for contrasting CPUs? Due to its connection to a particular task as well as the time it takes to accomplish it, power is generally a more appropriate measure. Especially, the electricity required to complete a volume of work is comparable to the average power times the duration of the volume of work.

And hence, users must make a comparison of energy usage (not power) for the task to be completed if it is to decide which of the processor cores is much more effective for an assigned activity. For instance, although CPU A uses 20% more energy on average than CPU B, if A accomplishes the assignment within just 70% of B's time, its energy usage would be 1.2 x 0.7 = 0.84, which is undoubtedly better.

It is incorrect to assert that in a big cloud or server in which the task is regularly obtained to be unlimited, it is acceptable to take average output into account. The volume of effort that our cloud may achieve using the same energy consumption may be reduced if it was made up of CPU B's as compared to A's.

By investing time into evaluating the options available, the above trap is prevented. The ideal method for evaluating CPU options when faced with fixed tasks, whether for a mobile phone or a cloud the size of a storage facility, would be by making comparisons of the power used, which includes both the power bill for the cloud and the battery life for the mobile phone depending on the amount of power used.

When is electricity usage an effective marker? The major legal implementation is a limitation; for example, in this case, a processor may have a 100-watt cap. If the volume of work is continuous, it might be used as a measure, in which case it is simply a distorted version of the actual unit of measure of electricity for every assignment.

KEYWORD

Complementary metal–oxide–semiconductor is a type of metal–oxide–semiconductor field-effect transistor fabrication process that uses complementary and symmetrical pairs of p-type and n-type MOSFETs for logic functions.

3.6.2. Trends in Power and Energy in Integrated Circuits

Switching transistors, also known as dynamic energy, typically consume the majority of the electricity in CMOS chips. The power necessary for each transistor is determined by the device of the capacitor load powered by the transistor and the square of the wattage. The above formula means that the power of the pulse of the logic transition is 010 or 101.

The energy requirement for each transistor is merely the product of the energy of a transition calculated by multiplying by the frequency of transitions. For a set assignment, limiting the pace of the clock speed decreases power, not energy. The voltages have gone down from 5V to less than 1V in the last 20 years due to the evidence that reducing the power output significantly reduces dynamic energy and power consumption.

The innovation also controls the capacitor of the wires as well as the transistors, and the volume of transistors attached to an output decides the voltage level. The number of transistors swapping and the regularity with which they swap outpace the reduction in resistive load and wattage as users progress from one process to the next, resulting in a rise in overall consumption of electricity and power.

A 3.3 GHz Intel Core i7 takes up 130 watts, especially in comparison to the initial microprocessors' usage with less than a watt and around two watts for the oldest 32-bit processors (such as the Intel 80386). Researchers have arrived at the point where a cooling system is no longer an option since this heat must be forced to remove from a chip that measures only 1.5 cm on an edge. Unless researchers can't decrease the power output or boost the ability of each chip, users might predict clock frequency expansion to slow down considering the formula previous section.

KEYWORD

Buffer is a software application for the web and mobile, designed to manage accounts in social networks, by providing the means for a user to schedule posts to Twitter, Facebook, Instagram, Instagram Stories, Pinterest, and LinkedIn, as well as analyze their results and engage with their community.

3.7. INTERRUPTS

Just about all computers offer a path for other components (I/O, memory, etc.) to halt the processor from conducting its routine activities. The primary function of interruptions is to increase processing effectiveness (Figure 3.2).

The user program processes information while also performing a number of WRITE calls. The terms "code segments 1, 2, and 3" designate sets of instructions without I/O. The actual I/O operation would be brought out by the system utility that receives the WRITE calls, which is an I/O program. There seem to be three components in the I/O program:

- To plan for the precise, I/O operating condition, a series of commands, denoted by the number 4 in the statistic, is used. This could involve establishing the settings for a device instruction and duplicating the information to output it into the specific buffer.
- The I/O self-instructs. Once an instruction is given, the software should pause for the I/O machine to carry out all the corresponding tasks in the absence of halts (or periodically poll the device). To check if the I/O action is

finished, the program could perhaps merely consistently run a test procedure.

- A set of commands to complete the process, denoted by the number 5 in the statistic. Creating a marker to imply if the function had been successful or not could be part of all this.

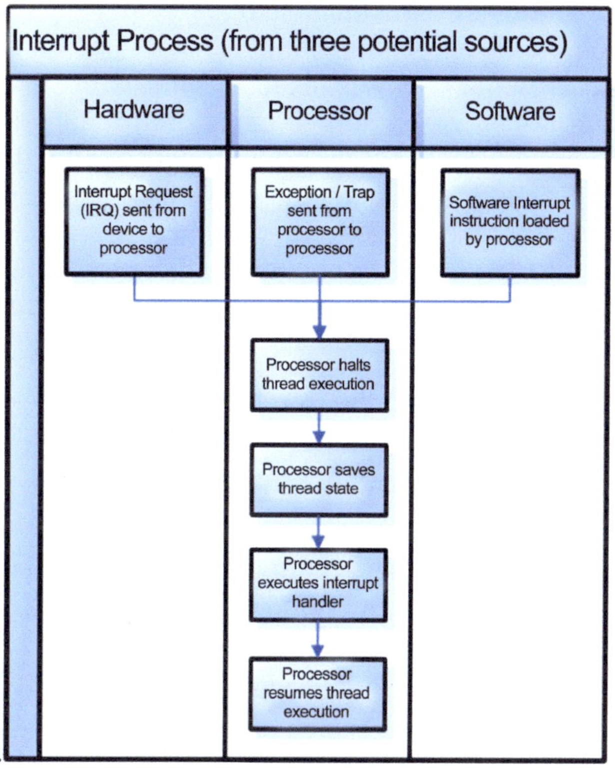

Figure 3.2. Interrupt process.

Source: Image by Wikimedia Commons.

3.7.1. The Instruction Cycle and Interrupts

The Instruction Cycle and Interruptions allow the CPU to work on certain commands whilst an I/O function is currently going on. Recalling the flow of control from previously, the user program ultimately reaches a stage where it issues a WRITE call to the device. Upon completion of these brief commands, regulation is transferred back to the user program.

While this is progressing, the external machine is effectively able to print information that is being acknowledged from memory storage. Simultaneous with the user program's commands being carried out is this I/O function. The I/O module for that external monitor transmits an alert command signal to the CPU whenever the external device is ready to receive further information from it.

When an error occurs, the CPU reacts by preventing the entire program, branching to the interrupt controller program to take care of such a precise I/O machine, and then beginning the initial version again after the machine has been repaired.

In Figure 1.9b, an exclamation mark is placed to signify the facts in which these disruptions happen. An obstruction of a regular implementation sequentially is exactly what it appears like from the user program's viewpoint: it kept interrupting the process. Implementation restarts the interrupt process after the interrupt procedure is finished, as well as the CPU tests to see whether any interruptions have taken place. The CPU moves onto the retrieve cycle and obtains the following commands from the running program if there are no waiting interrupts. When there is an impending interrupt, the CPU seems to do the following procedure:

- It assists in saving the current program's background and pausing its execution.
- It begins a routine that controls interrupts at the program counter's address.

TIPS

There are some interesting non-Von Neumann architectures, such as the massively parallel Connection Machine and the nascent efforts at building biological and quantum computers, or neural networks.

The processor now proceeds to the fetch cycle and fetches the first instruction in the interrupt handler program, which will service the interrupt. When the interrupt handler routine is completed, the processor can resume execution of the user program at the point of interruption.

Which is a timing diagram based on the flow of control indicates this state of affairs. In this case, the user program reaches the second WRITE call before the I/O operation spawned by the first call is complete. The result is that the user program is hung up at that point.

When the preceding I/O operation is completed, this new WRITE call may be processed, and a new I/O operation may be started. The timing for this situation with and without the use of interrupts. We can see that there is still a gain in efficiency because part of the time during which the I/O operation is underway overlaps with the execution of user instructions.

3.7.2. Multiple Interrupts

Multiple interrupts can occur. Two approaches can be taken to dealing with multiple interrupts. The first is to disable interrupts while an interrupt is being processed. A disabled interrupt simply means that the processor can and will ignore that interrupt request signal. Thus, when a user program is executing and an interrupt occurs, interrupts are disabled immediately.

After the interrupt handler routine completes, interrupts are enabled before resuming the user program and the processor checks to see if additional interrupts have occurred. This approach is nice and simple, as interrupts are handled in strict sequential order. The drawback to the preceding approach is that it does not take into account relative priority or time-critical needs a second approach is to define priorities for interrupts and to allow an interrupt of higher priority to cause a lower-priority interrupt handler to be itself interrupted.

> **KEYWORD**
>
> **User program** is a program that must communicate with a resource manager for some or all of its processing.

As an example of this second approach, consider a system with three I/O devices: a printer, a disk, and a communications line, with increasing priorities of 2, 4, and 5, respectively. A user program begins at t = 0. At t = 10, a printer interrupt occurs; user information is placed on the system stack and execution continues at the printer interrupt service routine (ISR).

While this routine is still executing, at t = 15, a communications interrupt occurs. Because the communications line has higher priority than the printer, the interrupt is honored. The printer ISR is interrupted, its state is pushed onto the stack, and execution continues at the communications Erstwhile this routine is executing, a disk interrupt occurs (t = 20).

Because this interrupt is of lower priority, it is simply held, and the communications ISR runs to completion. When the communications ISR is complete (t = 25), the previous processor state is restored, which is the execution of the printer ISR. However, before even a single instruction in that routine can be executed, the processor honors the higher-priority disk interrupt and control transfers to the disk ISR. Only when that routine is complete (t = 35) is the printer ISR resumed. When that routine completes (t = 40), control finally returns to the user program.

3.8. PERFORMANCE MEASURES

In this section, we consider the important issue of assessing the performance of a computer. In particular, we focus our discussion on a number of performance measures that are used to assess computers. Let us admit at the outset that there are various facets to the performance of a computer. For example, a user of a computer measures its performance based on the time taken to execute a given job (program).

KEYWORD

Performance Analysis is a specialised discipline that provides athletes and coaches with objective information that helps them understand performance.

On the other hand, a laboratory engineer measures the performance of his system by the total amount of work done in a given time. While the user considers the program execution time a measure for performance, the laboratory engineer considers the throughput a more important measure for performance.

A metric for assessing the performance of a computer helps comparing alternative designs. Performance analysis should help answering questions such as how fast can a program be executed using a given computer? In order to answer such a question, we need to determine the time taken by a computer to execute a given job.

We define the clock cycle time as the time between two consecutive rising (trailing) edges of a periodic clock signal. Clock cycles allow counting unit computations, because the storage of computation results is synchronized with rising (trailing) clock edges. The time required to execute a job by a computer is often expressed in terms of clock cycles.

We denote the number of CPU clock cycles for executing a job to be the cycle count (CC), the cycle time by CT, and the clock frequency by f ¼ 1/CT. The time taken by the CPU to execute a job can be expressed as CPU time ¼ CC CT ¼ CC = f. It may be easier to count the number of instructions executed in a given program as compared to counting the number of CPU clock cycles needed for executing that program.

Therefore, the average number of clock cycles per instruction (CPI) has been used as an alternate performance measure. The following equation shows how to compute the CPI. CPI ¼ CPU clock cycles for the program Instruction count CPU time ¼ Instruction count CPI Clock cycle time ¼ Instruction count CPI Clock rate. It is known that the instruction set of a given machine consists of a number of instruction categories: ALU (simple assignment and arithmetic and logic instructions), load, store, branch, and so on.

In the case that the CPI for each instruction category is known, the overall CPI can be computed as CPI = Pn i=1 CPIi Ii Instruction count where Ii is the number of times an instruction of type i is executed in the program and CPIi is the average number of clock cycles needed to execute such instruction.

3.9. DESIGN OF PRACTICAL MACHINES

A broad picture of a practical machine has emerged from our discussion. We have summarized the basic structure of such a machine. Let us call this machine as the concept machine. Ideas similar to our concept machine were beginning to circulate in the computer science community after Alan Turing published his research paper proposing the Turing machine in 1936. Several scientists got inspired by his ideas, and started pursuing efforts to design practical machines.

3.9.1. Harvard Architecture

One of the earliest efforts in this direction was the Harvard Mark-I. The Harvard architecture is very similar to our concept machine. Its block diagram there is separate structures for maintaining the instruction table and the memory. The former is also known as instruction memory because we can think of it as a specialized memory tailored to hold only instructions.

The latter holds data values that programs need. Hence, it is known as the data memory. The engine for processing instructions is divided into two parts – control and ALU. The job of the control unit is to fetch instructions, process them, and co-ordinate their execution. ALU stands for arithmetic-logic-unit. It has specialized circuits that can compute arithmetic expressions or logical expressions (AND/OR/NOT, etc.).

Note that every computer needs to take inputs from the user/programmer and needs to finally communicate results back to the programmer. This can be done through a multitude of methods. Today we use a keyboard and monitor. Early computers used a set of switches and the final result was printed out on a piece of paper (Figure 3.3).

KEYWORD

Instruction memory is the memory that instructions are fetched from, and data memory is the memory where the data is written to and read from.

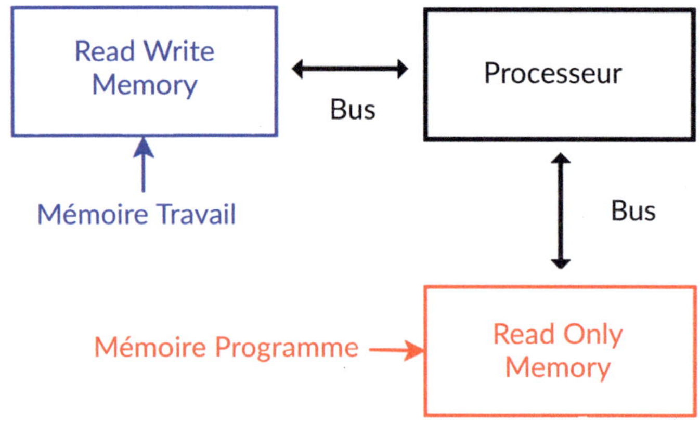

Figure 3.3. Harvard architecture.

Source: Image by Wikimedia Commons.

3.9.2. Von Neumann Architecture

John von Neumann proposed the Von Neumann architecture for general purpose Turing complete computers. Note that there were several other scientists such as John Mauchly and J. Presper Eckert who independently developed similar ideas.

Eckert and Mauchly designed the first general purpose Turing complete computer(with one minor limitation) called ENIAC (Electronic Numerical Integrator and Calculator) based on this architecture in 1946. It was used to compute artillery firing tables for the US army's ballistic research laboratory.

This computer was later succeeded by the EDVAC computer in 1949, which was also used by the US army's ballistics research laboratory. The basic Von Neumann architecture, which is the basis of ENIAC and EDVAC. This is pretty much the same as our concept machine.

The instruction table is saved in memory. The processing engine that is akin to our modified Turing machine is called the CPU (central processing unit). It contains the program counter. Its job is to fetch new instructions, and execute them. It has dedicated functional units to calculate the results of arithmetic functions, load and store values in memory locations, and compute the results of branch instructions. Lastly, like the Harvard architecture, the CPU is connected to the I/O subsystem.

The path breaking innovation in this machine was that the instruction table was stored in memory. It was possible to do so by encoding every instruction with the same set of symbols that are normally stored in memory. For example, if the memory stores decimal values, then each instruction needs to be encoded into a string of decimal digits.

A Von Neumann CPU needs to decode every instruction. The crux of this idea is that instructions are treated as regular data(memory values). We shall see in later chapters that this simple idea is actually a very powerful tool in designing elegant computing systems. This idea is known as the stored program concept.

The stored program concept tremendously simplifies the design of a computer. Since memory data and instructions are conceptually treated the same way, we can have one unified processing system and memory system that treats instructions and data the same way.

From the point of view of the CPU, the program C counterpoints to a generic memory location whose contents will be interpreted as that of an encoded instruction. It is easy to store, modify, and transmit programs. Programs can also dynamically change their behavior during runtime by modifying themselves and even other programs.

This forms the basis of today's complex compilers that convert high level C programs into machine instructions. Furthermore, a lot of modern systems such as the Java virtual machine dynamically modify their instructions to achieve efficiency.

Lastly, astute readers would notice that a Von Neumann machine or a Harvard machine do not have an infinite amount of memory like a Turing machine. Hence, strictly speaking they are not exactly equivalent to a Turing machine. This is true for all practical machines. They need to have finite resources. Nevertheless, the scientific community has learnt to live with this approximation (Figure 3.4).

KEYWORD

Virtual Machine (VM) is a compute resource that uses software instead of a physical computer to run programs and deploy apps.

Figure 3.4. Von Neumann architecture

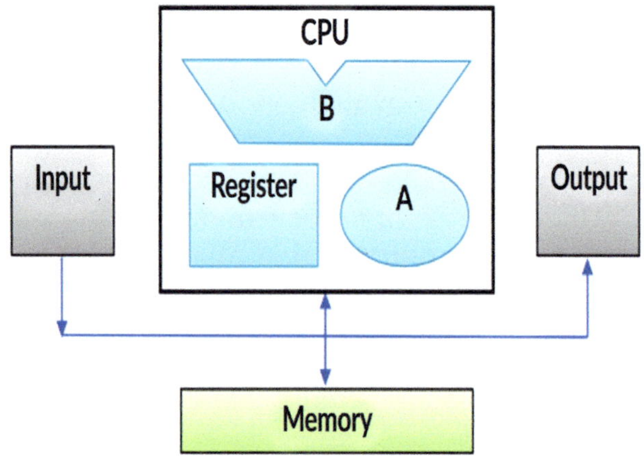

Source: Image by Wikimedia Commons.

3.9.3. Towards a Modern Machine with Registers and Stacks

Many extensions to the basic Von-Neumann machine have been proposed in literature. In fact, this has been a hot field of study for the last half century. We discuss three important variants of Von Neumann machines that augment the basic model with registers, hardware stacks, and accumulators.

The register-based design is by far the most commonly used today. However, some aspects of stack-based machines and accumulators have crept into modern register-based processors also. It would be worthwhile to take a brief look at them before we move on.

3.9.4. Von-Neumann Machine with Registers

The term "register machine" refers to a class of machines that in the most general sense contain an unbounded number of named storage locations called registers. These registers can be accessed randomly, and all instructions use registers names as their operands. The CPU accesses the registers, fetches the operands, and then processes them.

However, in this section, we look at a hybrid class of machines that augment a standard Von Neumann machine with registers. A register is a storage location that can hold a symbol. These are the same set of symbols that are stored in memory.

For example, they can be integers. Let us now try to motivate the use of registers. The memory is typically a very large structure. In modern processors, the entire memory can contain billions of storage locations. Any practical implementation of a memory of this size is fairly slow in practice. There is a general rule of thumb in hardware, "large is slow, and small is fast." Consequently, to enable fast operation, every processor has a small set of registers that can be quickly accessed.

However, it sometimes becomes necessary to bring in memory locations into registers or write back values in registers to memory locations. In those cases, we use dedicated load and store instructions that transfer values between memory and registers. Most programs have a majority of pure register instructions.

The number of load and store instructions is typically about a third of the total number of executed instructions. Let us give an example. Assume that we want to add the cubes of the numbers in the memory locations b and c, and we want to save the result in the memory location a. A machine with registers would need the following instructions. Assume that r1, r2, and r3 are the names of registers. Here, we are not using any specific ISA (the explanation is generic and conceptual).

Here, mem is an array representing memory. We need to first load the values into registers, then perform arithmetic computations, and then save the result back in memory. We can see in this example that we are saving on memory accesses by using registers. If we increase the complexity of the computations, we will save on even more memory accesses. Thus, our execution with registers will get even faster. The resulting processor organization.

Remember

The number of registers is typically between 8 and 64. Most of the operands in arithmetic and branch operations are present in these registers. Since programs tend to use a small set of variables repeatedly at any point of time, using registers saves many memory accesses.

3.9.5. Von-Neumann Machine with a Hardware Stack

A stack is a standard data structure that obeys the semantics – last in, first out. Readers are requested to lookup a book on data structures such as for more information. A stack-based machine has a stack implemented in hardware. First, it is necessary to insert values from the memory into the stack.

After that arithmetic functions operate on the top k elements of the stack. These values get replaced by the result of the computation. For example, if the stack contains the values 1 and

2 at the top. They get removed and replaced by 3. Note that here arithmetic operations do not require any operands.

If an add operation takes two operands, then they do not need to be explicitly specified. The operands are implicitly specified as the top two elements in the stack. Likewise, the location of the result also does not need to be specified. It needs to be inserted at the top of the stack.

KEYWORD

Java is a high-level, class-based, object-oriented programming language that is designed to have as few implementation dependencies as possible.

Even though, generating instructions for such a machine is difficult and flexibility is an issue, the instructions can be very compact. Most instructions other than load and store do not require any operands. We can thus produce very dense machine code. Systems in which the size of the program is an issue can use a stack-based organization.

They are also easy to verify since they are relatively simpler systems. A stack supports two operations – push and pop. Push pushes an element to the top of the stack. Pop removes an element from the top of the stack. Let us now try to compute w = x + y/z − u ∗ v using a stack based Von Neumann machine, we have:

- push u // load u
- push v // load v
- multiply // u*v
- push z // load y
- push y // load z
- divide // y/z c
- subtract // y/z – u*v
- push x // load x
- add // x + y/z – u*v

Pop w // store result in w. It is clearly visible that scheduling a computation to work on a stack is difficult. There will be many redundant loads and stores. Nonetheless, for machines that is meant to evaluate long mathematical expressions, and machines for which program size is an issue, typically opt for stacks.

There are few practical implementations of stack-based machines such as Burroughs Large Systems, UCSD Pascal, and HP 3000 (classic). The Java language assumes a hypothetical stack-based machine during the process of compilation.

Since a stack-based machine is simple, Java programs can virtually run on any hardware platform. When we run a compiled

Java program, then the Java Virtual Machine (JVM) dynamically converts the Java program into another program that can run on a machine with registers.

3.9.6. Accumulator-Based Machines

Accumulator based machines use a single register called an accumulator. Each instruction takes a single memory location as an input operand. For example, an add operation adds the value in the accumulator to the value in the memory address and then stores the result back in the accumulator. Early machines in the fifties that could not accommodate a register file used to have accumulators.

Accumulators were able to reduce the number of memory accesses and speed up the program. Some aspects of accumulators have crept into the Intel x86 set of processors that are the most commonly used processors for desktops and laptops as of 2012. For multiplication and division of large numbers, these processors use the register eux as an accumulator. For other generic instructions, any register can be specified as an accumulator.

KEYWORD

Accumulator is an energy storage device: a device which accepts energy, stores energy, and releases energy as needed.

3.10. HOW TO ENSURE THAT AN ISA IS COMPLETE?

This is a very interesting, difficult, and theoretically profound question. The problem of finding if a given ISA is complete for a given set of programs, is a fairly difficult problem, and is beyond the scope of the book. The general case is far more interesting.

3.10.1. Towards a Universal ISA

Assume that we are given an ISA that contains the basic instructions adding, and multiply. Can we use this ISA to run all possible programs? The answer is no, because we cannot subtract two numbers using the basic instructions that we have. If we add the subtract instruction to our repertoire of instructions, can we compute the square root of a number? Even if we can, is it guaranteed that we can do all types of computations?

It is a machine that can execute all programs. We can treat each basic action of this machine as an instruction. Thus, the set of actions of a universal machine is its ISA, and this ISA is complete. Consequently, when we say that an ISA is complete, it is the same as saying that we can build a universal machine exclusively based on the given ISA.

Hence, we can solve the problem of completeness of an ISA by solving the problem of designing universal machines. They are dual problems. It is easier to reason in terms of universal machines. Hence, let us delve into this problem. Computer scientists started pondering at the design of universal machines at the beginning of the 20th century.

KEYWORD

Turing machine is a mathematical model of computation describing an abstract machine that manipulates symbols on a strip of tape according to a table of rules.

They wanted to know what is computable, and what is not, and the power of different classes of machines. Secondly, what is the form of a theoretical machine that can compute the results of all possible programs? These fundamental results in computer science form the basis of today's modern computer architectures. Alan Turing was the first to propose a universal machine that was extremely simple and powerful.

This machine is aptly named after him, and is known as the Turing machine. This is merely a theoretical entity, and is typically used as a mathematical reasoning tool. It is possible to create a hardware implementation of a Turing machine. However, this would be extremely inefficient, and require a disproportionate amount of resources.

Nonetheless, Turing machines form the basis of today's computers and modern ISAs are derived from the basic actions of a Turing machine. Hence, it is very essential for us to study its design. Note that we provide a very cursory treatment in this book. Interested readers are requested to take a look at the seminal text on the theory of computation by Hopcroft, Motwani, and Ulmann.

3.10.2. Turing Machine

The general structure of a Turing machine. A Turing machine contains an infinite tape that is an array of cells. Each cell can contain a symbol from a finite alphabet. There is a special symbol $ that works as a special marker. A dedicated tape head points to a cell in the infinite tape. There is a small piece of storage to save the current state among a finite set of states. This storage element is called a state register. The operation of the Turing machine is very simple.

In each step, the tape head reads the symbol in the current cell, its current state from the state register, and looks up a table that contains the set of actions for each combination of symbol and state. This dedicated table is called a transition function table or action table.

Each entry in this table specifies three things – whether to move the tape head one step to the left or right, the next state, and the symbol that should be written in the current cell. Thus, in each step, the tape head can overwrite the value of the cell, change its state in the state register and move to a new cell. The only constraint is that the new cell needs to be to the immediate left or right of the current cell. Formally, its format is (state, symbol) → ({L, R}, new state, new symbol). L stands for left, and R stands for right.

Remember

A dedicated tape head points to a cell in the infinite tape. There is a small piece of storage to save the current state among a finite set of states. This storage element is called a state register. The operation of the Turing machine is very simple.

Turing machines from them. We can immediately conclude that designing Turing machines for even simple problems is difficult, and cryptic. The action table can contain a lot of states, and quickly blow out of size. However, the baseline is that it is possible to solve complex problems with this simple device. It is in fact possible to solve all kinds of problems such as weather modeling, financial calculations, and solving differential equations with this machine!

This observation is captured by the Church-Turing thesis, which basically says that all functions that are computable by any physical computing device are computable by a Turing machine. In lay man's terms, any program that can be computed by deterministic algorithms on any computer known to man is also computable by a Turing machine. This thesis has held its ground for the last half century.

Researchers have up till now not been able to find a machine that is more powerful than a Turing machine. This means that there is no program that can be computed by another machine, and not by a Turing machine. There are some programs that might take forever to compute on a Turing machine. However, they would also take infinite time on all other computing machines.

We can extend the Turing machine in all possible ways. We can consider multiple tapes, multiple tape heads, or multiple tracks in each tape. It can be shown that each of these machines is as powerful as a simple Turing machine (Figure 3.5).

Figure 3.5. Turing machine.

Source: Image by Wikimedia Commons.

3.10.3. Universal Turing Machine

The Turing machine is not a universal machine. This is because it contains an action table, which is specific to the function being computed by the machine. A true universal machine will have the same action table, symbols, and also the same set of states for every function. We can make a universal Turing machine, if we can design a Turing machine that can simulate another Turing machine.

This Turing machine will be generic and will not be specific to the function that is being computed. Let the Turing machine that is being simulated be called M, and the universal Turing machine be called U. Let us first create a generic format for the action table of M, and save it in a designated location on the tape of U.

This simulated action table contains a list of actions, and each action requires the five parameters – old state, old symbol, direction (left or right), new state, and new symbol. We can use a common set of basic symbols that can be the 10 decimal digits (0–9). If a function requires more symbols then we can consider one symbol to be contained in a set of contiguous cells demarcated by special delimiters.

Let such a symbol be called a simulated symbol. Likewise, the state in the simulated action table can also be encoded as a decimal number. For the direction, we can use 0 for left, and 1 for right. Thus, a single action table entry might look something like. Here the '@' symbol is the delimiter. This entry is saying that we are moving from state 1334 to 1335 if symbol 34 is encountered.

We move left (0), and write a value of 10. Thus, we have found a way of encoding the action table, set of symbols, and states of a Turing machine designed to compute a certain function. Similarly, we can designate an area of the tape to contain the state register of M. We call this the simulated state register. Let the tape of M be given a dedicated space in the tape of U, and let us call this space the work area.

The tape is thus divided into three parts. The first part contains the simulated action table, the second part contains the simulated state register, and the last part contains the work area that contains a set of simulated symbols. The universal Turing machine (U) has a very simple action table and set of states. The idea is to find the right entry in the simulated action table that matches the value in the simulated state register and simulated symbol under the tape head.

Then the universal Turing machine needs to carry out the corresponding action by moving to a new simulated state, and overwriting the simulated symbol in the work area if required. The devil is in the details. For doing every basic action, U needs to do tens of tape head movements. The details are given in Hopcroft, Motwani, and Ulmann. However, the conclusion is that we can construct a universal Turing machine.

3.10.4. Turing Completeness

Since the 1950s, researchers have devised many more types of hypothetical machines with their own sets of states and rules. Each of these machines has been proven to be at most as powerful as the Turing machine. There is a generic name for all machines and computing systems that are as expressive and powerful as a Turing machine. Such systems are said to be Turing complete. Any universal machine and ISA are thus Turing complete.

3.11. SUMMARY

1. Computer Architecture and Historical Context

In this chapter, basics of computer architecture have been explained which emphasizes on the historical context of the computer architecture, architectural development and styles. It also discussed about the concept of the instructional language. This chapter also addresses that computers are dumb machines. It also provides highlights on the power and the energy trends in the integrated circuits.

2. Design of Practical Machine

It also discussed about the various design of practical machines such as Harvard architecture, von Neumann architecture, towards a modern machine with registers and stacks, von-Neumann machine with registers, von-Neumann machine with a hardware stack, and accumulator-based machines.

3.12. REVIEW QUESTIONS

1. What do you understand by the term computer architecture?
2. What is architectural development and styles?
3. How, do we make a dumb machine do intelligent things?
4. What do you understand by the instructional language?
5. Explain power and energy trends in integrated circuits
6. What do you understand by performance measures in computer architecture?
7. What is the difference between the Harvard architecture and Von Neumann architecture?
8. Explain the importance of computer architecture.

3.13. MULTIPLE CHOICE QUESTIONS

1. When the mainframe computers and minis did have been initiated to be supplanted by local-area networks?

a. 1991

b. 1980

c. 1995

d. 1990

2. Which of the following is a type of architecture used in the computers nowadays?

a. Micro architecture

b. Harvard Architecture

c. Von-Neumann Architecture
d. System Design

3. What does JVM stands for?

a Java Virtual Memory
b. Java Virtual Machine
c. Java Virtual Management
d. Java Virtual Mechanism

4. What is the full form of ISA?

a. Industry Standard Architecture
b. International Standard Architecture
c. International American Standard
d. None of the mentioned

5. Turing machine consist of:

a. Input tape
b. Blank symbol
c. Tape head
d. All of these

Answers to Multiple Choice Questions

1. (d) 2. (c) 3. (b) 4. (c) 5. (a)

REFERENCES

1. Abd-El-Barr, M., & El-Rewini, H., (2005). *Fundamentals of Computer Organization and Architecture*. Hoboken: Wiley.
2. Ahmet, B., (2017). *Fundamentals of Computer Architecture and Design*. [online] Academia.edu. Available at: https://www.academia.edu/41536175/Fundamentals_of_Computer_Architecture_and_Design (accessed on 03 March 2023).
3. Douglas Comer, (2017). *Essentials of Computer Architecture* (2nd edn.). CRC Press Taylor & Francis Group.
4. Ideen, S., (2022). *Basics of Computer Architecture & HPC as Related to CFD*. ResearchGate.
5. Mostafa Abd-El-Barr & Hesham El-Rewini, (2005). *Fundamentals of Computer Organization and Architecture* (pp. 1–29). [e-Book] New Jersey: John Wiley & Sons, Inc., Hoboken. Available at: https://download.e-bookshelf.de/download/0000/5841/11/L-G-0000584111-0002361063.pdf (accessed on 03 March 2023).

6. Smruti, R. S., (2021). *Basic Computer Architecture*. [e-Book] Available at: https://www.cse.iitd.ac.in/~srsarangi/archbook/archbook.pdf (accessed on 03 March 2023).

CHAPTER 4

COMPUTER PROGRAM AND LANGUAGES

UNIT INTRODUCTION

Consider a few of the various computer application areas. Learners use computer systems at school to complete assignments, conduct research studies, write e-mails, as well as take part in virtual learning. Computer systems are used by employees in the workplace for a variety of purposes, such as data processing, presentation creation, commercial activities, employee and customer connectivity, machine control in manufacturing operations, and many others.

Individuals use personal computers to perform activities like internet purchases, payment services, direct messages with dear ones, as well as playing video games. Keep in mind that numerous other gadgets, such as cellular telephones, iPods, Blackberries, GPS technologies, and numerous others, are also computer systems. Nearly all aspects of our daily lives can benefit from computer systems.

Due to their programming capabilities, machines are capable of a huge assortment of tasks. Accordingly, computer systems are created to complete any activity that one's program instructs them to, instead of being intended to perform a single task.

To carry out an assignment, a computer must implement a set of commands known as a program. Screenshots from Microsoft Word and Adobe Photoshop, two widely used program, as an illustration. Using the device to create, modify, and print documents is possible with the word processing application called Microsoft Word.

Users can modify graphic images, such as pictures taken with their digital cameras, using Adobe Photoshop. Software is a term that is quite often used to describe programs. A computer cannot perform without software since it directs all of its operational processes. Coders and software engineers are also the people who generate all of the software that users use to operate their computer systems.

An individual who has the knowledge and experience required to develop, produce, and check software programs is known as a programmer or software engineer. A profession in computer engineering is exciting and fulfilling. Presently, programming is employed in a broad range of industries, such as business, government, police departments, agriculture, academia, amusement, and numerous others. This book offers an introduction to Python programming as well as its basic theories. Users must grasp a few fundamental aspects regarding computer systems and their implementation in order to discover those suggestions in more detail.

Students would then constantly draw on the understanding students acquire in this book as they learn about computer science. Let's start off by conversing about the exact parts of which computer systems are normally made of. Then they analyze how computer systems store information and run programs. After that, the software that readers will use to create Python programs will be briefly described.

Learning Objectives

After completing this chapter, you should be able to understand the following:

- Understand the definition of computer program
- Identify the nature and characteristics of basic programming
- Understand the components of computer hardware
- Educate about the different types computer programming languages
- Give advice about the C language
- Understand the concept of looping
- Give advice about the importance of machine language

Key Terms

- Computer Program
- Hardware
- Machine Language
- Programming Languages
- Software

4.1. DEFINITION OF CONCEPTS PROGRAM, PROGRAMMER, AND PROGRAMMING LANGUAGE

A program is a sequence of commands written in a programming language that a person can understand and use to accomplish a specific task. A software package which is designed primarily for resolving a particular kind of software glitch might be created by using a well-written program that has been carefully packaged.

A software engineer is a computer programmer who has perfected the application of computer language concepts to create executable and respectable software applications. A professional programmer is a software engineer. On big ventures, system developers and software developers frequently collaborate closely.

In order to format computer-programmed commands for subsequent implementation by the computer, scripting languages were established or formed as artificial mathematical formalism languages. They typically contain a set of syntax guidelines which define how to employ certain words and how to interpret the meaning of written expressions. Every programming language has an interpreter, also known as an interpreter or compiler, depending on the scenario. Computer programmers who exercise coding practice the technique of creating computer programs using a chosen programming language. The achievement of the resulting program or software provides a criterion for assessing this rare ability. Coding steps, from problem identification to maintenance, should be strictly implemented (Figure 4.1).

Figure 4.1. Top programming languages in the world.

Source: Image by Flickr.

4.2. THE NATURE AND CHARACTERISTICS OF BASIC PROGRAMMING

An abbreviation for a complete beginner's all-purpose symbolic instruction code is BASIC. The language was designed to be among the simplest computer languages to gain knowledge and to instruct students on the basic fundamentals of coding. Since BASIC is a high-level programming language, it must first be transformed to its equivalent in machine code in order to run on a computer.

This requires the use of a BASIC interpreter, or translator, program. Prior to being transcribed by the translator, the program's source code is termed as such, whereas an interpreted version which is prepared for implementation is referred to as object code. There are other interpreters being used in coding besides interpreters, however. The usage of assemblers by assembly languages stands in contrast to the adoption of compilers by many other high-level programming languages, including C++, Pascal, and so on. Java has a code editor and a translator which translates this same source code line by line and statement by statement without creating intermediate object code. It simultaneously equates and runs the source code.

Did you Know?

The high-level programming language known as BASIC was created at Dartmouth College in New Hampshire, USA, between the academic periods of 1963 and 1964, under the direction of university professors John G. Kemeny and Thomas E. Kutz.

4.3. HARDWARE

The term "hardware" refers to all of the physical objects, or parts, that make up a computer (Figure 4.2). Computers are systems of interconnected devices, not just one machine. Every element of a desktop has a specific function to play, similar to the multiple instruments in a symphony orchestra. If users ever purchased a desktop, likely viewed sales literature listing products like microprocessors, memory, disc drives, video displays, graphics cards, and other parts.

Recognizing how these various elements interact could be complicated, except if users are very savvy about computer systems or at least have a friend who is. Key components of a standard computer system include a number of things:

- The central processing unit (CPU)
- Main memory
- Secondary storage devices
- Input devices
- Output devices

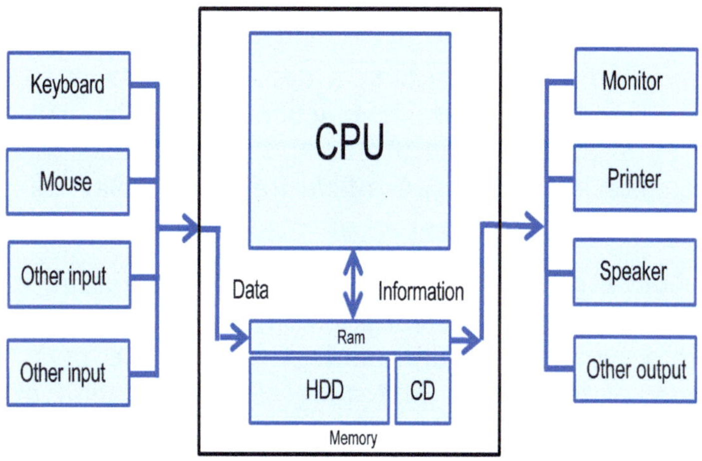

Figure 4.2. Computer hardware.

Source: Image by Wikimedia Commons.

4.3.1. The Processor (CPU)

When a computer follows the instructions provided by a program, this is referred to as operating or implementing the program. The element of a computer which basically implements programs is known as the central processing unit, or CPU. In order for a computer to operate software, its central processing unit (CPU) is extremely important. The central processing units (CPUs) in the oldest computer systems were large systems built from both electrical and mechanical parts like vacuum tubes and switches.

The historic ENIAC computer is being operated by the two female subjects in the picture. The ENIAC, generally regarded as the first configurable electronic digital computer ever made, was created in 1945 for the U.S. Army to quantify artillery ballistic tables. This device was 100 feet long, 8 feet in height, and weighed 30 tons. Its key part was indeed a large CPU.

Nowadays, CPUs are tiny chips called microprocessors. a photo of a lab technician managing a modern microprocessor. Microprocessors are markedly more potent than the old electro-mechanical CPUs found in early computer systems, and they are also becoming considerably smaller.

4.3.2. Main Memory

The computer's working space is depicted by its main memory. The data that the program is functioning with is also saved in this when it is operating on the computer. Let's take the situation in which users are writing an article for a particular course using word processing software.

The word processor and the write-up would both be kept in the main memory as you do this. Random-access memory, or RAM, is the word most frequently used to refer to the main memory. As a result of the CPU's fast access to information maintained in just about any arbitrarily defined place in RAM, this capacity is recognized as "quick access." RAM is generally primarily used for temporary backups whereas a program is operating and is a potentially volatile kind of memory. The information in RAM is removed whenever the computer is switched off. RAM is kept in chips within the computer.

KEYWORD

Random-access memory is a form of computer memory that can be read and changed in any order, typically used to store working data and machine code.

4.3.3. Devices Used for Secondary Storage

A sort of memory recognized as a storage device could remain capable of storing information even if the desktop is not powered. Typically, programs are held in secondary memory and added to the main memory as required. Vital information also ends up saved for secondary storage, along with word processing documents, payroll data, and inventory records.

Disk drives are among the most pervasive types of secondary storage devices. By magnetically encoding information onto a spherical disc, a disc drive stores it. A disc drive is usually installed in the case of computer systems. There are additional external sources available on disc drives that attach to a computer's communication port. External disc drives can be used to create backup copies of critical information or to transfer data to another desktop.

There are numerous different devices that can be employed to duplicate information and transfer it to other computer systems besides external disc drives. Disk drive drives have been broadly used for a long period of time. A small, removable floppy disc is used in floppy disc drives to store information. Floppies, nevertheless, have numerous downsides.

They are prone to errors, obtain information gradually, and are unable to store a small amount of information. Floppy disc drives have become significantly less popular in recent years, even though advanced devices like USB drives have gained in popularity. A USB drive is a miniature device that is attached to the computer's USB (universal serial bus) port and replicates a disc drive for the system.

But there is no disc in these drives. They use flash memory, a distinctive kind of memory, to store information. Memory sticks, flash drives, and USB drives are now all cost-effective, trustable, and compact enough to fit in one's pocket.

Lasers are used on CD and DVD drives to find the pits and decode the information by reading them. Optical discs are suitable for making backup duplicates of information since they can store large quantities of information and video recording CDs and DVD drives have become commonly accessible.

Remember

A further common method for storing data is with optoelectronic components, just like CDs (compact discs) and DVDs (digital versatile discs). On an optical disc, the information is encoded as a pattern of pits on the disc surface instead of being stored magnetically.

4.3.4. Input Devices

Input is any data the computer collects from people and from other devices. The component that collects the data and sends it to the computer is called an input device. Common input devices are the keyboard, mouse, scanner, microphone, and digital camera. Disk drives and optical drives can also be considered input devices because programs and data are retrieved from them and loaded into the computer's memory.

4.3.5. Output Devices

Output is any data the computer produces for people or for other devices. It might be a sales report, a list of names, or a graphic image. The data is sent to an output device, which formats and presents it. Common output devices are video displays and printers. Disk drives and CD recorders can also be considered output devices because the system sends data to them in order to be saved.

4.4. SOFTWARE

If a computer is to function, software is not optional. Everything that a computer does, from the time you turn the power switch on until you shut the system down, is under the control of software. There are two general categories of software: system software and application software. Most computer programs clearly fit into one of these two categories. Let's take a closer look at each (Figure 4.3).

Figure 4.3.
Computer software.

Source: Image by the blue diamond gallery.

4.4.1. System Software

The programs that control and manage the basic operations of a computer are generally referred to as system software. System software typically includes the following types of programs: Operating systems an operating system is the most fundamental set of programs on a computer.

The operating system controls the internal operations of the computer's hardware, manages all of the devices connected to the computer, allows data to be saved to and retrieved from storage devices, and allows other programs to run on the computer.

Screens from three popular operating systems: Windows Vista, Mac OS X, and Linux. Utility programs a utility program performs a specialized task that enhances the computer's operation or safeguards data. Examples of utility programs are virus scanners, file compression programs, and data backup programs. Software Development Tools Software development tools are the programs that programmers use to create, modifies, and test software. Assemblers, compilers, and interpreters are examples of programs that fall into this category.

4.4.2. Application Software

Programs that make a computer useful for everyday tasks are known as application software. These are the programs that people normally spend most of their time running on their computers.

TIPS

In 1965, Intel cofounder Gordon Moore introduced Moore's Law which predicted that the number of transistors on a chip would double every two years while the costs would be halved.

4.5. COMPUTING ENVIRONMENTS

In computing, the transition of information into data is referred to as computing. Distinct computing environments have been needed as a result of many new varieties of computers. Listed below are the various computing environments that are obtainable.

1. Personal Computing Environment
2. Time Sharing Environment
3. Client/Server Environment
4. Distributed Computing Environment

4.5.1. The Personal Computer Environment

The essential parts of the central processing units were merged into the microprocessor by Marcian E. Hoff in 1971 while Hoff was continuing to work for INTEL. Each part of computer hardware is linked when people use a personal computer. An individual user who has used the computer for personal purposes employs this type of computer technology to meet their requirements.

4.5.2. Time-Sharing Environments

The theory behind time-sharing in computer science is to divide up data processing in accordance with a time-based criterion. The central computer is required to carry out all computations in this set-up. The central computer manages each aspect of computation. The computers that demand computation are merely ineffective connectors.

4.5.3. Client/Server Configuration

The processing is performed by two devices in client/server computing. A client machine is a computer that creates a processing request. The device that gives computation is the server machine. As a consequence, the client is competent to handle the computation. Clients handle some of the handlings, while the server manages the vital (core) processing (Figure 4.4).

Figure 4.4. Computer server.

Source: Image by Flickr.

4.5.4. Distributed Processing

When using a dispersed computing environment, numerous servers and clients could easily integrate their processing needs. A client is more than simply one who requests that the server process their requests for data. Data processing is another capacity of the client. The handling action is distributed among all clients and servers on the machine.

4.6. A COMPREHENSIVE LIST OF COMPUTER PROGRAMMING LANGUAGES

In order to give a computer commands, application programs are used. Each of the computer language constructs' definitions is determined by a set of syntactic and semantic guidelines. Below is the put-together list of all programming languages as of late, separated into the following areas:

- Scripting Programming Languages
- Markup Programming Languages

- Logic-Based Programming Languages
- Concurrent Programming Languages
- Object-Oriented Programming Languages
- Interpreted Programming Languages
- Functional Programming Languages
- Compiled Programming Languages
- Procedural Programming Languages

4.7. PROGRAMMING LANGUAGES THAT CAN BE INTERPRETED

An understandable language is a programming language for which a large percentage of applications undertake commands before even completing a program into machine-language instructions. By converting each statement into a series with one or more subroutines that have already been gathered into assembly language, the translator straightforwardly performs the operation.

KEYWORD

Assembly language is a type of low-level programming language that is intended to communicate directly with a computer's hardware.

1. APL

   A programming language for arrays with the same title was released in 1962 by Kenneth E. Iverson. It is able to handle numerous information arrays at once. It is a functional programming language that is descriptive, immersive, and adaptable.

2. AutoIt

   It is capable of automating window frames by using free software languages. Its major objective is to allow the advancement of automation scripts for Windows that may be utilized to perform specific routine assignments.

3. BASIC

   For a Complete beginner, All-purpose Representational Instruction Code is the word of the abbreviation that John George Kemeny and Thomas Eugene Kurtz created in 1964 at Dartmouth. Its aim was to enable the use of computers for those who didn't acquire scientific knowledge.

4. Eiffel

   It is an object-oriented language of programming which has obtained ISO certification and is therefore implemented to create reusable and expandable software. It serves as a development platform for a wide range of businesses, including video games, aviation, and financial services.

5. Forth

   It is an imperative language of programming that is organized and utilizes stacks as the foundation of its execution. Both compiling control segments and engaging control implementation are supported.

6. Frink

   It is designed by Alan Eliasen, and decided to name it after the well-known character in a book, Professor John Frink. It has an engineering and scientific focus and is based on the Virtual Machine for Java. Perhaps the most remarkable characteristic is how it keeps a record of the measuring system across all the estimations, which allows amounts to possess their own measuring system.

7. Language of Game Maker

   It is a programming language that interprets computer systems developed to be used in combination with the game-making program Game Maker. This language was devised by Dutch computer scientist Mark Overmars.

8. ICI

   ICI is a multi-purpose understandable programming language for computers that Tim Long developed in 1992. It claims to support adaptable data types, dynamic typing, as well as other C-like linguistic features.

9. J

   Its founders, J Ken Iverson and Roger Hui, just needed the essential ASCII character set to build this computer language. The ephemeral programming language it utilizes is efficient for both statistical and mathematical operational processes.

10. Lisp

    Nowadays, the most broadly utilized high-level programming language is Lisp, being the second-oldest language overall. The List Processing Language is the origin of the name Lisp. Linked lists are some of the critical information systems that Lisp facilitates. Programs are written in Lisp and consider the source code as a data model.

11. Lua

    The 1993 release of Lua has been made available by members of the Computer Graphics Technology Group. This was formed as a scripting language and is both an

KEYWORD

Programming language is a system of notation for writing computer programs. Most programming languages are text-based formal languages, but they may also be graphical.

absolutely crucial and formal language of programming. This is famous because it is simple and clear but quite impactful.

12. M

The acronym M originally stood for MUMPS; a computer language intended for the medical sector. The M language was invented by colleagues of the founding father of healthcare information technology, named Neil Pappallardo.

13. Pascal

The objective of this procedural programming language was to employ structured programming and data collection procedures. This language was developed by Swiss computer scientist Niklaus Wirth and given the name by French mathematician and scholar Blaise Pascal.

14. PCASTL

The parent and child form Philippe Choquette created the Available Syntax Tree Language, also known as PASTL, an elevated coding language for computers. This falls within the category of interpreted programming languages. It was specifically developed for self-modifying code.

15. Perl

Perl is an elevated, dynamically-programable interpretive language. Larry Wall, a linguist and former network engineer for NASA, created it. It provides text processing tools for software developers and integrates characteristics from a range of programming languages, such as C, Lisp, and Ask.

16. PostScript

It is used in the desktop publishing field and is known as a page description language. It is a dynamically typed stack-based programming language developed by John Warnock, an American computer scientist and Charles Geschke, a notable figure in the field of computer science. These developers went on to found the very well-known company, Adobe Systems.

17. Python

It is a high-level programming language that supports imperative, object-oriented, and functional programming paradigms. In its features like the dynamic type system and automatic memory management, it is similar to Perl. Originally released in 1991 by Guido van Rossum, a Dutch

ACTIVITY 4.1.

Find out the clock speed of the microprocessor of your computer and compare with that of your peers?

computer programmer, Python is an open community-based language whose development is managed by the Python Software Foundation.

18. REXX

Short for Restructured Extended Executor, REXX is an interpreted language developed by IBM. It was designed with intent to be an easily learnable and readable language. NetRexx is the IBM's implementation of REXX that offers object-oriented programming. Object REXX is an object-oriented scripting language that is based on REXX.

KEYWORD

Object-oriented programming is a programming paradigm based on the concept of "objects", which can contain data and code.

19. Ruby

The efforts for developing this language initiated in Japan in the 1990s. Similar to Perl, it has a dynamic type system and an automatic memory management. It supports multiple programming paradigms and is a dynamic object-oriented language.

20. S-Lang

Originally developed as a stack-based language, S-Lang has evolved as a language similar to C. It was developed by John E. Davis.

21. Spin

It is a multitasking object-oriented programming language whose compiler converts the Spin code into byte codes. Multiple Spin code threads can run at a time, thus enabling multitasking. Spin was developed by Chip Gracey of Parallax.

4.8. CREATING AND RUNNING PROGRAMS

The procedure for turning a program written in C into machine Language. The process is presented in a straightforward, linear fashion but you should recognize that these steps are repeated many times during development to correct errors and make improvements to the code. The following are the four steps in this process:

- Writing and editing the program
- Compiling the program
- Linking the program with the required modules
- Executing the program

4.8.1. Writing and Editing Programs

The software used to write programs is known as a text editor. A text editor helps us enter, change and store character data. Once we write the program in the text editor we save it using a filename stored with an extension of .C. This file is referred as source code file.

4.8.2. Compiling Programs

The code in a source file stored on the disk must be translated into machine language. This is the job of the compiler. The Compiler is a computer program that translates the source code written in a high-level language into the corresponding object code of the low-level language.

This translation process is called compilation. The entire high-level program is converted into the executable machine code file. The Compiler which executes C programs is called as C Compiler. Example Turbo C, Borland C, GC, etc. The C Compiler is actually two separate programs: The Preprocessor the Translator the Preprocessor reads the source code and prepares it for the translator.

While preparing the code, it scans for special instructions known as preprocessor commands. These commands tell the preprocessor to look for special code libraries. The result of preprocessing is called the translation unit.

After the preprocessor has prepared the code for compilation, the translator does the actual work of converting the program into machine language. The translator reads the translation unit and writes the resulting object module to a file that can then be combined with other precompiled units to form the final program. An object module is the code in the machine language.

KEYWORD

Compiler is a special program that translates a programming language's source code into machine code, bytecode or another programming language.

4.8.3. Linking Programs

The Linker assembles all functions, the program's functions and system's functions into one executable program.

4.8.4. Executing Programs

To execute a program, we use an operating system command, such as run, to load the program into primary memory and execute it. Getting the program into memory is the function of an operating system program known as the loader. It locates the executable program and 14 read it into memory. When everything is loaded the program takes control and it begins execution (Figure 4.5).

KEYWORD

Primary memory is a segment of computer memory that can be accessed directly by the processor.

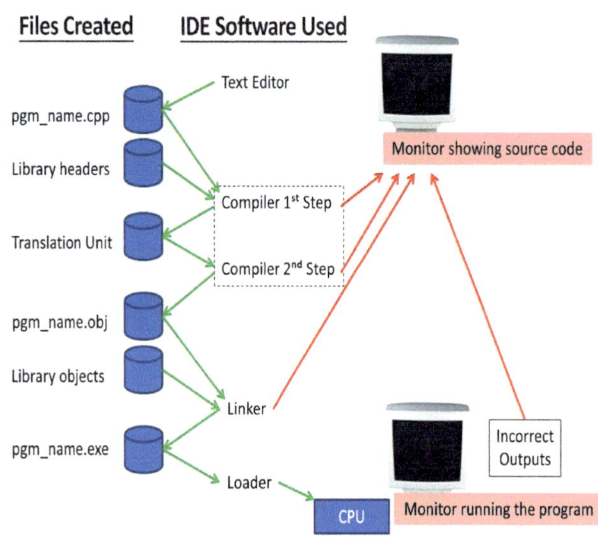

Figure 4.5. Software IDE process.

Source: Image by Wikimedia Commons.

4.9. C LANGUAGE OVERVIEW

The programming language C empowers a rather effective technique for developing and placing into practice computer programs. The historical record of C began with Dennis M. Ritchie's initiative to employ this language at Bell Laboratories in the United States in 1972. The American National Standards Institute (ANSI) set up a group in 1983 with the purpose of developing "an unequivocal and machine-independent description of the language C" while conserving its enthusiasm.

One of the most commonly used programming languages connected to UNIX is C. Although since the 1970s, C has served as the primary programming language used to develop both the UNIX operating system and its software. One of the earliest and most compact operating systems has been UNIX since the C programming language doesn't quite depend solely on any particular hardware architecture.

To look at it another way, the vast significant proportion of the program which helps make up UNIX are oblivious to and unconcerned with the computer on which they are effectively functioning. The UNIX kernel's isolation of machine-specific characteristics into a small set of components allows it to be simple to alter them once they are transferred to a distinct hardware structure.

Dennis Ritchie originally developed C to collaborate with UNIX on DEC PDP-11 computers. The BCPL of Martin Richard was the starting point for the language, and one of its earliest iterations was indeed the B language made by Ken Thompson for the DEC PDP-7. The C Programming Language, authored by Brian Kernighan and Dennis Ritchie, was the initial read on C. This was launched in 1978. In standardizing the definition of C, the American National Standards Institute (ANSI) created an advisory board in 1983.

Remember

It seems that a new ANSI C standard, presently referred to as "C9X," would be published with an official launch date of 1999 or at the beginning of 2000.

The final outcome is a good benchmark for language, grammar, and the basic establishment of libraries, recognized as ANSI C. The original C language, typically referred to as Kernighan and Ritchie or K&R, does have a bit of a distinct syntax.

Furthermore, there is also an ISO standard that is extremely exactly equivalent to the ANSI benchmark.

4.10. THE C LANGUAGE'S FUNDAMENTAL STRUCTURE

This represents the fundamental framework accompanied by the C language program. The segments' order ought to follow that of the fundamental principle. A C program must include segments, and the segments must be in the proper order.

- The documentation segments
- The connecting segment
- Segment on interpretations
- Segment on the global declaration
- Executable segment of the main controller segment
- Program or function segment.

4.10.1. Documentation Section

The first section, "Documentation," explains how your application uses logic and rationalization. It has the ability to clarify the program's goal, founder, and logic. The information is written in C using the /* and */symbols. Comment threads are anything written in between these two.

KEYWORD

Rationalization is the process of changing a pre-existing workflow into one that's more goal-oriented and based on a specific set of rules.

4.10.2. Linking Section

This line directs the code editor to connect particular examples of the operations or search terms in one program to the header files mentioned in this. e.g., #include.

4.10.3. Definition Section

A few components are proclaimed and granted the values that use it. containing # describe MAX 25In this, #explain directs the code editor to substitute MAX to 25 once it appears in the program.

4.10.4. Section on the Global Declaration

The factors that are employed across the entire program, such as the primary purpose as well as other features, are proclaimed below in a manner that makes them global (i.e., available to all areas of the program), such as int I (before main ()).

4.10.5. Main Function Section

It commands the optimizer on where it should begin the implementation.

Main ()

{Point from execution starts}

The main function is divided into two sections:

1. **Declaration section:** The factors and their different data are revealed in the first segment, known as the declaration section.
2. **Executable section:** This segment of the program contains the code that usually carries out the assignment that users require.

4.11. Segment of a Sub-Program or Function

This includes every purpose or sub-program that our program requires.

4.11.1. C-Tokens

A C program can be subdivided into tokens, which are individual words and punctuation in paragraphs written in the English language. No matter how big the program is, a programming language must include at least three C tokens.

KEYWORD

Rationalization is the process of changing a pre-existing workflow into one that's more goal-oriented and based on a specific set of rules.

4.11.2. Key Terms

The "C" language has some words that are identified as keywords (reserved words) and also have predetermined meanings.

These keywords must only be applied to the particular function for which they were aimed, not even as signifiers.

4.12 Identifier

Identifiers are commonly used to refer to the identities of factors as well as other program components like functions, arrays, and so on. The naming of factors is controlled by a set of guidelines (identifiers).

1. Identifiers can be given the name to use the alphabetic, numeric, and digit A-Z, a-z, 0–9, and _ (underscore) combinations.
2. An underscore or an alphanumeric character should serve as the first letter of the identifier. Digit is prohibited.

It shouldn't have a keyword in it. like name, ptr, and sum Users must tell the code editor what information type a factor is after naming it. Declaring a parameter is done in the following format:

Data-types id_1, id_2, ..., id_n;

Float, int, char, and any other data type may be used as the data type. These same variables that users utilize have the identities id_1, id_2, and id_3. There is no need for commas when only one variable is used. For instance, float a, b, c; int e, f, grand total;

Char present_or_absent;

4.13. THE CODE SEGMENT

The term "code segment" describes the logical program segment. If a program is connected, the linker continues to add a note explaining the destination of the code segment to the program's executable file. When the DOS loads an executable file into memory, the loader gets to read that note.

As it loads the program into memory, the loader also makes notes to itself of precisely where in memory it currently locates each of the program's other logical segments. As the loader transmits control of implementation to the program it has just loaded, the CS record is established to point to the foundation of the segment assigned by the linker as that of the code segment.

Each instruction in the code segment is now directly accessible in segment relative terms using the format CS:. The first instruction in the code segment is also assumed to be the initial command to be performed by the linker by proxy.

The linker provides the loader with this data by having left a second note in the top corner of the program's executable file. This instruction would then show up in memory at an offset of 0000H from the segment's base. That value is entered by the loader in the IP (Instruction Pointer) record. This changes CS: IP to the program's first instruction segment relative address (Figure 4.6).

Figure 4.6. Programming language.

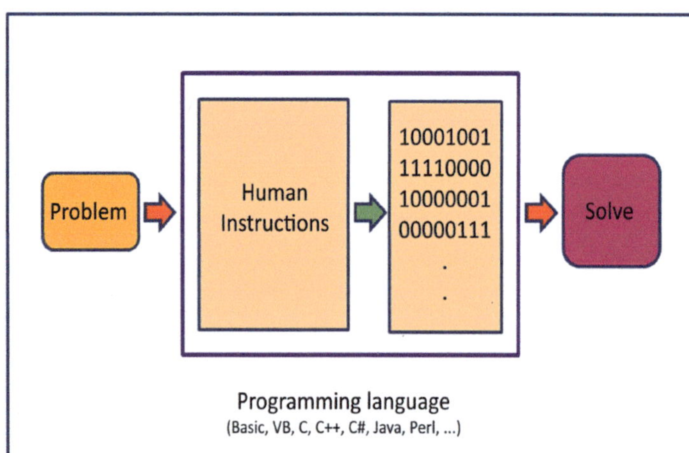

Source: Image by Wikimedia Commons.

4.14. STACK SEGMENT

8086 Microprocessor supports the Word stack. The stack segment parameters tell the assembler to alert the linker that this segment statement defines the program stack area. A program must have a stack area in that the computer is continuously carrying on several background operations that are completely transparent, even to an assembly language programmer, for example, a real time clock.

Every 55 milliseconds the real time clock interrupts and for every 55 milliseconds, the CPU is interrupted. The CPU records the state of its registers and then goes about updating the system clock. When it finishes servicing the system clock, it has to restore the registers and go back to doing whatever it was doing when the interruption occurred.

All such information gets recorded in the stack. If your program has no stack and if the real time clock were to pulse while the CPU is running your program, there would be no way for the CPU to find the way back to your program when it was through updating the clock. 0400H byte is the default size of allocation of stack. Please note if you have not specified the stack segment it is automatically created.

TIPS

Operating system is called resource manager as it manages different resources like main memory, CPU, I/O devices, so that each resource is used optimally and system performance does not deteriorate.

4.15. DATA SEGMENT

It contains the data allocation statements for a program. This segment is very useful as it shows the data organization.

4.16. MACHINE LEVEL LANGUAGE

Although computers can be programmed to understand many different computer languages, there is only one language understood by the computer without using a translation program, this language is called the machine language or the machine code of the computer. Machine code is the fundamental language of a computer and is normally written as strings of binary 1s and 0s.

The circuitry of a computer is wired in such a way that it immediately recognizes the machine language and converts it into the electrical signals needed to run the computer. An instruction prepared in any language has a two-part format. The first part is command or operation, and it tells the computer what function to perform. Every computer has an operation code or opcode for each of its functions.

The second part of the instruction is the operand, and it tells the computer where to find or store the data or other instructions that are to be maintained. Thus, each instruction tells the control unit of the CPU what to do and the length and location of the data field are involved in the operation. Typical operations involve reading, adding, subtracting, writing and so on.

When stored inside the computer, the symbols which make up the machine language program are made up of 1s and 0s this is obviously not a very easy language to learn, partly because it is difficult to read and understand and partly because it is written in a number system with which we are not familiar.

But it will be surprising to note that some of the first programmers, who worked with the first few computers, actually wrote their programs in binary form as above. Since human programmers are more familiar with the decimal number system, most of them preferred to write the computer instructions in decimal, and leave the input device to convert these to binary. In fact, without too much effort, a computer can be wired so that instead of using long numbers.

Did you Know?

All commuters use binary digits (0s and 1s) for performing operations. Hence, most computers machine language consists of strings of binary numbers and is the only one the CPU directly understands.

The set of instruction codes, whether in binary or decimal, which can be directly understood by the CPU of a computer without the help of a translating program, is called a machine code or machine language. Thus, a machine language program need not necessarily be coded as strings of binary digits (1s and 0s). It can also be written using decimal digits if the circuitry of the computer being used permits this.

4.17. ADVANTAGES AND LIMITATIONS OF MACHINE LANGUAGE

Programs written in machine language can be executed very fast by the computer. This is mainly because machine instructions are directly understood by the CPU writing a program in machine language has several disadvantages which are discussed below.

- **Machine dependent:** Because the internal design of every type of commuter is different from every other type of computer and needs different electrical signals to operate, the machine language also is different from computer to computer.

It is determined by the actual design or construction of the LU, the control unit, and the size as well as the word length of the memory unit. Hence, suppose after becoming proficient in the machine code of a particular computer, a company decides to change to another computer, the programmer may be required to learn a new machine language and would have to rewrite all the existing programs.

- **Difficult to program:** Although easily used by the computer, machine language is difficult to program, it is necessary for the programmer either to memorize the dozens of code numbers for the commands in the machine's instruction set or to constantly refer to keep track of the storage location of data and instructions.

Moreover, a machine language programmer must be an expert who knows about the hardware structure of the computer.

- **Error code:** For writing programs in machine language, since a programmer has to remember the opcode and he must also keep track of the storage location of data and instructions, it becomes very difficult for him to concentrate fully on the logic of the problem. This frequently results in program errors. Hence, it is easy to make errors while using machine code.
- **Difficult to modify:** It is difficult to correct or modify machine language programs. Checking machine instructions to locate errors is about as tedious as writing them initially. Similarly, modifying a machine language program at a later date is so difficult that many programmers would prefer to code the new logic afresh instead of incorporating the necessary modifications in the old program.

KEYWORD

Machine code is computer code consisting of machine language instructions, which are used to control a computer's central processing unit.

4.18. HIGHER LEVEL LANGUAGES

We have talked about programming languages as COBOL, FORTRAN and BASIC. They are called high level programming languages. The program shown below is written in BASIC to obtain the sum of two numbers.

```
LET X = 7

LET Y = 10
```

```
LET sum = X+Y

PRINT SUM

END
```

The time and cost of creating machine and assembly languages was quite high. And this was the prime motivation for the development of high-level languages.

Because of the difficulty of working with low-level languages, high-level languages were developed to make it easier to write computer programs. High level programming languages create computer programs using instructions that are much easier to understand than machine or assembly language code because you can use words that more clearly describe the task being performed.

KEYWORD

Computer program is a sequence or set of instructions in a programming language for a computer to execute.

4.19. COMPILING HIGH LEVEL LANGUAGE

Since a high-level source program must be translated first into the form the machine can understand, this is done by a software called Compiler which takes the source code as input and produces as output the machine language code of the machine on which it is to be executed. During the process of translation, the Compiler reads the source programs statement-wise and checks the syntax (grammatical) errors.

If there is any error, the computer generates a printout of the errors it has detected. This action is known as diagnostics. A compiler is a computer program (or set of programs) that transforms source code written in a computer language (the source language) into another computer language (the target language, often having a binary form known as object code).

The most common reason for wanting to transform source code is to create an executable program. The name "compiler" is primarily used for programs that translate source code from a high-level programming language to a lower-level language (e.g., assembly language or machine code). A program that translates from a low-level language to a higher level one is a decompile.

A program that translates between high-level languages is usually called a language translator, source to source translator, or language converter. A language rewriter is usually a program that translates the form of expressions without a change of language. There is another type of software, which also does the translation. This is called an Interpreter. The Compiler and Interpreter have different approaches to translation. The following table lists the differences between a Compiler and an Interpreter.

TIPS

In case you're feeling overwhelmed by all this, relax! You will not have to actually convert numbers to binary while programming. Knowing that this process is taking place inside the computer will help you as you learn, and in the long term this knowledge will make you a better programmer.

4.19.1. Advantages of High-level Programming Language

The various advantages of high-level programming language are:

- Readability: Programs written in these languages are more readable than assembly and machine language.
- Portability: Programs could be run on different machines with little or no change. We can, therefore, exchange software leading to creation of program libraries.
- Easy debugging: Errors could easily be removed (debugged).
- Easy Software development: Software could easily be developed. Commands of programming language are similar to natural languages (ENGLISH).

4.20. LOOPING

Iteration statements are also known as loops or looping statements because the program execution typically loops through the statement more than once. In this category, C provides the following statement or you call loops.

- for loop
- while loop
- do-while loop

Looping must not continue indefinitely as an analogy to real life you would not like to crack the same joke again and again, so a mechanism is required to break out the loop and to allow the executives of the next set of statements. Therefore, a general structure has been devised for the implementation of a loop statement. Which can be more understood by understanding the various elements/ parts/components of a loop that controls the number of repetitions as given below?

- **Initial Expression(s):** Initial expression(s) is usually an assignment expression(s) which initializes the control variable(s) of a loop, as they must be initialized before entering in a loop. The initial expression(s) is executed only once, in the beginning of the loop. But if this expression(s) occurs in the loop body, control variable(s) would be reassigned to initial values with every loop pass, and the condition expression would never fail.
- **Condition Expression:** Conditional expression is typically a relational expression that is set up to terminate the execution of a loop. If the condition expression evaluates, to true i.e., 1, the loop body gets executed, otherwise the loop is terminated.

KEYWORD

Exit controlled loop is a loop in which the loop body is executed first and then the given condition is checked afterwards.

A condition expression may be evaluated before entering in to a loop or before exiting from the loop called as entry-controlled loop and exit controlled loop respectively. In C, the for loop and while loop are entry-controlled loops whereas do while loop is exit-controlled loop.

- **Update Expression(s):** The update expression(s) is essentially an increment expression or decrement expression that changes the value(s) of loop variable(s), so that they could come to the boundary values. The update expression(s) normally execute at the end of the loop body. It may appear in the body of loop as it is updating expressions that assign the variable a new updated value every time the loop passes.
- **The Loop Body:** The loop body consists of statement(s) that is supposed to be executed again and again as long as the condition expression evaluator to true i.e., 1. In an entry-controlled loop, the condition expression evaluated first and if it evaluates to true, the loop-body is executed and if it evaluates to false, the loop-body is terminated.

Whereas, in exit-controlled loop, the loop body executed first and then the condition expression are evaluated. It is evaluated to false i.e., o, the loop is terminated, otherwise repeated.

The above-mentioned components are the essential component of a statement to be called as a loop statement. Messing any of them may change the basic meaning of a perfect loop. For, while and do-while statements of C, comprises of all these essential components, hence referred to as loop statements.

4.20.1. For Loop

For loop in C is the simplest, fixed and entry-controlled loop. It is simplest as the structure of for loop is divided into two segments i.e., control statement and the body of the loop. All its loop control elements are placed together in the control statement whereas body of the loop consists of statements to be executed repeatedly. It is fixed as number of repetitions is known is advance and can be useful in a situation when you want to do something a fixed number of times.

KEYWORD

Iteration is the repetition of a process in order to generate a sequence of outcomes.

4.20.2. While Loop

The second type of loop, the while loop is an entry-controlled loop as it tests the conditions first and if the condition is true, then only the control will enter into the loop body. When each iteration of the loop is finished, the control returns to the while statement which perform the condition test again as so on.

But if the condition in false the first time, no iteration of the loop executes and control passes to the statement next to loop statement. In this way, it is a sort of variable loop as we do not know the exact number of iteration. The statements repeat over and over until certain specified conditions are met.

Where the loop-body may contain a single statement, a compound statement or an empty statement. The while loop iterates the loop body as long as the specified condition expression evaluates to true. The while loop doesn't explicitly contain the initialization expression and update expressions of the loop.

These two expressions are normally provided by the programmers as the initialization expression(s) should be placed before the loop begins and updating expression(s) should be inside the loop body.

4.20.3. Do-While Loop

C's third loop statement is the do-while loop, is an exit-controlled loop i.e., it tests the conditions after having executed the statement with in loop body. This means unlike the for and while loops, a do while loop always executes at least once. The braces { } can be discarded when the loop-body contains a single statement.

The do-while loop iterates the loop body as long as the specified condition is true while testing the condition at the end of the loop each time, rather than at the beginning, as is done by the for and the while loop. Like while loop, do-while loop also doesn't contain the initialization and updating expression as part of loop statement.

KEYWORD

Do/while loop is a variant of the while loop. This loop will execute the code block once, before checking if the condition is true, then it will repeat the loop as long as the condition is true.

However, these expressions can be associated with do-while loop by the programmer according to required logic. The do-while loop resembles the while loop in both syntax and operation. All the variations that could be implemented with while loop may also be applied on do-while loop. But still do-while loop is used less frequently than while and for loops as it is most appropriate when the statement(s) associated with the loop must be executed at least once.

The most common of the do-while loop is to write the menu selection program, where the menu is appeared on the monitor at least once. And then depending upon the user's response it is either repeated or terminated. The following program is an example of menu selection program using do-while loop. This program provides a menu with three choices. The user has to select one of the three choices, and then the program performs the selected operation. This process will be continuing until user selects the particular choice to terminate the loop.

4.21. SUMMARY

1. Definition and nature of Computer Program

In this chapter, definition of concept program, programming language, and the role of a programmer. It also discussed about the nature and characteristics of basic programing. It also addresses the role of hardware in computer hardware and computer software.

2. Computer Languages

This chapter explains the significance of C language along with the comprehensive list of computer programing language. It also discussed about the fundamental structure of C language. Towards the end of the chapter, it discussed about the machine level language, advantages and limitations of the machine language, higher level languages, and compiling high level languages.

4.22. REVIEW QUESTIONS

1. What do you understand by the term computer program?
2. Name the software required to make a computer functional.
3. How does the computer understand a program written in high level language?
4. What are the advantages of high-level language?
5. What is the limitation of machine level language?
6. What do you understand by terms 'For loop,' 'Do while' and 'While loop' in a Looping?
7. What is the need for secondary memory?
8. Explain the importance of machine level language.

4.23. MULTIPLE CHOICE QUESTIONS

1. Who is the father of C language?

a. Steve Jobs

b. James Gosling

c. Dennis Ritchie

d. Rasmus Lerdorf

2. ANSI full form is ______.

a. American National Standards Institute

b. African National Standards Institute

c. Australian National Standards Institute

d. None of these

3. **The factors and their different data are revealed in the first segment, known as the ________.**
   a. Call function
   b. declaration section
   c. insertion section
   d. tokens
4. **There is only one language understood by the computer without using a translation program, this language is called __________.**
   a. python
   b. java
   c. C language
   d. machine language
5. **Find which is not the loop case?**
   a. For loo
   b. While loop
   c. Do-while loop
   d. If loop

Answers to Multiple Choice Questions

1. (c) 2. (a) 3. (b) 4. (d) 5. (d)

REFERENCES

1. (n.d). *Computer Programming*. [e-Book] Hyderabad: Institute of Aeronautical Engineering. Available at: https://www.iare.ac.in/sites/default/files/lecture_notes/C%20LECTURE%20NOTES%20FULL_1.pdf (accessed on 03 March 2023).
2. Pandey, R., (2017). *A Complete List of Computer Programming Languages*. [online] Academia.edu. Available at: https://www.academia.edu/40362143/A_Complete_List_of_Computer_Programming_Languages (accessed on 03 March 2023).
3. Sharma, D., (n.d). *Basic Programming Skills/ Foundations of Computer Programming*. [e-Book] ebooks.lpude. Available at: https://ebooks.lpude.in/computer_application/mca/term_1/DCAP102_BASIC_PROGRAMMING_SKILLS_DCAP401_FOUNDATIONS_OF_COMPUTER_PROGRAMMING.pdf (accessed on 03 March 2023).
4. Usman, O. L., Akeem, O., Abimbola, B. L., & Gbenga, O., (2016). *Introduction to Computer Programming*. [online] Available at: https://www.researchgate.net/publication/317182495_INTRODUCTION_TO_COMPUTER_PROGRAMMING_BASIC (accessed on 03 March 2023).

5. (n.d). *Programming for Problem Solving* (pp. 4–74). [e-Book] Malla Reddy College of ENGINEERING & Technology. Available at: https://mrcet.com/downloads/digital_notes/HS/Programming%20for%20Problem%20Solving.pdf (accessed on 03 March 2023).

CHAPTER 5

ROLE OF ARTIFICIAL INTELLIGENCE IN COMPUTER SCIENCE

UNIT INTRODUCTION

Artificial intelligence (AI) refers to the capabilities of computers to mimic or improve human mental abilities like rational thought and experience-based learning. While it has long been incorporated into computer software, machine intellectual ability is now employed in a broad range of other services and goods.

For example, in this case, a few modern cameras use machine intelligence software to identify the objects depicted in an image. Experts also anticipate that artificial intelligence will be put to use in smart electric grids and many other novel applications in the future.

To fix real-world issues, AI employs methods from statistical inference, economics, and algorithm design. Furthermore, computer science, mathematics, psychology, and linguistics are all used in the AI field.

The tools for creating and implementing algorithms that emerge from computer science, as well as the tools for modeling techniques and fixing the optimal control issues that arise from those models, come from mathematics.

Even though Alan Turing first suggested a "imitation game" to measure machine intelligence in the 19th century, the idea of artificial intelligence (AI) didn't become a reality until recent times because of the increased availability of computer resources and information to train AI systems.

The investigation into this field's priority is the automation of work that requires intelligent human behavior. Regulation, time management, the capacity to respond to consumer and lab test inquiries, writing skills, voice recognition, and the ability to transport and manipulate objects are a few examples.

Consider what distinguishes human intelligence from that of other organisms: our ability to draw lessons from our past and apply them to current situations. This will help users grasp the concept behind AI. Humans are able to accomplish this because and are highly intelligent and possess the most neurons of any life form.

Modern machines fall far short of the biological neural system of a human being. They do, however, have one significant advantage over us: they can process massive amounts of information and perspectives far faster than we could ever hope. With AI, users can concentrate on the most important responsibilities and make more informed decisions based on data gathered about a use case. It may be implemented for challenging tasks, such as figuring out the best path for a delivery van and forecasting maintenance needs. In other words, artificial intelligence can computerize a wide range of business procedures, enabling users to focus on their fundamental competencies (Figure 5.1).

Figure 5.1. Artificial intelligence.

Source: Image by Wikimedia Commons.

Well, nearly every industry currently uses AI, offering businesses that implement it broadly a challenging technical advantage. In contrast to certain other advanced analytics, artificial intelligence has the ability to add 50% more added value to the financial sector, or 600 billion U.S. dollars, says McKinsey. The potential income increase is 89% greater in the transportation and logistics sectors. Conclusively, implementing repetitive and tedious activities is feasible if an organization needs AI for its marketing division. This frees up the sales representative to remain focused on relationship-building, lead nurturing, and so forth. A business by the title of Gong provides a program for conversation intelligence. Every time a salesperson conducts a telephone conversation, the device records a summary of the conversation and evaluates it.

A victorious plan may be created by the VP by utilizing AI analytics and suggestions. To make it short, artificial intelligence offers state-of-the-art technology to solve multiple informational problems which a person cannot manage and control. AI automates repetitive tasks so that a worker can focus solely on high-level, value-added duties. AI execution at scale results in reducing costs and increasing revenues.

Learning Objectives

After completing this chapter, you should be able to understand the following:

- Understand the meaning and definition of artificial intelligence
- Identify the different nature, and subfields of artificial intelligence
- Understand the pros and cons of artificial intelligence
- Educate about the role of artificial intelligence
- Give advice about artificial intelligence in future technology
- Understand the types of AI classification
- Give advice about the importance of artificial intelligence

Key Terms

- Artificial Intelligence
- Chatbots
- Deep Learning
- Image Recognition
- Machines Intelligent
- Neural Networks
- Semantic Analysis
- Supervised Learning
- Unsupervised Learning

5.1. HISTORY OF ARTIFICIAL INTELLIGENCE

Because of the emphasis on contemporaneous artificial intelligence, it really is simple to ignore that the sector is not entirely new. Obviously, it depends if the primary objective was to demonstrate rational theory or attempt to replicate human ideas utilizing neurology, AI has also been through a number of distinct stages.

The next 20 years have seen a concentration of scientific studies on the application of artificial intelligence in attempting to solve practical issues. This technology gave rise to automated systems, that enable computers to learn from past errors and draw conclusions from the collected information. Even though expert systems lack the complexity found in human brains, they can be trained to spot patterns in the information and draw conclusions from it. Presently, they are often used in industrial production and pharmaceutics.

KEYWORD

Robotics is a branch of engineering that involves the conception, design, manufacture and operation of robots.

The creation of programs like Shakey the Robot and ELIZA, which automated basic human-machine communication, marked a second significant turning point in history in 1965. These pioneering applications helped pave the way for more sophisticated voice recognition technology, which finally gave rise to Siri and Alexa.

Approximately ten years were spent during the initial wave of excitement surrounding artificial intelligence. It resulted in important developments in robotics, theorem proving, and computer language design. However, it also sparked a backlash against exaggerated assertions made about the sector, and financing was significantly reduced around 1974.

The late 1980s saw a resurgence of curiosity after ten years of little advancement. The findings that computers were outdoing people at "narrow" activities like playing solitaire or board games, as well as advancements in computer vision and voice recognition, have been the main drivers of this re-emergence. The focus this time was on creating a system that required very little human contact to grasp and gain knowledge from actual statistics.

Such changes occurred gradually until 1992, when participation began to rise once more. The interest in artificial intelligence research was first sparked by technological developments in calculating power and data space.

Another significant boom followed in the middle of the 1990s, this time fueled by significant advancements in computer hardware that had been made since the early 1980s. As a consequence, there have been notable enhancements in performance for a number of important benchmark issues, including image processing, in which computers are now nearly as proficient as people in certain sectors.

AI made significant breakthroughs in the first decade of the 21st century. The creation of the self-learning neural network was the first significant development. In many specific areas, its achievements had indeed exceeded those of living creatures by 2001.

The research team increased its achievement over the years, which followed a wide range of tasks due to advancements in the core technologies.

Conceptual prototype validation learning algorithms have been created during this time, resulting in the second major development. In order to learn complex activities from scant information, generative models could develop new instances from the specific class. For instance, they can be used to teach people how to operate a vehicle after just 20 minutes of practice.

There have been a number of other considerable events in AI over the past ten years along with these two breakthroughs. Deep neural systems have been receiving more attention lately when it comes to computer vision tasks like object acknowledgement and scene ability to comprehend.

Likewise, there has been a lot more emphasis on the use of machine learning algorithms for projects that necessitate the handling of natural language, like extracting data and data retrieval. Last but not least, there has been a rise in interest in applying these very same tools to speech pattern recognition like speaker identification (SID) and automatic speech recognition (ASR).

KEYWORD

Prototype validation comes in when you've determined what user problem you need to solve, but you haven't yet figured out how to solve it.

5.2. VARIOUS TYPES OF ARTIFICIAL INTELLIGENCE

Creating computers and other machines as smart as people is the focus of the multiple-disciplinary artificial intelligence field.. It is designed to potentially replicate human thinking processes and outperform them even further than living beings. "Artificial General Intelligence" is the name given to this artificially intelligent hypothesis. From a conceptual standpoint, AI is still in its infancy. But besides this, AI is currently commonplace in almost all industries.

The outcome of big data has contributed to the development and significance of AI over the past ten years. The significance of data has been made clear by search engines, social media, e-commerce, the internet of things, and online company data analysis.

Institutions require fast information and insight from the huge amount of information that the web has created, instantly obtainable from everywhere and everywhere. Of that kind, repetitive, data-intensive tasks are practically impossible for humans to complete, and computer systems absent the intellectual capabilities necessary to process data independently. The only alternative is to give computers intelligence similar to that of humans to enable them to gain knowledge from information rather than from explicitly programmed instructions.

TIPS

A knowledge base is a store of information consisting of facts, assumptions and rules which an AI system can use for decision making.

Machine learning and deep learning are two instances of how AI is developing and being used. The main goal of machine learning is to learn from historical data by spotting data patterns and relationships between data and results. Deep learning is centered on deriving truly representative ideas directly from the information. The foundation of modern artificial intelligence is machine learning and deep learning.

The categorization of artificial intelligence could assist us in better comprehending its development and uses. Artificial intelligence is categorized according to its capabilities to show how AI is developing. There seem to be three main categories of artificial intelligence predicated on functionality.

1. Specific AI (Weak AI)
2. AI in general (Strong AI)
3. Super AI

Now let us examine the various categories of artificial intelligence.

5.2.1. Weak/Narrow AI

The most well-known and efficient type of artificial intelligence is narrow AI, also termed "weak AI." In order to accomplish a single particular task within a constrained context, narrow AI imitates human intellect. It has the capacity to use just one set of cognitive skill sets to succeed at one specific project.

The same subset cannot be applied to another task, i.e., narrow AI only operates in a limited predefined range and cannot be generalized to perform other tasks. Some examples of Narrow AI are virtual personal assistants (like Siri, Alexa, etc.), Image recognition programs, self-driving cars, IBM's Watson, Google's page ranking algorithm, Google translate, recommendation engines, Chatbots, spam filtering, etc.

For example, face recognition software can recognize a familiar face, but it cannot respond to a voice command. A virtual personal assistant can respond to a voice command, but it cannot perform anything else. Much of the weak AI is the implementation of machine learning or deep learning.

KEYWORD

Deep learning is a machine learning technique that teaches computers to do what comes naturally to humans: learn by example.

5.2.2. General AI/Strong AI

General AI, also known as Strong AI or Artificial General Intelligence, is a term for implementing a full set of cognitive abilities that is not limited by any context. It aims at making machines capable of applying human-level intelligence to any task. It focuses on deriving a universal algorithm for learning and acting in any environment.

The researchers have not been able to achieve strong AI yet. In theory, a strong AI program must pass the Turing Test and the Chinese room test. Many different artificial intelligence technologies are under development to achieve AGI.

This includes computer vision, natural language processing, fuzzy logic, robotics, machine learning, deep learning, etc. A human brain is estimated to do one billion calculations per second, and even the fastest supercomputer takes 40 minutes to perform the same number of calculations. Therefore, Strong AI doesn't seem to be possible soon.

5.2.3. Super AI

Super AI refers to artificial intelligence that may be superior to human-level intelligence. It envisions machines capable of learning, reasoning, and problem-solving even better than humans.

Artificial Super Intelligence (ASI) is the hypothetical AI, i.e., we have not been able to achieve it but we know what will happen if we achieve it. So basically, it is the imaginary AI which not only interprets or understands human-behavior and intelligence, but ASI is where machines will become self-aware/self-vigilant enough to surpass the capacity of human intelligence and behavioral ability.

With Super intelligence, machines can think of the possible abstractions/interpretations which are simply impossible for humans to think. This is because the human brain has a limit to the thinking ability which is constrained to some billion neurons.

Super intelligence has long been the muse around the dystopian science fiction which showed how robots overrun, overpower or enslave humanity. In addition to the replication of multi-faceted human behavioral intelligence, the concept of artificial super intelligence focuses on the perspective of not just being able to understand/interpret human emotions and experiences, but instead, it must also evoke emotional understanding, beliefs and desires of its own, based on its understanding functionality.

KEYWORD

Cognitive ability refers to the ability of the human brain to process, store, and extract information, including attention, memory, and reasoning ability.

ASI would be exceedingly far-far better at everything or whatever we do, whether it be in math's, science, arts, sports, medicine, marketing strategies, hobbies, emotional relationship, or applying a precise human intellect to a particular problem.

ASI would have a greater memory with a faster ability to process and analyze situations, data, and stimuli actions. Due to this fact, we can rest assured that the decision-making and problem-solving capabilities of super-intelligent beings/machines would be far superior and precise as compared to those of human beings.

The possibility and potential of having such powerful machines at our disposal may seem appealing, but this concept itself is a fold of unknown consequences. What impact it will have on humanity, our survival, our existence is just a myth or pure speculation.

Engineers and scientists are still trying to achieve full artificial intelligence, where computers can be considered to have the apt cognitive capacity as that of a human. Although there have been surprising developments like IBM's Watson supercomputer and Siri, still the computers have not been able to fully simulate and achieve the breadth and diversity of cognitive abilities that a normal adult human can easily do.

However, despite the achievements, there are a lot of theories that predict artificial super intelligence coming sooner than later. With the emerging accomplishments, experts say that full artificial intelligence could manifest within a couple of years, and artificial super intelligence could exist in the 21st century possibly.

In the book Super intelligence, Nick Bostrom describes the initials with "The Unfinished Fable of Sparrows." The idea was basically that some sparrows wanted to control an owl as a pet. The idea seemed awesome to all except one of the skeptical sparrows who raised her concern as to how they can control an owl.

This concern was dismissed for the time being in a "we'll deal with that problem when it's a problem" matter. Elon Musk has similar concerns regarding the super-intelligent beings and considers that humans are the sparrows in Bostrom's metaphor and the owl is the future ASI. As it was in the case of sparrows, the "control problem" is seemingly concerning because we might only get one chance to solve it if a problem arises.

When considering how AI might become a risk, two key scenarios have been concluded to occur most likely:

Remember

The danger is in the fact of "whatever it takes" to complete a given task. Super intelligent AI would be at utmost efficiency to achieve a given goal, whatever it may be, but we'll have to ensure that the goal completion is done in correspondence to all the needed rules to be followed to maintain some level of control.

5.3. TYPES OF AI CLASSIFICATION (BASED ON FUNCTIONALITIES)

The classification of AI is based on functionalities highlights its technical applicability. This classification was given by Arend Hintze, an assistant professor of integrated biology and computer science at Michigan State University, in a 2016 article. Based on functionalities, there are four types of artificial intelligence.

- reactive machines;
- limited memory;
- theory of mind; and
- self-awareness.

Since AI research purports to make machines emulate human-like functioning, the degree to which an AI system can replicate human capabilities is used as the criterion for determining the types of AI. Thus, depending on how a machine compares to humans in terms of versatility and performance, AI can be classified under one, among the multiple types of AI.

Under such a system, an AI that can perform more human-like functions with equivalent levels of proficiency will be considered as a more evolved type of AI, while an AI that has limited functionality and performance would be considered a simpler and less evolved type.

Based on this criterion, there are two ways in which AI is generally classified. One type is based on classifying AI and AI-enabled machines based on their likeness to the human mind, and their ability to "think" and perhaps even "feel" like humans. According to this system of classification, there are four types of AI or AI-based systems: reactive machines, limited memory machines, theory of mind, and self-aware AI (Figure 5.2).

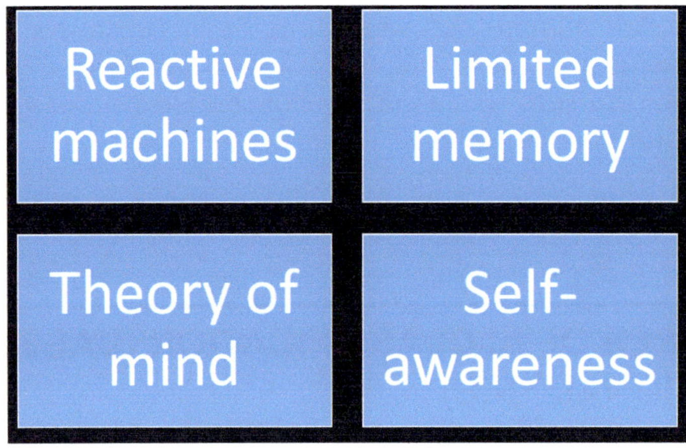

Figure 5.2. Categories of AI classification.

5.3.1. Reactive Machines

These are among the earliest varieties of artificial intelligence systems, and they possess very little authority. They replicate the capability of the human brain to actually respond to various stimuli. These devices don't have memory-based functionalities. This indicates that such computers lack the capacity to "learn," or to use past events to guide the way they act in the present. These devices were only capable of reacting automatically to a small number of different inputs or combinations. They cannot be created to depend on memory to enhance the same operational processes. IBM's Deep Blue, a responsive AI machine that defeated chess Grandmaster Garry Kasparov in 1997, is a well-known instance.

One of the foundational varieties of artificial intelligence is a responsive device.

It has no memory to hold previous events. As a result, it only uses data that is current. It collects input and responds to it in order to carry out a particular task. The functionality of this kind of artificial intelligence is constrained, and the algorithm is intended to accomplish a specific goal. Nothing else or even an assignment that is comparable could be done by employing the same algorithm. IBM's Deep Blue is an exceptionally reactive machine. A chess-playing supercomputer is Deep Blue. It is a memoryless, reactive machine. It pertains its algorithm to the bits of the chess game at the point in time to evaluate its opposing player and potential successful moves. Since it has no memory usage,

it is incapable of progressing through repetition or learning from mistakes. It only responds to the latest game and selects the most effective moves. Deep Blue is highly regarded for beating Garry Kasparov in the 1990s at the chess board game.

Alpha Go by Google is yet another popular instance of a reactive machine. Considering that it uses neural network models to assess the game, it represents a more enhanced application of artificial intelligence. But besides becoming an entirely reactive machine that is incapable of preparing itself in any manner, Alpha Go is known worldwide for defeating the best human Go players.

KEYWORD

Dynamic memory is a type of computer memory storage in which the size of the allocated memory can be changed relative to the data being handled.

Reactive machines function in exceptional conditions and are built to accomplish certain tasks faster; even so, they lack any depiction of their surroundings. Numerous researchers contend that AI should only advance toward reactive machines; these machines should not be given a predetermined depiction of the world and must communicate with their environment actively. Moreover, it is basically impossible to create any general artificial intelligence without the need for an appropriate environmental portrayal.

5.3.2. Memory Limitations

A momentary memory is a characteristic of this kind of machine learning. This can obtain expertise in a particular task by gaining knowledge from recent experiences, it is unable to accrue considerable experience libraries.

To hold a specific version of the globe that is meaningful to one's assignment, such machines have fixed memories. Furthermore, they have such a dynamic memory that only stores recent events or short attention spans. They thrive at a particular task by envisioning a representation of the surroundings from static memory and implementing correlations with the aid of short-term memories.

Self-driving vehicles are an exceptional type of artificial intelligence with limited memory. To acknowledge road signs, traffic lights, and lane markers, the vehicles have a fixed memory. They have such a dynamic memory that they employ to access data about the pace and direction of the automobiles around them.

They test with self-driving and along with other vehicle types and human drivers by employing the guidelines and expertise saved in static memory and analyzing their immediate area through short-term memories. They only maintain sufficient data about the speed and driving patterns of other vehicles to get them where they're headed at the moment. Through repetitive self-driving, they cannot enhance their driving ability or acquire new ones.

KEYWORD

Machine learning model is similar to computer software designed to recognize patterns or behaviors based on previous experience or data.

Limited memory the use of artificial intelligence in machine learning is widespread. A large percentage of the software for machine learning presently being used uses artificial intelligence with limited memory. Long Short-Term Memory (LSTM), Evolutionary Generative Adversarial Networks (E-GAN), and Reinforcement Learning are three main categories of machine learning models that employ a restricted size of memory (E-GAN).

Through countless processes of trial and error, Reinforcement Learning utilizes short-term memories to maximize forecasts and complete work well. The most popular machine learning model is LSTM. With little focus on past data, it uses recent historical information.

It creates estimates based on its short-term memories or attempts to predict results from the most recent data trends. E-GAN is an evolutionary model within which the computer consistently learns from its most recent memories and findings to enhance its achievement. Assumptions made based on earlier results are used to create the new findings. The design keeps changing all throughout the course through a process of constant learning.

5.3.3. Theory of Mind

Given that they all have limited memory or are reactive, the present generation of artificial intelligence systems is categorized as narrow AI. Based on the philosophy of mind, people's opinions, emotions, and choices are defined in the world by computers.

In the coming years, this is what needs to be accomplished. Robotic systems like Kismet and Sophia are creating some actual initiatives in this direction. Sophia is a robot with fully advanced machine vision functionality that can identify people, converse with others, and follow faces. The robotic head Kismet is made to imitate and acknowledge human feelings.

The third category of artificial intelligence, or the next level of AI systems, is named the Theory of Mind.

This sort of AI participates in human sentiments and thoughts. One such AI would then primarily concentrate on individuals whose perceptions could be influenced by a wide range of variables, such as human comprehension.

By comprehending the needs, thinking patterns, emotional responses, and belief systems of the entities they communicate with, theory of mind AI will have a greater understanding of those entities. The Theory of Mind's central idea is "comprehension." It might touch on a range of topics, including behavior, emotions, human nature, and feelings, among many others.

KEYWORD

Artificial intelligence is the simulation of human intelligence processes by machines, especially computer systems.

Among the most important technological advancements that categories people's feelings, emotions, and opinions are these. Scientists are working to develop computers which can gain knowledge from different aspects of human thinking patterns and comprehend them effectively.

Researchers can observe an emotional intelligence machine interacting with individuals in order to imitate a proper conversation. The Theory of Mind AI is designed to address this. It will enable computers to make choices that are equivalent to those of humans. The will have a serious influence and can be used to research people's behavior and build a precise computer which can predict human mood and emotions.

5.3.4. Self-Awareness

This is the highest goal of artificial intelligence, which is to make machines have a proper representation of the world on their own and have an awareness of them. It envisions machines to be aware of their traits, conditions, and internal states with their feelings, faith, and beliefs. A self-aware machine would not need to borrow consciousness from a model. Instead, have its consciousness. It will know what it wants and what it has to do. Such a machine will be a living creature in itself.

All the current artificial intelligence applications fall under narrow AI and have functionalities of either reactive nature or limited memory. These applications with no representation of the world or a limited and specific representation are so valuable and reliable that they can best perform in data-heavy and detail-oriented tasks that normal humans cannot. Even these primitive and limited forms of artificial intelligence have proved their worth in a new world where data is the new oil.

The field of artificial intelligence envisions machines to have far superior consciousness where they have their representation of the world and may have a representation of their own all on their own. Though researchers are concentrating their efforts on computer vision, natural language processing, robotics, sensor technology, artificial emotional intelligence, etc., creating a living creature from metal is still a faraway dream.

TIPS

Robotics is an interdisciplinary branch of technology requiring applications of mechanical engineering, electronics, and computer science, among others. Robotics is primarily concerned with the design, fabrication, operation, and application of robots.

5.4. PROS AND CONS OF ARTIFICIAL INTELLIGENCE

Artificial intelligence (AI) is a wide-ranging branch of computer science concerned with building smart machines capable of performing tasks that typically require human intelligence. The use of AI is gradually growing all over the world and it has both advantages and disadvantages that one should be aware of.

5.4.1. Advantages

a. **Available 24*7:** Without breaks, an average human will labor for 4–6 hours every day. Humans are created in such a way that they can take time off to replenish themselves and prepare for a new day at work, and they even have weekly off days to keep their professional and home lives separate. But, unlike humans, we can use AI to make machines work 24 hours a day, seven days a week with no breaks, and they don't get bored.

b. **Reduction in Human error:**Because humans make mistakes from time to time, the term "human error" was coined. Computers, on the other hand, do not make these errors if they are correctly programmed. Artificial intelligence makes choices based on previously obtained data and a set of algorithms. As a result, errors are decreased, and the prospect of achieving better precision and accuracy is increased.

d. **Daily Applications:** Apple's Siri, Microsoft's Cortana, and Google's OK Google are all commonplace in our daily lives, whether it's for finding a location, taking a selfie, making a phone call, or responding to an e-mail.

e. **Faster Decisions**: We can make computers make decisions and carry out activities faster than humans by combining AI with other technologies. While a human will consider numerous aspects, both emotionally and practically, before making a decision, an AI-powered machine will focus on what it has been designed to do and will produce results more quickly.

f. **Digital Assistance:**Utilizing digital assistants rather than human employees, a few of the most technologically superior organizations communicate with their clients. Numerous web pages require digital helpers to produce consumer information. They are accessible to chat about our quest. It may be difficult to distinguish between such a human and a chatbot when using some chatbots because of their design.

   Every company, as everyone understands, has a customer service department that must respond to the inquiries and troubles of its clients. Commercial enterprises could use AI to develop a chatbot or voice bot which can reply to all of their customers' queries.

g. **Take chances rather than human beings:** This represents one of the major benefits of AI technology. Humans could conquer many more of humankind's dicey limitations by creating an artificial intelligence-based robot that can undertake dangerous tasks for us. Missions to Mars, disarming a bomb, diving to the deepest ocean depths, and mining for fossil fuels and oil—it can be used successfully in any natural or man-made disaster.

h. **Supporting Repeated Tasks:** In the course of our everyday chores, humans will perform various routine tasks, including sending e-mails of gratitude and double-checking paperwork for mistakes, among other things. Machine intelligence may be used to efficiently computerize such repetitive tasks and perhaps even delete "monotonous" roles and responsibilities from the human work schedule, freeing them up to participate in more creative projects.

Excellent demonstration: In financial institutions, gaining a loan commonly requires multiple record verifications, which would be time-consuming for the bank's owner. Using AI and cognitive automation, the owner could speed up the file verification system to the benefit of both the customers and the owner.

KEYWORD

Voice bot is artificial intelligence (AI) powered software used in contact centers that can interact with inbound callers.

i. **New Discoveries:** Machine learning has greatly assisted in the formation of novel innovations to address challenging problems in almost every field. The latest finding has enabled doctors to anticipate the initial phases of breast cancer in women by employing cutting-edge machines. The latest finding has enabled doctors to anticipate the initial phases of breast cancer in women by employing cutting-edge AI learning technologies.

j. **The lack of emotions in AI machines:** Apart from Chitti, the robot whose fascination with the female protagonist Sana genuinely left us so baffled, computers are emotionless. Users could really address complaints from customers more steadily by leveraging this one function of AI-enabled machines. Take into account software features and functions that abruptly stop functioning, inconveniencing ones, consumers. Without a doubt, they'll e-mail you, chat with your support team, and submit tickets. Many people choose to use "live chat" instead of waiting for an e-mail or a ticket to be responded to. Imagine getting a person who is tirelessly addressing thousands of complaints on the opposite end and who really is fully mindful of the issues.

That person will end up losing it. There's a decent possibility that language responsiveness will be thrown out the window in discussions. It's among the least risky remedies even though computers do not however suffer pain. They would also easily investigate the words in the question, compare those with the pre-loaded knowledge, and give appropriate and important alternatives (Figure 5.3).

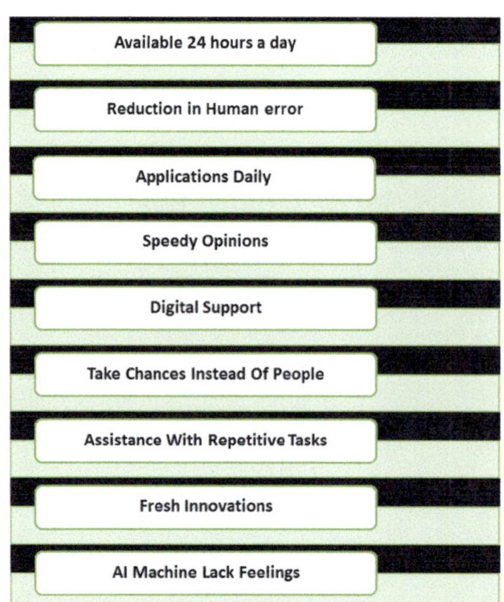

Figure 5.3. Benefits of artificial intelligence.

5.4.2. Negative Aspects

a. **High Implementation Costs:** Since artificial intelligence is changing all the time, both hardware and software must always be frequently updated to fulfill the most current norms. Systems require servicing and repairs, each of which comes at a heavy cost. They demand a huge amount of money to operate due to their highly complex equipment.

b. **Unemployment:** Even though AI substitutes a large percentage of routine work as well as other activities with robotic systems, human influence is reducing, which presents a significant matter for employment norms. Every company seeks to swap over to automation and artificial intelligence, which can accomplish comparable tasks faster in place of staff members who only possess the bare basic qualifications. The major cause of the GDP stagnating or not rising as rapidly as anticipated is the loss of jobs. People are lacking the highly sought-after skills that are needed. As a consequence, there exists a substantial disparity in both demand and supply.

c. **A lack of imagination:** The AIs are not meant to carry out imaginative activities. Therefore, it must be pretty apparent that AIs are not creative or imaginative. They aren't going to be able to meet the human mind, perhaps if they manage to help users develop something original. The one who programs them and provides them with commands restricts their ability to create. Human brains are incredibly susceptible and possess a highly emotional factor. In simplest terms, AIs could develop into skillful robotic systems, yet they will never compare to a human brain's intellectual capabilities. This happens because, unlike abilities, which are learned and perfected, skill sets are inherent and must be developed.

d. **Lack of Improvement with Practice:** Among the most incredible characteristics of organisms is how the human mind can get stronger as it matures and experiences more. AIs, in contrast, cannot be described as computers that seem to get better with use; rather, they become worse over time. Since they are still unable to fully comprehend moral or legal notions, computers are not able to figure out what is right or wrong. They are incapable of making choices when faced with an unexplainable (non-programmed-for)

KEYWORD

Automation is the use of technology to perform tasks with where human input is minimized.

circumstance because they are developed for particular instances.

e. **Humans cannot be replaced by AI:** There is no question that computers work rather more efficiently than people. Human intellect is a natural ability that can't be coded into the computer, so substituting humans with AIs still seems to be extremely hard, at least for the foreseeable future.

Consequently, a computer will not be capable of completely substituting a human being, irrespective of how smart it becomes. Although the idea of being supplanted by computers makes us cringe, it remains a long way off. Computers are rational, but they don't have feelings or ethical beliefs. They lack the interpersonal skills needed for managing a group of individuals since they are unable to develop relationships with others.

f. **No morals:** It might be difficult to bring moral principles and ethical standards important human qualities—into machine learning. The fast development of AI has led to rising concerns that it may suddenly grow out of control and eventually exterminate humanity. The term employed to define this period of time is "AI singularity."

g. **Lacking Feelings:** Even though it is among the key benefits of artificial intelligence, it has downsides as well. Machines are not able to communicate with individuals since they are completely devoid of empathy and emotions. While machine learning and language understanding processing have managed to help business, owners establish preliminary customer service through chat portals with bots, a real person still needs to step in to fix a persistent concern at a certain point.

KEYWORD

AI singularity is a hypothetical concept where artificial intelligence exceeds human intelligence.

Consumer experience will struggle worldwide when everything is left to chatbots. Chatbots are able to handle the preliminary touch basing. If a consumer's issue could be resolved using pre-fed guidance transcripts, that's great.

If this is not the situation, a ticket will be brought up by the bot for manual follow-up by a human. A bot might be unable to apprehend a suffering user since it is not psychologically driven like users are. Users always require a human ear to hear what needs to be accomplished (Figure 5.4).

- High costs of implementation
- Unemployment
- Lack of creativity
- Not Improving with Experience
- AI can't replace Humans
- No ethics
- No emotions

Figure 5.4. Disadvantage of AI.

5.5. ROLE OF ARTIFICIAL INTELLIGENCE

Artificial intelligence (AI) makes it possible for machines to learn from experience, adjust to new inputs and perform human-like tasks. Most AI examples that you hear about today – from chess-playing computers to self-driving cars – rely heavily on deep learning and natural language processing. Using these technologies, computers can be trained to accomplish specific tasks by processing large amounts of data and recognizing patterns in the data.

Every industry has a high demand for AI capabilities – including systems that can be used for automation, learning, legal assistance, risk notification and research.

5.5.1. AI in Cyber Security

Since more industries are harnessing the power of digitalization, people share more information with companies compared to the past. As the amount of data stored and processed in companies grows exponentially, companies feel more responsible for keeping them secure.

However, with the advent of cloud technology and cheaper computing power, mass cyber-attacks, often using thousands of bots, have become possible. A small-scale cyber-attack can cost millions of dollars and cause companies to lose their reputation. As a popular field, cyber security can deal with such problems.

Unfortunately, users appear to be the weakest link in the security chain because hackers can easily trick them using various methods. Nonetheless, thanks to the novel research field of AI in cyber security, the cyber-defense has been strengthened with the applications of AI.

A study by Pranav Patil states that in cyber security, it is critical to have the power to use higher AI than offenders. Hence, the development of intelligent cyber security methods is of capital importance in cyber defense.

KEYWORD

Digitization is the process of converting information into a digital format. The result is the representation of an object, image, sound, document, or signal obtained by generating a series of numbers that describe a discrete set of points or samples.

5.5.2. AI for Healthcare

The digitization of healthcare data and the expectation among increasingly engaged patients for personalized and virtual care are introducing unprecedented opportunities to disrupt the way healthcare is delivered.

Meanwhile, healthcare systems are overwhelmed by the flood of new, rich data sources – such as social determinants, genetic and imaging data, data from medical devices and wearable's, and social media data. Healthcare organizations must adapt the way they use and share data to relieve pressure on healthcare systems and improve medical decision making to ensure greater patient satisfaction and better outcomes.

AI capabilities – such as machine learning, computer vision, natural language processing, and forecasting and optimization – can unleash the full potential of data to improve population health and solve some of the greatest healthcare challenges. This necessary evolution will enable healthcare organizations to:

- **Improve patient outcomes**. Empower physicians with more accurate diagnostics and targeted prevention capabilities.
- **Control costs**. Improve the operational performance of hospitals by optimizing staffing resources and taking action to reduce the number of hospital readmissions.

5.5.3. AI for Retail and Consumer Goods

Mobile devices, conversational commerce, social networking and other technologies have shifted the behavior of the connected customer – and retailers and consumer goods companies need to shift accordingly.

Customers can quickly research products and compare prices through multiple channels, and you must be ready to respond with relevant offers, competitive prices and the right merchandise. That means moving beyond spreadsheets, using data from every conceivable source to understand your customer's relationship with your brand so you can influence it in real time.

And then there are the challenges facing the supply side of your business. In an effort to support unified commerce, supply chain networks are becoming increasingly complex and high-speed, making them almost impossible to track or optimize.

KEYWORD

Assortment is a collection of things that aren't the same.

Advances in AI for retail and consumer goods have made it possible to automate complex tasks through constant learning, enabling retailers to improve operations – and customer experiences – by breaking down departmental silos and applying omnichannel analytics to every step of the customer journey. Understanding where customers are in their journeys – and optimizing each interaction – drives longevity, loyalty and growth by turning data into action. In turn, you collect more data and learn more, so you can:

- **Replace search with conversational commerce**: Natural language processing and cognitive computing have given rise to conversational computer interfaces and Chatbots that enable customers to shop anywhere, anytime – giving you the opportunity to better understand customers and unify commerce.
- **Tailor efforts to specific customers:** Uncover precise consumer needs by tapping into where and at what price customers shop across all channels and devices. Rule-based systems can't handle the sheer number of products, customers and touch points in real time. But when driven by machine learning, you're pricing, assortment and marketing are always on target down to the micro market level.
- **Anticipate your customer's next move**: For every customer, AI uses thousands of pieces of text and digital data to develop a next-best action and drive recommendation engines. And you can use this insight to predict future buying behaviors, shape demand and seize opportunities to maximize margins.
- **Optimize inventory and fulfillment for online or in-store shoppers:** Planning and adjusting the movement of merchandise can be overwhelming. AI techniques can learn and correct supply chain issues while reducing the

need for human intervention. And by adding in machine-to-machine IoT analytics and RFID data streams, you can achieve real-time inventory transparency.

- **Control fraud and shrinkage**: As the volume of digital transactions with customers and vendors continues to rise, analytic anomaly detection is the only way to keep an eye on what's happening. Deep learning algorithms can uncover and adapt to new fraud vectors, enabling you to address money laundering, vendor procurement fraud, cashier fraud and returns abuse.
- **Power the store of the future today with analytics at the edge:** Your physical stores have untapped potential to connect with customers. Wi-Fi foot-traffic sensors, video cameras, electronic shelf labels, and warehouse and in-aisle robotics can transform how you use every square foot. Deep learning algorithms, computer vision technology and real-time decisioning enable you to bake the art and science of retail and consumer goods into the customer experience.

Remember

Cyber security is expected to remain popular in the decades. International Data Corporation (IDC) predicts the expenditure in (cyber) security to reach $174.7 billion in 2024, with a compound annual growth rate (CAGR) of 8.1% over the 2020–2024 forecast periods.

5.5.4. AI for Manufacturing

In manufacturing, you're under pressure to continuously improve quality while reducing costs and increasing productivity. You also strive to right-size inventory and boost profitability while driving year-over-year cost improvements. Finding new ways to extract value from the deluge of sensor and IoT data would enable you to move from a reactive to a proactive approach to minimizing unplanned downtime, reducing scrap and rework, and developing innovative new revenue streams.

Managing the unexpected is a constant challenge. Traditional approaches – Six Sigma, line-level reporting, and MES systems – are no longer sufficient for gaining insights from data to improve decision making. Finding new ways to harness the value of industrial data is essential to enabling modern manufacturers to manage today's data volume, velocity and variety.

Advances in AI enable us to automate complicated tasks and find useful signals in data that was previously too large or complex to tackle. From quality and equipment performance, to supply chain and spare parts optimization, to service improvements and monetization of IoT data, AI techniques can unlock new insights across the spectrum of manufacturing data, enabling you to:

- **Find early indicators of potential quality issues**: AI capabilities go far beyond what simple rule-based systems can do, continuously learning to automatically detect patterns in data that a human would likely never see.
- **Avoid costly scrap and rework**: Use image recognition to identify flaws during the manufacturing process so you can address them promptly.
- **Identify areas for improvement**: Text analytics, including natural language processing, lets you link customer sentiment, service comments and other written records to quality and production variables to identify areas for improvement.
- **Improve yield**: Apply deep learning in industrial operations to optimize product composition and production techniques, combining audio, video, text and other data at efficiency levels that were previously unimaginable.

KEYWORD

Regulatory risk is the risk that a change in laws and regulations will materially impact a security, business, sector, or market.

5.5.5. AI for Banking

Changing regulatory compliance requirements and shifting customer demands mean a bank's survival hinges on its ability to glean relevant insight from all available data. In fact, the efficient and effective use of data is critical to addressing many issues today's banks face – combating fraud and financial crimes, managing credit and regulatory risk, enhancing the customer experience and generating sufficient capital.

A partnership between humans and machines – each augmenting the other – holds the most promise for successfully achieving compliance and meeting customer needs, but knowing where and how to start isn't always easy.

- From fraud to credit to risk to customer experience, artificial intelligence (AI) can enhance the speed, precision and effectiveness of human efforts, which results in a more responsive, more profitable bank.
- **Turn customer experience into customer engagement**. With embedded AI tools, you can stitch data together from all sources, providing an accurate and evolving view of the customer journey. You can then optimize customer journeys across all channels to maximize engagement and enable real-time decisioning.

- **Quickly identify fraudulent transactions**. Use AI and machine learning techniques to identify which types of banking transactions are likely to be fraudulent. AI techniques, including adaptive machine learning and unsupervised intelligent agents, can predict fraudulent transactions in real time – and reduce false positives – based on changes and inconsistencies in customer behavior patterns. Reducing false positives boosts customer satisfaction, protects revenue and lowers costs.
- **Adopt fast, accurate credit scoring policies**. When a potential customer applies for a loan or credit card, use AI and machine learning techniques to analyze alternative data sources – like utility payments, mobile phone use and text message activity – for improved loan rating accuracy to give good customers faster access to credit using real-time decisioning.

KEYWORD

Commercialization is the process of bringing new products or services to market.

5.5.6. AI in Pharma

The digitization of healthcare data has introduced unprecedented opportunities to disrupt the way new and innovative therapies are delivered. There is increasing pressure on life sciences companies from the market and regulatory agencies to incorporate real world data throughout the pharmaceutical life cycle, from clinical trials through the commercialization of drug products. That means adapting the way they use and share data to get innovative therapies to patients faster.

AI capabilities – such as machine learning, computer vision, natural language processing, and forecasting and optimization – can unleash the full potential of data to solve some of our greatest health challenges and dramatically change the way therapies are delivered. This necessary evolution will enable life sciences organizations to:

- **Ensure drug safety**: Enable pharmaceutical companies to quickly determine the quality, efficacy and safety of new product candidates.
- **Get new therapies to market faster**: Accelerate clinical trials using real-world data sources, and develop fit-for-future trial designs, e.g., virtual, pragmatic and adaptive trials.

- **Uncover manufacturing issues with greater speed and accuracy**: Uncover potential issues earlier than ever and proactively take corrective action to improve outcomes.

5.6. THE ROLE OF ARTIFICIAL INTELLIGENCE IN FUTURE TECHNOLOGY

Artificial intelligence has changed the world a lot and will bring many more changes in the coming days. AI is already embedded in our daily lives. Let's take an example: many of us use virtual assistants like Google Assistant, Alexa, Siri, etc. to help us. It is predicted that in the near future, AI will be more embedded in our daily lives and that upcoming AI-based innovations will change the world forever.

Artificial intelligence (AI) is the science and technology concerned with the computational understanding of intelligent behavior and, thereby, the creation of intelligent machines.

These core areas are showing exponential growth and are having a significant impact on fields such as healthcare, space, robotics, and the military. With the ever-growing amount of data, ubiquitous connectivity, high-performance computing, and algorithms now available to us, AI will bring new levels of efficiency and sophistication to future technologies.

One of the main goals of the AI field is to produce fully autonomous agents that interact with their environment, discover optimal behaviors, and improve over time through trial and error, almost like humans. It's a long-standing challenge that ranges from robots that can sense and respond to the world around them to purely software-based agents that can interact with natural language and multimedia.

AI is ubiquitous and not just limited to computers, but has expanded into other areas such as health, safety, education, music, art, and business applications. Many AI applications are deeply embedded in the infrastructure of every industry.AI and are expected to touch almost every industry within a few years, and there are many ways AI can transform specific industries.

AI is currently being used for a variety of applications, such as medical diagnostics, e-commerce platforms, robotic control, and remote sensing. It has been used to develop and advance numerous fields and industries, including finance, healthcare, education, transportation, and robotics.

Did you Know?

The oldest known studies of artificial intelligence were performed in the late 1940s by computer innovators like Alan Turing and John von Neumann. In 1956, research teams demonstrated that a computer might solve any issue when it was given additional memory, marking an important turning point in the field of artificial intelligence. The outcome was software known as the General Problem Solver (GPS).

Researchers have developed many tools to solve the toughest problems in computer science and other fields. Current AI performance varies between subhuman, optimal, and superhuman performance. AI applications can solve a variety of tasks, including face recognition, speech recognition, object recognition, image classification, and overcoming human intelligence in the games of Go, Chess, Dota 2, and Star Craft II.

Another focus of AI technologies lies somewhere between healthcare and privacy, with the advancement of federated learning and privacy-aware machine learning. You can even produce music that can be used in a medical setting, using computer-generated music to relieve stress and pain.

Additionally, initiatives like Google Magenta, led by the Google Brain team, are looking to see if AI might be able to create compelling art and music. Another active field of AI research is the use of AI to create other AI. This includes Google's AutoML project to develop new neural network topologies with new architectures and topologies that surpass any previously released ImageNet performance.

> **KEYWORD**
>
> **Neutrality** is the tendency not to side in a conflict, which may not suggest neutral parties do not have a side or are not a side themselves. In colloquial use neutral can be synonymous with unbiased.

This applies to the current research on Generative Adversarial Networks and the work of the research teams of the Visual Computing Groups of the Technical University of Munich and Stanford University, which has developed Face2Face, a program that animates the subject's face with facial expressions transposed from an external source.

Since then, other methods based on deep neural networks have been demonstrated, from which the name "Deep Fake" was derived. Recently, new research directions, approaches, and initiatives have emerged, including research in quantum machine learning, hierarchical reinforcement learning, Bayesian deep learning, human-centered affective computing and artificial intelligence, neuroscience, self-driving cars, and conversational agents.

AI can only detect basic human emotional states like anger, joy, sadness, stress, pain, fear, and neutrality. Emotional intelligence is one of the next frontiers for higher levels of personalization. It is important to understand its impact not only from a technological point of view but also from a social, ethical, and legal perspective.

AI will change the way we live and work. It improves our productivity by helping us in many ways and saves us a lot of time doing monotonous tasks at home as well as at work. For example, now we can program the robot vacuum cleaner to clean the floor, so we can save some time and energy.

With the help of artificial intelligence, the vacuum robot avoids collisions with obstacles and effectively cleans the surface. In the same way, AI plus innovations will allow us to eliminate the need for repetitive work. Driverless vehicles will reduce the burden of driving on us and will most likely reduce the likelihood of vehicle accidents by eliminating the possibility of human error.

KEYWORD

Repetitive work refers to work that involves performing the same simple operation over and over.

Autonomous vehicles will improve the way we travel. Today's websites and apps use artificial intelligence to deliver experiences. For example, YouTube offers personalized suggestions based on what we watch. More personalized services will come in the future, including health services. The joint use of 5G and artificial intelligence will enable doctors to perform robotic surgeries, which will be very helpful in increasing access to healthcare services. Humans and machines can work wonders together with artificial intelligence.

AI will help people with special needs and the elderly live independently. With the advances that AI brings, there will be more security and privacy issues. And laws will come to deal with it. Ethical concerns will also arise.

Artificial intelligence has already improved many industries and has the potential to revolutionize all industries by reducing monotonous work, improving employee efficiency, and also thanks to the possibilities for rapid decision-making. As AI becomes more integrated into our lives, we must keep it that way by discussing ethical and safety concerns and taking the right steps.

5.7. SUMMARY

1. Artificial Intelligence and its Types

In this chapter, role of Artificial Intelligence in the field of computer science have been explained. It also mentions about the history of artificial intelligence. This chapter also emphasizes on the various types of artificial intelligence such as weak AI, Strong AI, and Super AI.

2. Role of AI and Its Pros/Cons

Towards the end of this chapter, it provides highlights to the role and different application of artificial intelligence in various industries such as AI in Cyber Security, AI for Healthcare, AI for Retail & Consumer Goods, AI for Manufacturing, AI for Banking, and AI in Pharma. In this chapter, relation of Artificial Intelligence In Future Technology also been explained

5.8. REVIEW QUESTIONS

1. What do you understand by the term artificial intelligence?
2. What is the history of artificial intelligence?
3. How is artificial intelligence important for the society?
4. How AI will replace humans?
5. Explain the pros and cons of artificial intelligence.
6. Discuss various types of AI.
7. How does the strong AI differ from the weak AI?
8. What is supervised versus unsupervised learning?

5.9. MULTIPLE CHOICE QUESTIONS

1. AI stands for.

a. Artificial Intelligence
b. Video Read
c. Virtual Reality
d. Virtual Record

2. What is the full form of ASR

a. Binocular Omni-Operating Monitor
b. Automatic Speech Recognition
c. Binocular Optical-Orientation Monitor Disk
d. Binocular Optical-Orientation Memory Disk

3. In how many category processes is Artificial Intelligence classified in?

a. Depends on the input nature
b. 5
c. 2
d. 3

4. Which is not the type of AI classification based on functionalities?

a. Reactive machines
b. Limited memory
c. Theory of mind
d. Super AI

5. What are the different types of Artificial Intelligence approaches?

a. Strong
b. Weak
c. Applied
d. All of the above

Answers to Multiple Choice Questions

1. (a) 2. (b) 3. (d) 4. (d) 5. (c)

REFERENCES

1. Abhishek, K., (2022). *Introduction to Artificial Intelligence* – Simple Talk. [online] Simple Talk. Available at: https://www.red-gate.com/simple-talk/development/data-science-development/introduction-to-artificial-intelligence/#:~:text=Artificial%20intelligence%20(AI)%20is%20the,many%20other%20products%20and%20services (accessed on 03 March 2023).
2. Agnihotri, N., (n.d). *What are Different Types of Artificial Intelligence?* [online] Engineers Garage. Available at: https://www.engineersgarage.com/what-are-different-types-of-artificial-intelligence/ (accessed on 03 March 2023).
3. GeeksforGeeks, (2020). *What is Artificial Super Intelligence (ASI)?* – GeeksforGeeks. [online] Available at: https://www.geeksforgeeks.org/what-is-artificial-super-intelligence-asi/ (accessed on 03 March 2023).
4. icertglobal.com (n.d). *Advantages and Disadvantages of Artificial Intelligence* | iCert Global. [online] Available at: https://www.icertglobal.com/advantages-and-disadvantages-of-artificial-intelligence/detail (accessed on 03 March 2023).

5. Jessica, (2022). *The Role of Artificial Intelligence in Future Technology* – Inventiva. [online] Inventiva. Available at: https://www.inventiva.co.in/trends/the-role-of-artificial-intelligence-in-future-technology/ (accessed on 03 March 2023).
6. Joshi, N., (2019). *7 Types of Artificial Intelligence*. [online] Forbes. Available at: https://www.forbes.com/sites/cognitiveworld/2019/06/19/7-types-of-artificial-intelligence/?sh=1450e9fb233e (accessed on 03 March 2023).

CHAPTER 6

DATA COMMUNICATION AND COMPUTER NETWORK

UNIT INTRODUCTION

Inside this modern world, interaction decides every aspect of development. The world keeps getting better because of interactions that are efficient, simple, comprehensible, and prompt. The advancement of the internet, the telecommunications sector, and messaging services have increased human interaction, enjoyment, and money.

Anywhere around the globe can receive updates on an incident that takes place in one location. For instance, audiences can watch a live sporting tournament that is going to take place in India from wherever they are on the globe.

By using one-to-one, one-to-many, or even all methods, the system allows individuals to exchange data with anyone on the planet. Students will research the emergence of connections, networking devices, internet applications, and network design in this section.

Humans are transforming their way of life and how they conduct business as a consequence of information communication and networking. Company decisions need to be made more rapidly than ever before, and the decision-makers want access to trustworthy data straight away.

Why wait a week for that report from Germany to show up in the mail if it can be obtained nearly instantly online? Computer systems and the internet are essential for modern business. Moreover, before users request information about how fast users can connect, people must first understand how connections work effectively, what kinds of innovations are accessible, and which design best fulfills which set of demands.

The desktop computer reinvented business, companies, scientific knowledge, and education in unexpected ways. A comparable reformation is presently taking place in information communications and networking. Communication channels nowadays can pass more and speedier transmissions due to advancements in technology.

In order to make the most of this enhanced bandwidth, facilities are modified. For instance, in this case, traditional phone features like incoming calls, conference calling, call waiting, and voicemail messages have continued to expand. Modern inventions are the outcome of data communications and networking studies. The ability to transmit information from any part of the globe, such as messages, sound recordings, and video, is one aim.

Users are required to have a connection to the Internet at all times to efficiently and precisely install and transmit files. Data transmission, networks, the Web, and protocols and guidelines are the four topics covered in this section.

The authors start by providing an overall definition of information communication. Networks are subsequently described as information highways. The case in point of the internetwork is the world wide web (i.e., a network of networks). Eventually, the authors explain the various types of guidelines, the variation between protocols and standards, and the institutions that set some of these benchmarks.

The term "computer network" describes a network of linked computers and associated electronic devices, like printers. The transfer of data between computer systems is made easier by such connectivity. Computer systems can interact with one another remotely or over wired broadband.

Learning Objectives

After completing this chapter, you should be able to understand the following:

- Understand the concept of data communication
- Identify the significance of data representation
- Understand the measuring capacity of communication media
- Educate about the concept of transmitting media and wired transmitting media
- Give advice about switching techniques, and its various kinds
- Understand the importance of network and history of networks
- Give advice about the various categories of network

Key Terms

- Analog Signal
- Computer network
- Data Communication
- Data Representation
- Digital Signal
- Network Criteria
- Switching Techniques
- Transmission Media

6.1. DATA COMMUNICATION

6.1.1. Data

The term "data" refers to the setup of data in a manner that the two parties that are generating and employing it can comprehend. Data is "information in digital form which can be transferred or filtered," according to the Online Dictionary. Whatever type of information may be used, such as messages, signs, photos, video files, indicators, and much more.

KEYWORD

Wireless device is a device that uses radio waves to send or receive information.

6.1.2. Communication

The transfer of data between two entities that are relevant is termed communication. The elements can be characterized as creatures like humans, computers, animals, birds, and so on. The two different groups are capable of communicating with one another. A provider must transport the data in order to deliver the interaction. The provider could be cordless or wired. Once two people speak orally, the wireless device acts as a conduit to transfer the data.

"The communication medium" is a definition used in computer technology to describe the provider. The source of the information in a computer network is the speaker, and the receiver or destination of the information is the listener.

Humans share data when they talk with one another. Local or remote sharing is both possible. Local interactions take place face-to-face among people, whereas distant communication is established across space.

The word "telecommunication" describes long-distance communication and involves telephone service, telegraphy, and television (tele is Greek for "far"). The information displayed in any format that is accepted by the parties who are generating and employing the information is termed "data. Through the use of data communications, the exchange of data between transmitter and receiver is possible over any kind of transmission channel, like a wire or cable.

Technology and communication need to be components of a communication network consisting of a combination of equipment (physical equipment) and applications for data transmission to take place (programs). Delivery, precision, promptness, and buffering are the four basic qualities that decide how well a data communications network performs.

6.1.3. Data Transfer

Information communication refers to the process of sharing information between devices via a medium of communication in a significant way, as demonstrated by the above-mentioned examples. The hardware has to be a component of the communication network.

The communication system is composed of both software and hardware components. The four essential regulations mentioned below must be abided by in order to create a successful communications network:

1. **Delivery:** The information that is required to be sent must reach its intended recipient.
2. **Accuracy:** The information must be supplied in its original, authentic manner.
3. **Timeliness:** The information must also be delivered promptly by the communication network.
4. **Jitter:** Information is broken down into smaller groups (packets) and then sent individually over the network. Jitter is a term used to describe the difference in arrival between two data packets.

Did you Know?

The definition of "meaningful way" signifies the requirement that the communication's purpose be clear to both parties. This is the pattern for two-person information exchange. The term "Hello" is used by the communicator (a person) to initiate oral communication with the hearer (another person) in the dialect "English."

6.2. COMPONENTS

- **Data/Message:** The communication system's main component
- **Data/message** refers to the information sent between the source and the destination.
- **Source**: The origin is the machine that creates and transmits the data to the target.
- **Destination**: The information's recipient is a machine.
- **Medium**: It is used to transport data from one location to another.
- **The transporter** appears to offer a wireless or wired path.
- **Protocol:** A protocol is a set of guidelines for exchanging data and information.

Computer systems, cellular phones, workspaces, servers, video recorders, and other gadgets could act as both the source and the destination. The procedure makes the communication efficient. This outlines the procedure for communicating with each other without having to suffer any loss or disruption.

TIPS

MBPS stands for Megabyte per second whereas Mbps stands for Megabit per second.

6.3. DATA REPRESENTATION

Presently, data is available in a variety of formats, including text, numbers, images, audio, and video.

6.3.1. Text

Text is depicted as a binary sequence, or a series of bits, in transmitting data (Os or is). To depict text symbols, various bit pattern sets have been developed. Coding is the method of portraying symbols, so each set is termed as a code. Unicode, the current standard coding system, uses 32 bits to represent any symbol or character found in any language across the globe. The first 127 characters in Unicode, also known as Basic Latin, are made up of the American Standard Code for Information Interchange (ASCII), which was created in the United States many years ago. Part of Appendix A is Unicode.

6.3.2. Numbers

Bit patterns can also be employed to show numbers. To make arithmetic simpler, a number is instantly transformed into a binary number instead of being represented by a code like ASCII. In Appendix B, various numbering strategies are mentioned.

6.3.3. Images

Bit patterns also serve as an image representation. An image is formed of a matrix of pixels, or "picture elements," in which each pixel is a tiny dot. The resolution affects how big a pixel is. An image could be split, for instance, into 1000 or 10,000 pixels. The best resolution and a good example of the image are present in the second scenario, but more memory is required to store the image.

Thus, every pixel is allotted a bit pattern after already being separated into individual pixels in an image. The image helps determine the pattern's size and valuation. An l-bit pattern is sufficient to depict a pixel for an image made up of nothing but black and white dots (such as a chessboard).

Users can expand the bit pattern by adding a gray scale if such an image is not entirely made of pure white and pure black pixels. Employ 2-bit patterns, for instance, to display grayscale in four different ways. The digits 00, 01, 10, and 11 could be used to symbolize black, dark gray, light gray, and white pixels, respectively. The ways of reflecting-colored images differ.

Red, green, and blue are the three main colors which are combined to produce each color. That also gives rise to the name RGB for one technique. Each color's intensity is determined, and a bit pattern is then designated for it. By combining these three additional primary colors—yellow, cyan, and magenta—one color is created using a different technique known as YCM.

KEYWORD

Electronic signal" is simply a general term for a signal that carries information.

6.3.4. Audio

The term "audio" describes the capturing or transmission of a song or audio. Audio differs from text, numbers, and visuals by its very nature. It is not distinct; it is ongoing. People still produce a constant signal even though they use a microphone to convert music or voice to an electronic signal. What people will study is the conversion of audio or music to a digital or analog stream.

6.3.5. Video

A picture or movie that has been captured or aired is known as a "video." Video can be made as a single cohesive object (for example, by a TV camera) or as a collection of separate images merged to create the illusion of motion. Once more, video can be transformed into a digital or analog signal.

6.4. MODE OF DATA FLOW

The data flow defines the flow direction of the data between source and destination. The data flow may be either simplex or half-duplex or full duplex. The three modes of the data flow.

- **Simplex:** In simplex mode, the direction of the data flow is unidirectional. One of the device can transmit the data and another device can

- **Half-Duplex:** In half-duplex mode, the data can be transmitted on both directions but not at the same time (device 1 to device 2 or device 2 to device 1). One device can send and another one can receive at a time. The example is walkie-talkie. The entire medium is used for the one-way transmission.
- **Full-Duplex:** In full-duplex mode, the data can be transmitted on both directions (device 1 to device 2 and device 2 to device 1) at the same time. One device can send and another one can receive at a time. The example is telephone communication. In this, the entire medium is divided for the two-way transmission.

KEYWORD

Microphone is a transducer that converts sound into an electrical signal.

6.5. ANALOG AND DIGITAL SIGNAL

The entire world is full of signals, both natural and artificial. Signals can be analog or digital. The term analog signal refers to signal that is continuous and takes continuous value.

Most phenomenon's in the world today are analog. There is an infinite amount of colors to paint an object (even if the difference is indiscernible to the eye), it is possible for us to hear different sounds and also smell different odors. The common theme among all of these analog signals is their infinite possibilities.

Typical representation of analog signal. Because the signal varies with time, time is plotted on horizontal (x-axis), and voltage on the vertical (y-axis). While this signals may be limited to a range of maximum and minimum values. There are still an infinite number of possible values within that range.

For example, the analog voltage that light the bulbs is clamped between –220V and +220V, but as you increase the resolution more and more, you discover an infinite number of values that the signal can be. For example, pure audio signals are analog.

The signal that comes out of a microphone is full of analog frequencies and harmonics, which combine to beautiful music. A digital signal is a physical signal that is a representation of a sequence of discrete values. The signal must have a finite set of possible values, the number of set which can be anywhere between two and very large number that is not infinity. Digital signal is one of two voltage value (0V or 5V) timing graphs of these signals look like square waves.

6.6. WHY DATA COMMUNICATION?

Data communication refers to the movement of encoded information from one point to another by means of electronic transmission system. It can also be defined as the exchange of data between two devices via some form of transmission medium which can be wired or wireless. Another definition for data communications simply means the transferring of digital information (usually in binary form) between two or more points (terminals).

At both the source and destination, data are in digital form; however, during transmission, they can be in digital or analog form Information is carried by signal, which is a physical quantity that changes with time. The signal can be a voltage proportional to the amplitude of the voice like in simple telephone, a sequence of pulses of light in an optical fiber, or a radio-electric wave radiated by an antenna.

The fundamental purpose of data communication is to exchange information which is done by following certain rules and regulations called protocols and standards. Communications between devices are justified for the following reasons:

- Reduces time and effort required to perform business task
- Captures business data at its source
- Centralizes control over business data
- Effect rapid dissemination of information
- Reduces current and future cost of doing business
- Supports expansion of business capacity at reasonably incremental cost as the organization
- Supports organizations objective in centralizing computer system
- Supports improved management control of an organization.

As a rule, the maximum permissible transmission rate of a message is directly proportional to signal power and inversely proportional to channel noise. It is the aim of any communications system to provide the highest possible transmission rate at the lowest possible power and with the least possible noise.

KEYWORD

Fiber Optics is the communications medium that works by sending optical signals down hair-thin strands of extremely pure glass or plastic fiber.

6.7. MEASURING CAPACITY OF COMMUNICATION MEDIA

ACTIVITY 6.1.

1. List various types of senders on a network.
2. Find out how many hertz is 10 Megahertz.

In data communication, the transmission medium is also known as channel. The capacity of a channel is the maximum number of signals or traffic that a channel can carry. It is measured in terms of bandwidth and data transfer rate as described below.

6.7.1. Bandwidth

Bandwidth of a channel is the range of frequencies available for transmission of data through that channel. Higher the bandwidth, higher the data transfer rate. Normally, bandwidth is the difference of maximum and minimum frequency contained in the composite signals. Bandwidth is measured in Hertz (Hz). 1 KHz = 1000 Hz 1 MHz = 1000 KHz = 1000000 Hz

6.7.2. Data Transfer Rate

Data travels in the form of signals over a channel. One signal carry one or more bits over the channel. Data transfer rate is the number of bits transmitted between source and destination in one second. It is also known as bit rate. It is measured in terms of bits per second (bps). The higher units for data transfer rates are: 1 Kbps=210 bps=1024 bps 1 Mbps=220 bps=1024 Kbps 1 Gbps=230 bps=1024 Mbps 1 Tbps=240 bps=1024 Gbps.

6.8. SWITCHING PROCEDURES

In order to establish one-to-one communication, humans are keen to understand how to join the transmitter and the receiver in a network using various technologies. One alternative is to establish a specific link (mesh topology) between every device and every other device, or between a central hub and every other device (a star topology).

Furthermore, it is clear that for large networks, such solutions are expensive. Data can also be sent across different network nodes using switching as an alternative to this. An interim transmission path for the data is created by this switching procedure. Circuit switching and packet switching are the second most frequently employed switching procedures.

6.8.1. Switching Circuits

In circuit switching, a designated route between both the sender and the recipient is specified before communication commences. A linked series of links connecting nodes in the network creates this route. Each packet follows the very same route that was set up during the connection. In the past, whenever people made a phone call, the telephone system's switching devices established a physical pathway or route from our house phone to the recipient's phone. An illustration of circuit-switched networks would be this.

6.8.2. Packet Switching

In packet switching, each piece of data or communication that needs to be sent between both the sender and the receiver is divided into smaller pieces termed packets. The network is then employed to send those packets individually. Based on accessibility, various packets containing the same information may travel down multiple pathways. A header carrying the address of the destination and other information, in addition to the main message portion, makes up each packet. While every packet has reached its final position, it is placed back together, and the recipient then gets the actual message. In contrast to circuit switching, packet switching only utilizes a route while a packet is being transmitted. After the transmission is finished, the channel is open for packet transfers from additional communication partners (Figure 6.1).

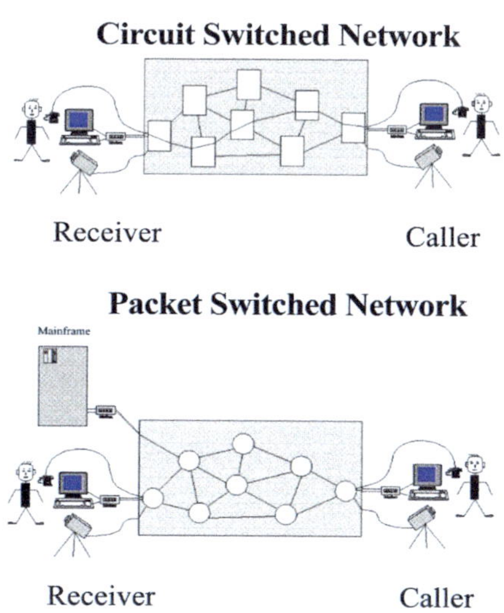

Figure 6.1. Circuit switching.

Source: Image by Wikimedia Commons.

6.9. TRANSMITTING MEDIA

Anything capable of sending signals or information between both the source (transmitter) and the location is a transmission technology (receiver). The electric cord, for instance, is the conduit through which electric current travels from the switch to the ceiling fan or bulb once turned on either one. Transmission media in information communication are indeed the pathways that transmit messages among two or even more communicators.

Depending on the categorization of communication media, transmission can be either directed or non-directive. In directed transmission, the nodes are linked physically by a cable or line over which messages carrying data are transmitted. Typically, these would be metal wiring, fiber-optic cables, and so on.

KEYWORD

Wireless media can send data through radio waves or infrared light on computers.

These go by the name "wired media" too.

Data is transmitted in the air using an antenna and electromagnetic waves during unsupervised transfer. These go by the name of wireless media as well. Longer-range data transmission and reception employ dish-shaped antennas. To ensure that they are in a line of sight, these antennas are positioned atop taller structures. After a given amount of airborne distance, waves start to weaken progressively. In order to renew the signals using the same strength, transmitters are placed.

6.10. WIRED TRANSMITTING MEDIA

The term "wired transmitting media" refers to any physical network that could also transmit data as signals. Coaxial cables, twisted pairs, and optical fiber are the three guided wired mediums of communication for transmitting data that are most regularly utilized. While fiber optic cables hold light signals, twisted-pair and coaxial cables pass electric signals.

6.10.1. Twisted-Pair Cable

The Twisted-pair is composed of two copper cables that have been twisted to imitate the DNA helix. Polycarbonate shields are being used to protect both copper cables. In most cases, several such pairs are bundled together and wrapped in external safety. One communication link is established through each of the twisted pair cables.

By employing a twisted setup, electronic intervention from nearby, comparable sets are kept to a bare minimum. Twisted pairs are more regularly used for LANs and landlines due to their lower cost. There are two distinct kinds of wires here: Unprotected twisted-pair (UTP) and protected twisted-pair (STP).

6.10.2. Coaxial Cable

An additional kind of data transfer type of media is a coaxial cable. In comparison to twisted-pair cable, it has a higher connection speed and is best protected. The wiring has an insulating layer covering a copper wire at its core. An external conductor is also placed on the insulator's side (usually a copper mesh).

A polycarbonate coat is placed over all this outer casing. The coaxial cable's protected construction, which enables the copper core to transmit information rapidly without intervention from the external world, is the secret to its victory. Higher frequency signals can be transported over longer distances using these kinds of wires (Figure 6.2).

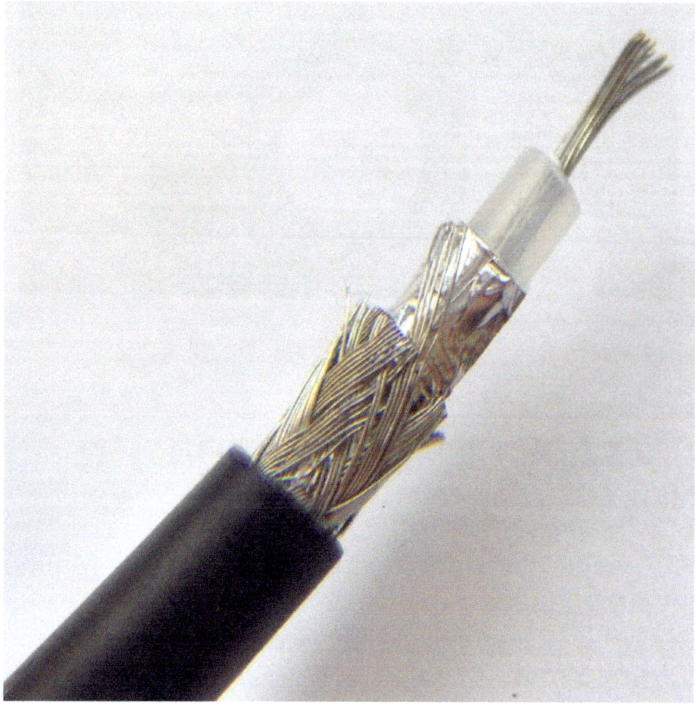

Figure 6.2. Coaxial cable.

Source: Image by Wikimedia Commons.

6.10.3. Fiber Optic

The data is transmitted over optical fiber wire as the light that needs to travel from the inside of a thin glass fiber. Refraction is a strategy used by optical fiber to guide light through a medium. A cladding-like layer of less dense glass surrounds a central thin transparent strand of glass. The entire setup is protected by a PVC or Teflon external shell.

Normally, backbone channels use these sorts of wires. The better bandwidth and lighter weight of these wires lead to a quicker rate of information transmission. Lengthier signal paths are possible, and the wire is unaffected by electromagnetic interference. Optic fibers cost a lot of money and are multidirectional. In order to communicate in full-duplex mode, two wires are necessary (Figure 6.3).

Figure 6.3. Internal structure of fiber optic cable.

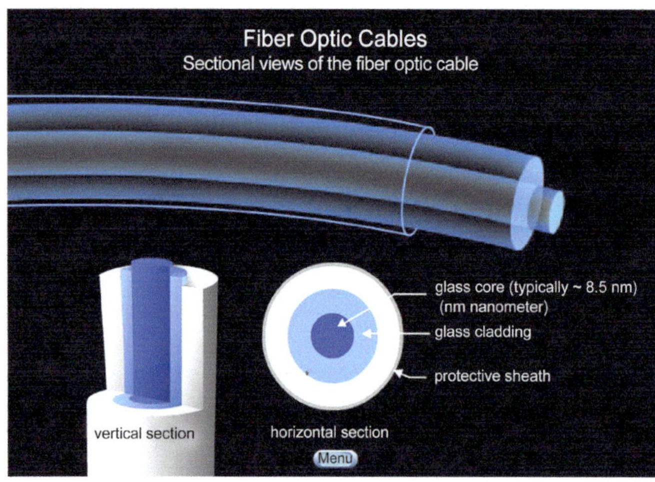

Source: Image by Flickr.

6.11 WIRELESS COMMUNICATION TECHNOLOGY

The electromagnetic signals used in wireless communication technology are the means by which information is transmitted over distances. Wireless technology can use electromagnetic waves at a frequency range from 3 kHz to 900 THz. Without the requirement for any physical medium, WiFi technologies enable interaction between two or more gadgets over short and long distances and time.

Bluetooth, Wi-Fi, Wireless LAN, as well as other technologies for wireless communications are just a few instances. As per their bandwidths, the electromagnetic frequency band (3KHz–900THz) could be divided into four types: radio waves, microwaves, infrared waves, and visible or light waves. The fact that each wave has three good qualities for wireless communication is one of those characteristics. The spectrum of electromagnetic waves.

6.11.1. Bluetooth

Bluetooth is a short-range wireless technology that can be used to connect mobile-phones, mouse, headphones, keyboards, computers, etc. wirelessly over a short distance. One can print documents with Bluetooth enabled printers without a physical connection. All these Bluetooth-enabled devices have a low-cost transceiver chip.

This chip uses the unlicensed frequency band of 2.4 GHz to transmit and receive data. These devices can send data within a range of 10 meters with a speed of 1–2 Mbps. In Bluetooth technology, the communicating devices within a range of 10 meters build a personal area network called piconet.

The devices in a piconet work in a master-slave configuration. A master device can communicate with up to 7 active slave devices at the same time. Bluetooth technology allows up to 255 devices to build a network. Out of them, 8 devices can communicate at the same time and remaining devices can be inactive, waiting for a response command from the master device.

KEYWORD

Bluetooth technology is a high-speed low powered wireless technology link that is designed to connect phones or other portable equipment together.

6.11.2. Wireless LAN

This is another way of wireless communication. Wireless LAN is a local area network (LAN), and it is a popular way to connect to the Internet. The international organization IEEE assigns numbers to each different standards of LAN. The wireless LAN is number as 802.11, and it is popularly known as Wi-Fi.

These networks consist of communicating devices such as laptops and mobile phones, as well as the network device called APs (access points) which is installed in buildings or floors. An access point is a device that is used to create a wireless local area network, by connecting to a wired router, switch, or hub.

The APs are connected to a wired network, and all the devices communicate or access the Internet through an access point. Wi-Fi gives users the flexibility to move around within the network area while being connected to the network. Following is some of the benefits of WLAN:

- Wireless connections can be used to extend or replace an existing wired infrastructure
- Resulted in increased access for mobile devices
- Provides easy access to the Internet in public places

KEYWORD

Data source is an object that represents a repository of data, such as an email archive, a fileshare, or a filing cabinet.

6.12. DATA COMMUNICATION AND TERMINAL EQUIPMENT

Communication facilities have an ancient history, but we tend to think of the advent of the telegraph and later the telephone as the beginning of modern communications. Extensive telegraph and telephone networks were established all over the world, decades before the emergence of computers.

Data communication equipment (DCE) is the hardware devices that can be used to establish, maintain and terminate communication between a data source and its destination. Data communications equipment is most used to perform signal exchange, coding and line clocking tasks as part of intermediate equipment or DTE. A typical example of data communication equipment is the modem.

Data terminal equipment (DTE) refers to the interface equipment which is source or destination in communication. The terminal equipment is capable of converting information to signals and also reconverting received signals. Data terminal equipment does communicate directly with each other. Communication between them is done by data communication equipment. Popular examples of data terminal equipment are computers, printers, routers, servers, etc. Data communication equipment and data terminal equipment are often confused with each other.

In fact, the confusion is more pronounce when data communication equipment is embedded in some data terminal equipment. The truth is that when the two are separated they are interlinked. Also, data terminal equipment and data communication connectors are wired differently if a single straight cable is employed. Data communication equipment generates internal clock signals, while data terminal equipment works with externally provided signals.

6.13. NETWORKS

A network is set of interconnected devices (sometime referred as nodes) which are used to transmit data between them with agreed protocols. The networks are used to connect the people, machines, devices to share the data anywhere in the world. The devices can be computers, printers, mobile phones, servers which are capable of sending and receiving data.

The data can be generated by a device. There is considerable confusion in the literature between a computer network and a distributed system. The key distinction is that in a distributed system, a collection of independent computers appears to its users as a single coherent system (Figure 6.4).

Usually, it has a single model or paradigm that it presents to the users. Often a layer of software on top of the operating system, called middleware, is responsible for implementing this model. A well-known example of a distributed system is the World Wide Web, in which everything looks like a document (Web page).

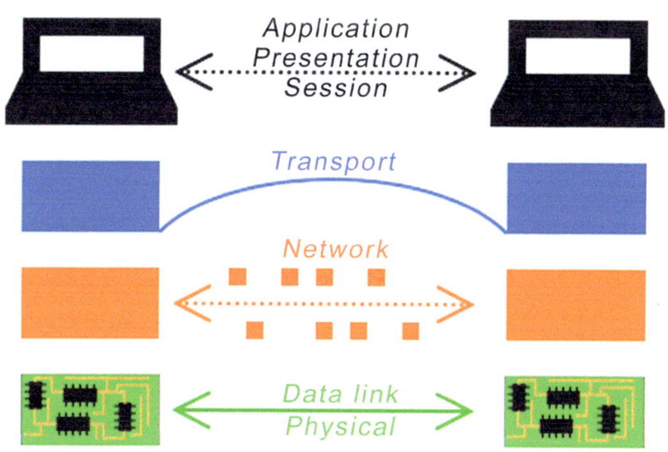

Figure 6.4. How do network work?

Source: Image by Explain that stuff.

6.14. HISTORY OF NETWORK

A computer network is a digital telecommunications network which allows nodes to share resources. In computer networks, computing devices exchange data with each other using connections (data links) between nodes. These data links are established over cable media such as wires or optic cables, or wireless media such as Wi-Fi.

Remember

Computer networking as we know it today may be said to have gotten its start with the Arpanet development in the late 1960s and early 1970s. Prior to that time there were computer vendor "networks" designed primarily to connect terminals and remote job entry stations to a mainframe.

In 1940, George Sit bit used a teletype machine to send instructions for a problem set from his model at Dartmouth college to his complex number calculator in New York and received results back by the same means. In 1950's, early networks of communicating computers included the military radar system Semi-Automatic Ground Environment (SAGE) was started.

Later, in 1960s, the notion of networking between computers viewing each other as equal peers to achieve "resource sharing" was fundamental to the Arpanet design. The other strong emphasis of the Arpanet work was its reliance on the then novel technique of packet switching to efficiently share communication resources among "bursty" users, instead of the more traditional message or circuit switching.

6.15. DISTRIBUTED PROCESSING

Most networks use distributed processing, in which a task is divided among multiple computers. Instead of one single large machine being responsible for all aspects of process, separate computers (usually a personal computer or workstation) handle a subset.

6.16. NETWORK PREREQUISITES

A network must therefore be capable of satisfying a range of requirements. The three which are the most crucial are safety, dependability, and effectiveness.

6.16.1. Execution

There are various approaches to examining the outcomes, such as transportation and processing times. The duration of time needed for a signal to transfer from one machine to another is known as the transit time. The time that passes between a request and a reaction is known as the response time.

Numerous variables, like the number of customers, the type of data transmission, the capabilities of the linked equipment, and the quality of the software, influence a network's performance. Throughput and delay are two networking measures that are frequently used to measure progress.

Fewer interruptions and increased bandwidth are usually required. And yet, these two requirements frequently conflict with one another. Users might be able to boost bandwidth by sending more data via the network, but the lag will increase as a result of traffic overcrowding.

6.16.2. Reliability

Delivery precision is influenced by the number of inadequacies, the pace at which a connection can be restored after a collapse, and the system's adaptability to major disasters.

KEYWORD

Bandwidth is the maximum rate of data transfer across a given path.

6.16.3. Safety

The safeguarding of information from unauthorized exposure, the protection of lost data and advancement, and the establishment of policies and procedures for recovering data from intrusions are all concerns related to network security.

6.17. PHYSICAL STRUCTURES

Users must first describe a few network attributes prior to actually talking about network systems.

6.17.1. Connection Type

When two or more pieces of equipment are linked together, they create a network. A connection is a communication medium that allows the transfer of data between two devices. The simplest and most effective way to illustrate any link is to think of it in terms of a line connecting the two points.

Two devices must be simultaneously connected to a single link in some sort of way to be able to communicate. Point-to-point and multipoint links are both possible options.

6.17.1.1. Point-to-Point

A dedicated link between two devices is supplied by a point-to-point connection. Transfer between these two devices can only be permitted at the link's highest output. Point-to-point links usually involve physical wires or cables operating between the opposite edges, but other possibilities exist as well, including microwave or satellite links.

By using an infrared remote controller to switch the channel on the television, users are creating a point-to-point linkage between both the remote control and the television's control method.

Multipoint In a multipoint linkage (also known as a multidrop connection), two distinct devices use the same channel. The channel's ability is shared, be it geographically or temporally, in the multipoint surroundings. It constitutes a spatially common linkage if various devices can use it at the same time. A timeshare linkage is one which consumer must alter.

KEYWORD

Topology is concerned with the properties of a geometric object that are preserved under continuous deformations, such as stretching, twisting, crumpling, and bending; that is, without closing holes, opening holes, tearing, gluing, or passing through itself.

6.17.2. Physical Topology

One or more devices may be connected to a connection, and two or more connections can make up a topology. This would be known as a physical topology. The spatial depiction of a network's topology demonstrates how each of the connections and connecting elements (commonly referred to as nodes) connect to each other. There are four potential fundamental topologies: ring, bus, star, and mesh.

6.17.2.1. MESH

Each device that is connected to another device in a mesh topology does have a unique point-to-point connection. Based on the definition of dedicated, a connection can only carry traffic in between two devices that it links. Users first take into account the necessity of how each node is linked to every other node in order to calculate the total quantity of physical links in a mesh network with n nodes.

Node 1 must be connected to n-l nodes, preceded by node 2, then node 1, and at last node n, all of which need to be linked to n-l nodes. n (n – 1) physical links are needed. As opposed to this, users could split the number of connections by two if each physical link continues to support duplex communication.

Optionally, users could conclude that duplex-mode connections are required in a mesh topology. Each network device must have n-1 input/output (VO) ports in order to communicate with the other n-1 stations and support as many linkages as possible.

When compared to other network topologies, a mesh has a number of benefits. Firstly, using dedicated links assures that each linkage can support its own collected data, exterminating any traffic issues that might arise when links are shared between multiple gadgets. A mesh topology is also reliable. The system is not rendered useless if just one connection breaks.

The positive impact of confidentiality or safety comes in third. Each message employs a distinct line to ensure that only the intended receiver can see it. Physical restrictions keep other users from accessing messages.

At last, failure isolation and fault diagnosis are made simple by point-to-point connections. Traffic could be detoured to avoid connections that might have issues. This facility gives the network manager the ability to pinpoint the fault precisely and helps in deciding its reason and fixing it. A large percentage of a mesh's drawbacks are linked to how much wiring and how many I/O access points are usually needed.

Setup and reconnecting are demanding since every system needs to be linked with every other machine. Second, there is a possibility that the setup will simply take up more area than the walls, ceilings, or floors can support. Finally, the equipment (I/O ports and cable) needed to link each connection may be impossible to afford.

Due to such factors, mesh topologies are typically only partially put in place. For instance, a mesh topology could act as the backbone linking the primary computer systems of a hybrid network that could also integrate other topologies. The linkage of phone line field offices, where each regional office must be attached to every other regional office, is a good demonstration of a mesh topology.

Star Topology In a star topology, each device has a dedicated point-to-point link only to a central controller, usually called a hub. The devices are not directly linked to one another. Unlike a mesh topology, a star topology does not allow direct traffic between devices. The controller acts as an exchange: If one device wants to send data to another, it sends the data to the controller, which then relays the data to the other connected device.

A star topology is less expensive than a mesh topology. In a star, each device needs only one link and one I/O port to connect it to any number of others. This factor also makes it easy to install and reconfigure. Far less cabling needs to be housed, and additions,

KEYWORD

Hybrid network is any network that can use more than one type of connecting technology.

moves, and deletions involve only one connection: between that device and the hub.

TIPS

An Internet service provider (ISP) is any organization that provides services for accessing the Internet.

Other advantages include robustness. If one link fails, only that link is affected. All other links remain active. This factor also lends itself to easy fault identification and fault isolation. As long as the hub is working, it can be used to monitor link problems and bypass defective links. One big disadvantage of a star topology is the dependency of the whole topology on one single point, the hub.

If the hub goes down, the whole system is dead. Although a star requires far less cable than a mesh, each node must be linked to a central hub. For this reason, often more cabling is required in a star than in some other topologies (such as ring or bus). The star topology is used in local-area networks (LANs). High-speed LANs often use a star topology with a central hub.

6.17.3. Bus Topology

The preceding examples all describe point-to-point connections. A bus topology, on the other hand, is multipoint. One long cable acts as a backbone to link all the devices in a network Nodes are connected to the bus cable by drop lines and taps. A drop line is a connection running between the device and the main cable.

A tap is a connector that either splices into the main cable or punctures the sheathing of a cable to create a contact with the metallic core. As a signal travels along the backbone, some of its energy is transformed into heat. Therefore, it becomes weaker and weaker as it travels farther and farther. For this reason, there is a limit on the number of taps a bus can support and on the distance between those taps.

Advantages of a bus topology include ease of installation. Backbone cable can be laid along the most efficient path, then connected to the nodes by drop lines of various lengths. In this way, a bus uses less cabling than mesh or star topologies. In a star, for example, four network devices in the same room require four lengths of cable reaching all the way to the hub.

In a bus, this redundancy is eliminated. Only the backbone cable stretches through the entire facility. Each drop line has to reach only as far as the nearest point on the backbone. Disadvantages include difficult reconnection and fault isolation. A bus is usually designed to be optimally efficient at installation. It can therefore be difficult to add new devices.

Signal reflection at the taps can cause degradation in quality. This degradation can be controlled by limiting the number and spacing of devices connected to a given length of cable. Adding new devices may therefore require modification or replacement of the backbone. In addition, a fault or break in the bus cable stops all transmission, even between devices on the same side of the problem.

The damaged area reflects signals back in the direction of origin, creating noise in both directions. Bus topology was the one of the first topologies used in the design of early local area networks. Ethernet LANs can use a bus topology, but they are less popular now for reasons.

KEYWORD

Bus topology, also known as line topology, is a type of network topology in which all devices in the network are connected by one central RJ-45 network cable or coaxial cable.

6.17.4. Ring Topology

In a ring topology, each device has a dedicated point-to-point connection with only the two devices on either side of it. A signal is passed along the ring in one direction, from device to device, until it reaches its destination. Each device in the ring incorporates a repeater.

When a device receives a signal intended for another device, its repeater regenerates the bits and passes them along A ring is relatively easy to install and reconfigure. Each device is linked to only its immediate neighbors (either physically or logically).

To add or delete a device requires changing only two connections. The only constraints are media and traffic considerations (maximum ring length and number of devices). In addition, fault isolation is simplified. Generally, in a ring, a signal is circulating at all times. If one device does not receive a signal within a specified period, it can issue an alarm.

The alarm alerts the network operator to the problem and its location. However, unidirectional traffic can be a disadvantage. In a simple ring, a break in the ring (such as a disabled station) can disable the entire network. This weakness can be solved by using a dual ring or a switch capable of closing off the break. Ring topology was prevalent when IBM introduced its local-area network Token Ring. Today, the need for higher-speed LANs has made this topology less popular (Figure 6.5).

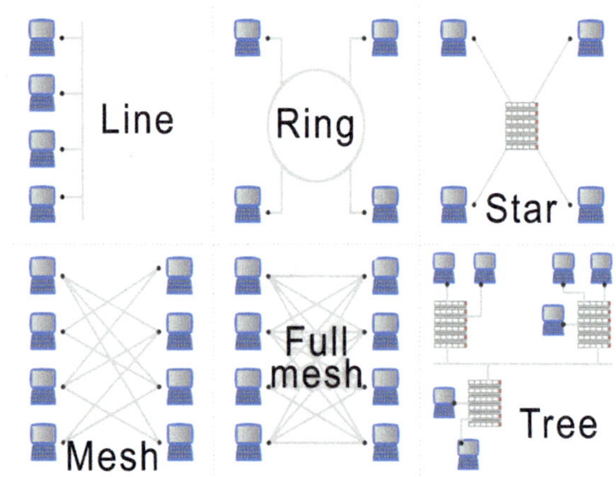

Figure 6.5. Types of topology.

Source: Image by Explain that stuff.

6.17.5. Hybrid Topology

A network can be hybrid. For example, we can have a main star topology with each branch connecting several stations in a bus topology.

Remember

The point-to-point WAN is normally a line leased from a telephone or cable TV provider that connects a home computer or a small LAN to an Internet service provider (ISP). This type of WAN is often used to provide Internet access.

6.18. NETWORK MODELS

Computer networks are created by different entities. Standards are needed so that these heterogeneous networks can communicate with one another. The two best-known standards are the OSI model and the Internet model. we discuss these two models. The OSI (Open Systems Interconnection) model defines a seven-layer network; the Internet model defines a five-layer network. This book is based on the Internet model with occasional references to the OSI model.

6.19. CATEGORIES OF NETWORKS

Today when we speak of networks, we are generally referring to two primary categories: local-area networks and wide-area networks. The category into which a network falls is determined by its size. A LAN normally covers an area less than 2 mi; a WAN can be worldwide. Networks of a size in between are normally referred to as metropolitan area networks and span tens of miles.

6.19.1. Local Area Network

A local area network (LAN) is usually privately owned and links the devices in a single office, building, or campus Depending on the needs of an organization and the type of technology used, a LAN can be as simple as two PCs and a printer in someone's home office; or it can extend throughout a company and include audio and video peripherals. Currently, LAN size is limited to a few kilometers. LANs are designed to allow resources to be shared between personal computers or workstations. The resources to be shared can include hardware (e.g., a printer), software (e.g., an application program), or data. A common example of a LAN, found in many business environments, links a workgroup of task-related computers, for example, engineering workstations or accounting PCs.

One of the computers may be given a large capacity disk drive and may become a server to clients. Software can be stored on this central server and used as needed by the whole group. In this example, the size of the LAN may be determined by licensing restrictions on the number of users per copy of software, or by restrictions on the number of users licensed to access the operating system.

In addition to size, LANs are distinguished from other types of networks by their transmission media and topology. In general, a given LAN will use only one type of transmission medium. The most common LAN topologies are bus, ring, and star. Early LANs had data rates in the 4 to 16 megabits per second (Mbps) range. Today, however, speeds are normally 100 or 1000 Mbps. LANs Wireless LANs are the newest evolution in LAN technology (Figure 6.6).

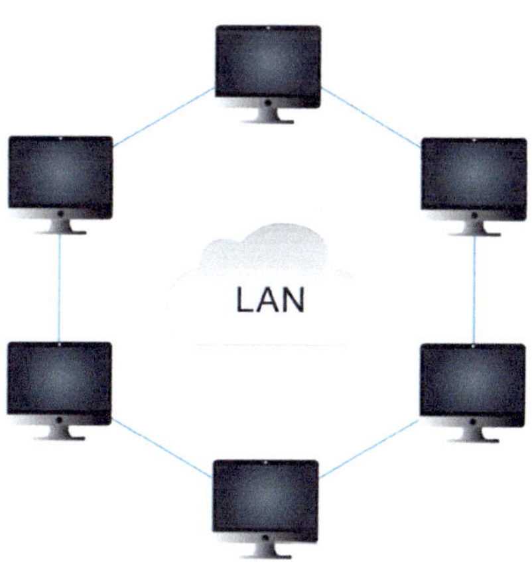

Figure 6.6. LAN.

Source: Image by Wikimedia Commons.

6.19.2. Wide Area Network

A wide area network (WAN) provides long-distance transmission of data, image, audio, and video information over large geographic areas that may comprise a country, a continent, or even the whole world. we discuss wide-area networks in greater detail. A WAN can be as complex as the backbones that connect the Internet or as simple as a dial-up line that connects a home computer to the Internet.

We normally refer to the first as a switched WAN and to the second as a point-to-point. The switched WAN connects the end systems, which usually comprise a router (internetworking connecting device) that connects to another LAN or WAN.

An early example of a switched WAN is X.25, a network designed to provide connectivity between end users. As we will see, X.25 is being gradually replaced by a high-speed, more efficient network called Frame Relay.

A good example of a switched WAN is the asynchronous transfer mode (ATM) network, which is a network with fixed-size data unit packets called cells. Another example of WANs is the wireless WAN that is becoming more and more popular. We discuss wireless WANs and their evolution (Figure 6.7).

Figure 6.7. WAN.

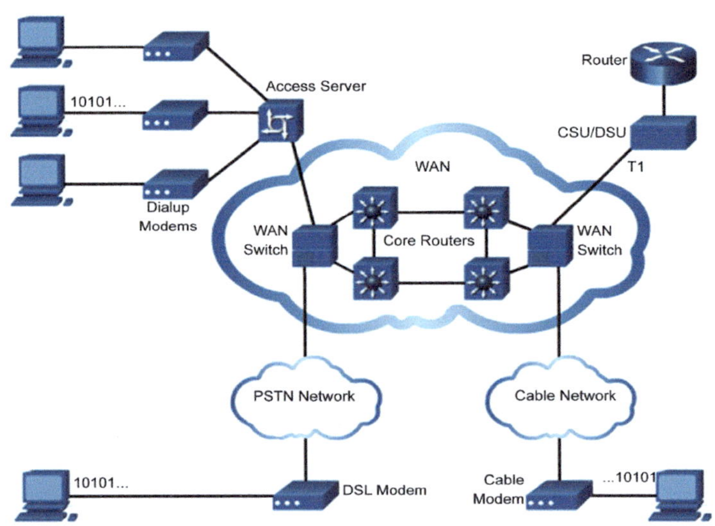

Source: Image by Wikimedia Commons.

6.19.3. Metropolitan Area Networks

A metropolitan area network (MAN) is a network with a size between a LAN and a WAN. It normally covers the area inside a town or a city. It is designed for customers who need a high-speed connectivity, normally to the Internet, and have endpoints spread over a city or part of city.

A good example of a MAN is the part of the telephone company network that can provide a high-speed DSL line to the customer. Another example is the cable TV network that originally was designed for cable TV, but today can also be used for high-speed data connection to the Internet. We discuss DSL lines and cable TV networks.

ACTIVITY 6.2.

1. Identify some other networks in the real world.
2. Create a hotspot using a Smartphone and connect other devices to it.
3. Find and list a few ISPs in your region.

6.20. INTERCONNECTION OF NETWORKS: INTERNETWORK

Today, it is very rare to see a LAN, a MAN, or a LAN in isolation; they are connected to one another. When two or more networks are connected, they become an internetwork, or internet. As an example, assume that an organization has two offices, one on the east coast and the other on the west coast. The established office on the west coast has a bus topology LAN; the newly opened office on the east coast has a star topology LAN.

The president of the company lives somewhere in the middle and needs to have control over the company from her Horne. To create a backbone WAN for connecting these three entities (two LANs and the president's computer), a switched WAN (operated by a service provider such as a telecom company) has been leased.

To connect the LANs to this switched WAN, however, three point-to-point WANs are required. These point-to-point WANs can be a high-speed DSL line offered by a telephone company or a cable modern line offered by a cable TV provider.

6.21. COMPUTER NETWORK MODELS

When dealing with networking, you may hear the terms "network model" and "network layer" used often. Network models define a set of network layers and how they interact. There are several different network models depending on what organization or company started them.

The Open Systems Interconnection model (OSI) is a conceptual model that characterizes and standardizes the internal functions of a communication system by partitioning it into abstraction layers. The model is a product of the Open Systems Interconnection project at the International Organization for Standardization (ISO), maintained by the identification ISO/IEC 7498–1. The model group communication functions into seven logical layers. A layer serves the layer above it and is served by the layer below it. For example, a layer that provides error-free communications across a network provides the path needed by applications above it, while it calls the next lower layer to send and receive packets that make up the contents of that path. Two instances at one layer are connected by a horizontal connection on that layer.

KEYWORD

Synchronization is the coordination of events to operate a system in unison.

6.22. PHYSICAL LAYER

The physical layer, the lowest layer of the OSI model, is concerned with the transmission and reception of the unstructured raw bit stream over a physical medium. It describes the electrical/optical, mechanical, and functional interfaces to the physical medium, and carries the signals for all of the higher layers. It provides:

- Data encoding: modifies the simple digital signal
- Pattern (1s and 0s) used by the PC to better accommodate the characteristics of the physical medium, and to aid in bit and frame synchronization. It determines: What signal state represents a binary 1 – How the receiving station knows when a “bit-time” starts – How the receiving station delimits a frame physical medium attachment, accommodating various
- Possibilities in the medium: Will an external transceiver (MAU) be used to connect to the medium? – How many pins do the connectors have and what is each pin used for? Transmission technique: determines whether:
- the encoded bits will be transmitted by baseband (digital) or broadband (analog) signaling.
- the physical medium transmission: transmits bits as electrical or optical signals appropriate for the physical medium, and determines: What physical medium options can be used – How many volts/db should be used to represent a given signal state, using a given physical medium.

6.23. SUMMARY

1. Data Communication and Data Representation

In this chapter, data communication and computer networks have been explained in detail. It also discusses about data representation, mode of data flow, difference between analog and digital signal. In this chapter, importance of data communication has also been explained.

2. Transmitting media

This chapter explains the measuring capacity of communication media such as bandwidth and rate of data transfer. It also addresses the concept of transmitting and wired transmitting media which includes twisted – pair cable, coaxial cable, and fiber optic.

3. Networks and Topologies

In this chapter, the significance of networks along with its history have been explained. It also consists different categories of networks such as local area network, wide area network, and metropolitan area network. Towards the end of the chapter, this chapter provides highlights on the different types of topologies which includes physical topology, bus topology, ring topology, and hybrid topology.

6.24. REVIEW QUESTIONS

1. What do you understand by the term data communication?
2. What is the difference between analog signal and digital signal?
3. Explain the concept of data representation.
4. What do you understand by the wireless communication technology?
5. Explain the significance of transmitting media.
6. What do you understand by a wired transmission media?
7. Define the term topology. What are the popular network topologies?
8. Explain the importance of network criteria.

6.25. MULTIPLE CHOICE QUESTIONS

1. LAN stands for _____.

a. Logic Area Network
b. Local Antenna Network
c. Local Area Network
d. Logic Antenna Network

2. Data communication system within a building or campus is ________.

a. LAN
b. WAN
c. MAN
d. PAN

3. Physical or logical arrangement of network is __________.

a. Topology
b. Routing
c. Networking
d. Control

4. _______ topology requires a multipoint connection

a. Star
b. Ring
c. Mesh
d. Bus

5. Data communication system spanning states, countries, or the whole world is ________.

a. LAN
b. WAN
c. MAN
d. PAN

Answers to Multiple Choice Questions

1. (c) 2. (a) 3. (a) 4. (d) 5. (b)

REFERENCES

1. Abhishek, K., (2022). *Introduction to Artificial Intelligence* – Simple Talk. [online] Simple Talk. Available at: https://www.red-gate.com/simple-talk/development/data-science-development/introduction-to-artificial-intelligence/#:~:text=Artificial%20intelligence%20(AI)%20is%20the,many%20other%20products%20and%20services (accessed on 03 March 2023).
2. Agnihotri, N., (n.d). *What are Different Types of Artificial Intelligence?* [online] Engineers Garage. Available at: https://www.engineersgarage.com/what-are-different-types-of-artificial-intelligence/ (accessed on 03 March 2023).

3. GeeksforGeeks, (2020). *What is Artificial Super Intelligence (ASI)?* – GeeksforGeeks. [online] Available at: https://www.geeksforgeeks.org/what-is-artificial-super-intelligence-asi/ (accessed on 03 March 2023).
4. icertglobal.com (n.d). *Advantages and Disadvantages of Artificial Intelligence* | iCert Global. [online] Available at: https://www.icertglobal.com/advantages-and-disadvantages-of-artificial-intelligence/detail (accessed on 03 March 2023).
5. Jessica, (2022). *The Role of Artificial Intelligence in Future Technology* – Inventiva. [online] Inventiva. Available at: https://www.inventiva.co.in/trends/the-role-of-artificial-intelligence-in-future-technology/ (accessed on 03 March 2023).
6. Joshi, N., (2019). *7 Types of Artificial Intelligence.* [online] Forbes. Available at: https://www.forbes.com/sites/cognitiveworld/2019/06/19/7-types-of-artificial-intelligence/?sh=1450e9fb233e (accessed on 03 March 2023).

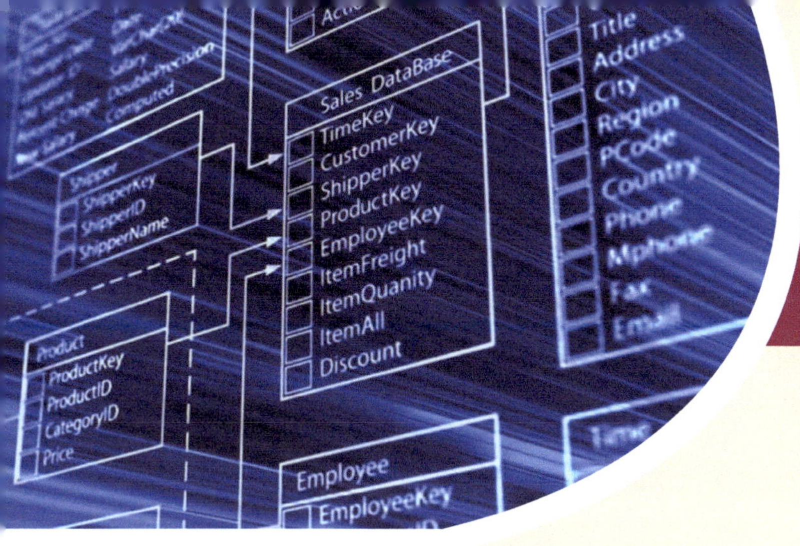

CHAPTER 7

FUNDAMENTALS OF DATABASE

UNIT INTRODUCTION

The increasing usage of computer systems has a massive effect on datasets and database management systems. It's correct to conclude that datasets seem to be vital for almost every profession that implements computer systems, such as corporate, electronic commerce, technology, biology, the legal system, education, and library and information science.

Because the term "database" is so often used, users must first explain what it means. Our traditional meaning is fairly broad. An assortment of linked data is known as a database. Data is established factual data that could be documented and has hidden importance.

Assume the titles, contact details, and addresses of the people you are familiar with. To use a laptop and programs like Microsoft Word or Excel, users might have managed to enter the above details in an index contact list or saved them on a hard disc drive.

A database refers to a collection of integrated data that has a hidden message. The meaning of the data supplied above is rather broad; for instance, users might say that perhaps the group of words that comprise this text page are linked information and, as an outcome, form a database.

The term "database" has a much narrower definition in normal conversation, though. These implied characteristics of a database are present:

- A database portrays a certain component of the actual world, also referred to as the mini world or the universe of discourse (UOD). The database updates in response to shifts in the mini world.
- A dataset is a group of logically related information that has some sort of underlying importance.
- A database is formed, crafted, and packed with information with a specific goal in mind; it may not be named a database if the information in it is randomized and organized.

It is designed for a specific user demographic and caters to some preconceived usage that all these consumers find interesting. To put it differently, a database has an origin from whom information is obtained, a few interactions with true events, and a customer base that's also extremely involved in its content and structure. The data held in a database could alter as a result of commercial transactions (such as a customer purchasing a webcam) or unexpected circumstances (such as a worker having children).

Adjustments must always be mirrored in the database as promptly as feasible in order for it to remain accurate and reliable, because a database must accurately reflect the mini world it reflects. A database could be of any shape or complexity. For example, in this case, the previously mentioned description of names and addresses might only contain a few hundred pieces of documentation, each having a straightforward system.

A sizable library's automated collection, in contrast, might have half a million records arranged in alphabetical order by topic, book title, and the final title of the main author. The Internal Revenue Service (IRS) manages a database that is even bigger and more complicated to track tax forms.

Users would possess a database of 100 106 400 5 characters (bytes) of data if the authors assumed that there existed 100 million tax-paying citizens and that every taxpayer filed an estimate of five types with about 400 characters of data on them. Whereas if the IRS retained the previous three rates of return of every taxpayer in place of the present return, people would be left with a database of 8,1011 bytes (800 gigabytes).

It is essential to control and coordinate this vast amount of data such that individuals can look for, retrieve, and keep updating the data required. Amazon.com is an illustrative example of a substantial advertising dataset. More than 20 million books, compact discs, video content, DVDs, games, electronic goods, clothes, and certain another products' information are included. The database is maintained on 200 distinct computers, or servers, and eats up more than 2 terabytes of storage (1012 bytes).

Amazon.com has approximately 15 million registered users who use its shopping dataset to buy goods. The database is upgraded often as new books and other products are uploaded to the inventory and stock levels are revised as transactions take place. The database on Amazon is updated by a team of around 100 employees.

A database could be created and upgraded manually or automatically. One database that can be manually built and maintained is a library card collection. A database administration system or a group of implementation software designed primarily for the purpose of creating and maintaining computerized databases could do either.

In this book, learners are only focused on computerized databases. A set of software applications called a database management system (DBMS) provides users with the ability to build and administer databases. The DBMS is a general-purpose software system that simplifies the ability for different users and programs to define, build, manipulate, and exchange data.

The procedures involved in establishing a database include identifying the types of data, structures, and restrictions of the information that will be saved therein. The database catalog or dictionary, often referred to as meta-data, is how the DBMS maintains the database description or relevant details. The act of placing the information on a storage device under the command of the DBMS is called creating the databases.

A database could be modified by performing operations like asking it to obtain certain information, upgrading it to respond to changes in the Databases and Database Users mini world, and creating reports from the records. When data is shared, numerous users and applications may utilize it simultaneously.

An application program can reach the database by issuing inquiries or information demands to the DBMS. A transfer might result in certain data being taken from the database and others being entered into it; a request normally results in some information being received. The DBMS also conducts additional crucial tasks such as keeping the database available for an extended period of time and securing it.

Security measures preventing unauthorized or malicious access are a part of safety, as is system security from hardware or software failure (or crashes). The lifetime of a normal massive database could be several years, so the DBMS has to be capable of managing the database system while also enabling it to develop as needed.

The application of a general-purpose DBMS (database management system) is not always required for the implementation of a computerized database.

One can create their own personal, custom DBMS software by writing their own set of programs to develop and manage the data. Whether one chooses a general-purpose DBMS or not, they often need to install a sizable number of advanced tools. However, the majority of DBMSs are incredibly complicated computer programs. So, one prefers to refer to the database and DBMS program as a database management system to enhance the original definitions. A number of ideas we've addressed thus far (Figure 7.1).

Figure 7.1. Lever arch file database.

Source: Image by Picserver.

Learning Objectives

After completing this chapter, you should be able to understand the following:

- Understand the fundamentals of database
- Identify the various feature of database strategy
- Understand the Advantages of using a DBMS
- Educate about the brief history of database application
- Give advice about the insulation between programs and data, and data abstraction
- Understand the database applications
- Give advice about the importance of MS-Access

Key Terms

- Client/Server
- Command
- Database
- Database Application
- Database Management System
- Document Store
- NoSQl

7.1. FEATURES OF THE DATABASE STRATEGY

The database approach is very different from the considerably earlier approach of programming using documents in a number of different ways. The documents necessary for a particular software application have been defined and executed by each consumer as components of the programming of the implementation in conventional data handling. A user could, for instance, maintain records of learners' marks, such as the grade reporting office.

Did you Know?

In the database method, data is specified once and thereafter maintained in a single repository for accessibility by many users. In file systems, any application has the ability to individually designate data items.

The application contains programs that can generate a student's record and update it with new marks. The accounts department, a second user, might monitor the costs and transactions that students have made. Regardless of the fact that both users are engaged in student information, they both retain individual files and programs to edit them as they both need certain information that databases and database users are unable to supply.

Due to the repeated definition and retention of data, storage capacity is lost and duplicate maintenance measures are taken to keep common information updated.

In comparison, databases, inquiries, trades, and programs regularly use identifiers or tags of information that have already been established. The following are the most important distinctions between the database strategy and the file-processing method:

- Self-descriptive properties of database systems
- Data abstraction and data insulating between programs and data
- The ability to accommodate multiple data views.
- Data sharing and multiple-user transaction handling in a separate section, let's go into further detail about each of these traits in their own area.

Added features of database systems would be discussed. Database systems have a self-descriptive structure. The idea that perhaps the database system typically includes a detailed definition or explanation of the database structure and limitations is a major element of the database approach.

This description is maintained in the database management system (DBMS) catalog, which also keeps track of numerous data restrictions and details about every file's structure, type, and storage formats. The catalogs are used by DBMS software and database users who need to know about database structure. The data held in the catalogs is termed "meta-data" and it defines the framework of the main database.

A general-purpose DBMS software package is not generated for particular database implementation. Consequently, it must review the catalogs to determine the filesystem in a particular database, including that of the sort and formatting of the information it would read.

As long as the database meaning is kept in the catalog, the DBMS software must function perfectly with just about any range of different database systems, including academic databases, financial databases, and business databases.

Data description is usually a feature of the software application itself in conventional data operations. As an outcome, these systems are restricted to working with a single, predetermined database, whose formation is specified in the software applications. For instance, a C++ application program may contain statements of classes or structures. Data division statements are used by COBOL programs to specify their folders.

TIPS

Some database management systems include a graphical user interface for users to create and manage databases. Other database systems use a command line interface that requires users to use programming commands to create and manage databases.

Although DBMS technology may access a wide range of databases by retrieving the database descriptions from the catalogs and to use them, file-processing applications must only handle a limited number of databases. Each document in the instance's meanings would be managed so that they could be saved in the DBMS catalog. A few examples of database catalogs records.

A codified type including all recognized majors is referred to as a major type. It is employed to describe a format that consists of four alphanumeric characters and then four digits. The developer clarifies these meanings, which are then kept in the catalog, before building the actual database.

The DBMS software collaborates with the catalog whenever a request is placed to connect, for example, the name of a STUDENT record to figure out the layout of the STUDENT folder and the location and size of the name data element within a STUDENT record.

In comparison, each software that retrieves this data element in a typical file-processing application already has the file structure and, in the worst-case scenario, the precise locations of the title within a STUDENT record programmed.

7.2. INSULATION BETWEEN PROGRAMS AND DATA, AND DATA ABSTRACTION

In traditional file processing, the structure of data files is embedded in the application programs, so any changes to the structure of a file may require changing all programs that access this file. By contrast, DBMS access programs do not require such changes in most cases. The structure of data files is stored in the DBMS catalog separately from the access programs.

We call this property program-data independence. For example, a file access program may be written in such a way that it can access only STUDENT records of the structure shown in If we want to add another piece of data to each STUDENT record, say the Birth Date, such a program will no longer work and must be changed.

KEYWORD

Program-data independence refers to the capability of leaving data intact and accessible regardless of modifications to the database that contains the data.

By contrast, in a DBMS environment, we just need to change the description of STUDENT records in the catalog to reflect the inclusion of the new data item Birth Date; no programs are changed. The next time a DBMS program refers to the catalog, the new structure of STUDENT records will be accessed and used.

In some types of database systems, such as object-oriented and object-relational systems, users can define operations on data as part of the database definitions. An operation (also called a function or method) is specified in two parts. The interface (or signature) of an operation includes the operation name and the data types of its arguments (or parameters).

The implementation (or method) of the operation is specified separately and can be changed without affecting the interface. User application programs can operate on the data by invoking these operations through their names and arguments, regardless of how the operations are implemented. This may be termed program-operation independence.

The characteristic that allows program-data independence and program-operation independence is called data abstraction. A DBMS provides users with a conceptual representation of data that does not include many of the details of how the data is stored or how the operations are implemented. Informally, a data model is a type of data abstraction that is used to provide this conceptual representation.

The data model uses logical concepts, such as objects, their properties, and their interrelationships, that may be easier for most users to understand than computer storage concepts. Hence, the data model hides storage and implementation details that are not of interest to most database users (Figure 7.2).

Figure 7.2. Data provider.

Source: Image by Justdial.

For example, consider again the internal implementation of a file may be defined by its record length-the number of characters (bytes) in each record-and each data item may be specified by its starting byte within a record and its length in bytes. The STUDENT record would thus be represented but a typical database user is not concerned with the location of each data item within a record or its length; rather, the concern is that when a reference is made to Name of STUDENT, the correct value is returned.

A conceptual representation of the STUDENT records many other details of file storage organization-such as the access paths specified on a file---can be hidden from database users by the DBMS; we discuss storage details. In the database approach, the detailed structure and organization of each file are stored in the catalog.

Database users and application programs refer to the conceptual representation of the files, and the DBMS extracts the details of file storage from the catalog when these are needed by the DBMS file access modules. Many data models can be used to provide this data abstraction to database users. A major part of this book is devoted to presenting various data models and the concepts they use to abstract the representation of data.

In object-oriented and object-relational databases, the abstraction process includes not only the data structure but also the operations on the data. These operations provide an abstraction of mini world activities commonly understood by the users. For example, an operation CALCULATE_CPA can be applied to a STUDENT object to calculate the grade point average.

Such operations can be invoked by the user queries or application programs without having to know the details of how the operations are implemented. In that sense, an abstraction of the mini world activity is made available to the user as an abstract operation.

KEYWORD

Virtual data room is an online repository of information that is used for the storing and distribution of documents.

7.3. SUPPORT OF MULTIPLE VIEWS OF THE DATA

A database typically has many users, each of whom may require a different perspective or view of the database. A view may be a subset of the database or it may contain virtual data that is derived from the database files but is not explicitly stored. Some users may not need to be aware of whether the data they refer to is stored or derived.

A multiuser DBMS whose users have a variety of distinct applications must provide facilities for defining multiple views. For example, one user of the database may be interested only in accessing and printing the transcript of each student; the view for this second user, who is interested only in checking that students have taken all the prerequisites of each course for which they register.

7.4. SHARING OF DATA AND MULTIUSER TRANSACTION PROCESSING

A multiuser DBMS, as its name implies, must allow multiple users to access the database at the same time. This is essential if data for multiple applications is to be integrated and maintained in a single database. The DBMS must include concurrency control software to ensure that several users trying to update the same data do so in a controlled manner so that the result of the updates is correct.

For example, when several reservation clerks try to assign a seat on an airline flight, the DBMS should ensure that each seat can be accessed by only one clerk at a time for assignment to a passenger. These types of applications are generally called online transaction processing (OLTP) applications. A fundamental role of multiuser DBMS software is to ensure that concurrent transactions operate correctly.

The concept of a transaction has become central to many database applications. A transaction is an executing program or process that includes one or more database accesses, such as reading or updating of database records. Each transaction is supposed to execute a logically correct database access if executed in its entirety without interference from other transactions.

KEYWORD

Database record is a collection of fields about the same person, item, or object in a database.

The DBMS must enforce several transaction properties. The isolation property ensures that each transaction appears to execute in isolation from other transactions, even though hundreds of transactions may be executing concurrently. The atomicity property ensures that either all the database operations in a transaction are executed or none are.

The preceding characteristics are most important in distinguishing a DBMS from traditional file-processing software. We discuss additional features that characterize a DBMS. First, however, we categorize the different types of persons who work in a database system environment.

7.5. ON-SCREEN ACTORS

One person normally describes, develops, and manages a small, private database, like a list of addresses, while there is no exchange involved. A large database with thousands of users is designed, used, and kept by countless individuals.

Researchers refer to these individual people as "actors on the scene" in this segment even though their work requires them to frequently use a substantial database. Researchers take into account individuals who could be referred to as "workers behind the scenes," i.e., those who keep the database system environment while not being extremely keen on the database itself.

7.5.1. Database Administrators

A chief administrator is needed to supervise and control resources in any organization where several people employ the same resources.

The database on its own serves as the main resource in a database environment, with the DBMS and associated software serving as the secondary resource. The database administrator is accountable for overseeing such resources (DBA).

KEYWORD

Database administrator is the information technician who directs and performs all activities related to maintaining a successful database environment.

The DBA is in control of authorizing access to the database, arranging and overseeing its use, and procuring the necessary equipment and software resources. The DBA's duty includes challenges like data leakage or slow system processing times. In big organizations, the DBA is backed by an employee who assists in conducting such responsibilities.

7.5.2. Designers of Databases

It is the duty of database developers to ascertain the information that will be saved in the database and also to choose the most suitable structures to reflect as well as store that information. The majority of these duties are performed prior to the database's execution and data loading. All potential database users must be approached in order for database administrators to fully comprehend their needs and develop a layout that aims to satisfy them (Figure 7.3).

Figure 7.3. Database designs.

Source: Image by Pix4Free.

The developers are usually applied by the DBA and might be given extra tasks once the database design has been finished. Each potential user group is typically interacted with by database designers, who would then build viewpoints of the database that fulfill their needs for handling as well as information. After that, each perspective is investigated and combined with the opinions of all other different users. The finished database layout must be competent to cater to all user groups' demands (Figure 7.4).

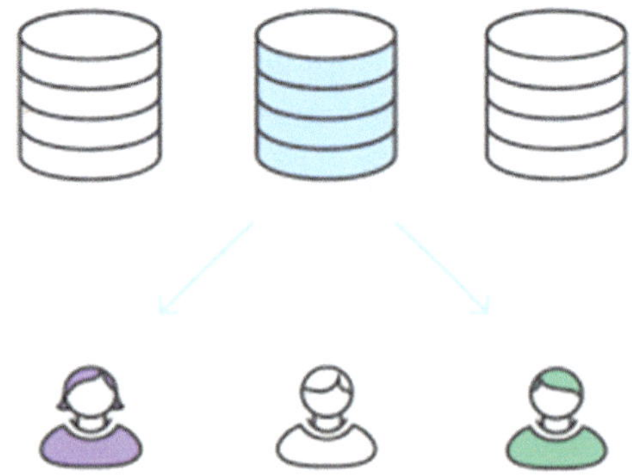

Figure 7.4. Database layout.

7.5.3. End Users

The individuals for whom the work requires them to have full rights to the information for query and analysis, upgrading, and creating documents are identified as end-users; the database is mainly there for their purposes. End users can be divided into different groups, such as:

- Casual users could occasionally browse the database, but each time individuals may require a different set of data. They are normally middle-or high-level executives or even infrequent internet explorers, and they explicitly state their queries using an advanced database query language.
- A large proportion of database end users are either correct or naive. Their primary responsibility is to continuously upgrade and request the database using checked and cautiously coded packaged transactions, which are frequent types of queries and alerts.

These users accomplish a number of tasks, which include checking account balances and uploading transfers, deposits, and cash withdrawals.

Reservation representatives for accommodations, flights, and car hire organizations search for availability and book reservations. To notify a central database of provided and in-transit deals, cashiers at parcel postal receiving stations feedback package identification documents through the use of barcode scanners and detailed descriptions through buttons.

- Advanced end users, such as technicians, researchers, industry experts, and many others, are those who are well-versed in the DBMS's features and can enforce their implementations to satisfy challenging needs.

- users People who work independently typically manage their own databases using pre-built software products with a simple menu- or graphic-based user interfaces. One illustration is a person who uses a tax package that maintains a record of various pieces of private financial information for tax reasons.

A normal DBMS offers several options for accessing a database. Simple end users only require to be familiar with the interactions of the basic transactions that have been developed and used for them to use; people are not required to grasp a lot about the benefits offered by the DBMS.

Just a few features that can be used frequently are learned by average users. Advanced users attempt to learn a large number of DBMS features in order to meet their demanding needs. Stand-alone users generally develop a high level of proficiency with a particular computer program.

Remember

In object-oriented and object-relational databases, the abstraction process includes not only the data structure but also the operations on the data. These operations provide an abstraction of mini world activities commonly understood by the users.

7.5.4. Application Programmers and System Analysts (Software Engineers)

System developers recognize the needs of the users, particularly naive as well as parametric users, and establish canned transaction standards that fulfill those needs. Software developers turn such requirements into working software, after which they assess, troubleshoot, record, and hold. To carry out their tasks, those kinds of experts and coders, alluded to as software developers must be knowledgeable about the entire scope of DBMS functionality.

7.6. WORKERS BEHIND THE SCENE

In addition to those who design, use, and administer a database, others are associated with the design, development, and operation of the DBMS software and system environment. These persons are typically not interested in the database content itself. We call them the workers behind the scene, and they include the following categories:

- DBMS system designers and implementers design and implement the DBMS modules and interfaces as a software package. A DBMS is a very complex software system that consists of many components, or modules, including modules for implementing the catalog, query language processing, interface processing, accessing and buffering data, controlling concurrency, and handling data recovery and security. The DBMS must interface with other system software such as the operating system and compilers for various programming languages.

- Tool developers design and implement tools—the software packages that facilitate database modeling and design, database system design, and improved performance. Tools are optional packages that are often purchased separately. They include packages for database design, performance monitoring, natural language or graphical interfaces, prototyping, simulation, and test data generation. In many cases, independent software vendors develop and market these tools.
- Operators and maintenance personnel (system administration personnel) are responsible for the actual running and maintenance of the hardware and software environment for the database system. Although these categories of workers behind the scene are instrumental in making the database system available to end users, they typically do not use the database contents for their own purposes.

TIPS

SQL is the standard language for RDBMS systems like MySQL.

7.7. ADVANTAGES OF USING A DBMS

In this section we discuss some of the advantages of using a DBMS and the capabilities that a good DBMS should possess. These capabilities are in addition to the four main characteristics. The DBA must utilize these capabilities to accomplish a variety of objectives related to the design, administration, and use of a large multiuser database.

7.7.1. Controlling Redundancy

In traditional software development utilizing file processing, every user group maintains its own files for handling its data-processing applications. For example, consider the UNIVERSITY database example of here, two groups of users might be the course registration personnel and the accounting office. In the traditional approach, each group independently keeps files on students.

The accounting office keeps data on registration and related billing information, whereas the registration office keeps track of student courses and grades. Other groups may further duplicate some or all of the same data in their own files. This redundancy in storing the same data multiple times leads to several problems.

First, there is the need to perform a single logical update—such as entering data on a new student—multiple times: once for each file where student data is recorded. This leads to duplication of effort. Second, storage space is wasted when the same data is stored repeatedly, and this problem may be serious for large databases.

Third, files that represent the same data may become inconsistent. This may happen because an update is applied to some of the files but not to others. Even if an update—such as adding a new student—is applied to all the appropriate files, the data concerning the student may still be inconsistent because the updates are applied independently by each user group.

For example, one user group may enter a student's birth date erroneously as 'JAN-19–1988,' whereas the other user groups may enter the correct value of 'JAN-29–1988.' In the database approach, the views of different user groups are integrated during database design. Ideally, we should have a database design that stores each logical data item—such as a student's name or birth date—in only one place in the database.

This is known as data normalization, and it ensures consistency and saves storage space However, in practice, it is sometimes necessary to use controlled redundancy to improve the performance of queries. For example, we may store Student_name and Course_number redundantly in a GRADE_REPORT file because whenever we retrieve a GRADE_REPORT record, we want to retrieve the student name and course number along with the grade, student number, and section identifier.

By placing all the data together, we do not have to search multiple files to collect this data. This is known as demoralization. In such cases, the DBMS should have the capability to control this redundancy in order to prohibit inconsistencies among the files.

This may be done by automatically checking that the Student_name–Student_number values in any GRADE_REPORT record in match one of the Name–Student_number values of a STUDENT record. Similarly, the Section_identifier–Course_number values in GRADE_REPORT can be checked against SECTION records.

KEYWORD

Data normalization is the practice of organizing data entries to ensure they appear similar across all fields and records, making information easier to find, group and analyze.

Such checks can be specified to the DBMS during database design and automatically enforced by the DBMS whenever the GRADE_REPORT file is updated. GRADE_REPORT record that is inconsistent with the STUDENT file this kind of error may be entered if the redundancy is not controlled. Can you tell which part is inconsistent?

KEYWORD

Authorization is the process that establishes whether a given identity or subject can perform a given function against a given object.

7.7.2. Restricting Unauthorized Access

When multiple users share a large database, it is likely that most users will not be authorized to access all information in the database. For example, financial data is often considered confidential and only authorized persons are allowed to access such data. In addition, some users may only be permitted to retrieve data, whereas others are allowed to retrieve and update.

Hence, the type of access operation—retrieval or update—must also be controlled. Typically, users or user groups are given account numbers protected by passwords, which they can use to gain access to the database. A DBMS should provide a security and authorization subsystem, which the DBA uses to create accounts and to specify account restrictions. Then, the DBMS should enforce these restrictions automatically. Notice that we can apply similar controls to the DBMS software. For example, only the dba's staff may be allowed to use certain privileged software, such as the software for creating new accounts. Similarly, parametric users may be allowed to access the database only through the predefined canned transactions developed for their use.

7.7.3. Providing Persistent Storage for Program Objects

Databases can be used to provide persistent storage for program objects and data structures. This is one of the main reasons for object-oriented database systems. Programming languages typically have complex data structures, such as record types in Pascal or class definitions in C++ or Java.

The values of program variables or objects are discarded once a program terminates, unless the programmer explicitly stores them in permanent files, which often involves converting these complex structures into a format suitable for file storage.

When the need arises to read this data once more, the programmer must convert from the file format to the program variable or object structure. Object-oriented database systems are compatible with programming languages such as C++ and Java, and the DBMS software automatically performs any necessary conversions.

Hence, a complex object in C++ can be stored permanently in an object-oriented DBMS. Such an object is said to be persistent, since it survives the termination of program execution and can later be directly retrieved by another C++ program. The persistent storage of program objects and data structures is an important function of database systems.

Traditional database systems often suffered from the so-called impedance mismatch problem, since the data structures provided by the DBMS were incompatible with the programming language's data structures. Object-oriented database systems typically offer data structure compatibility with one or more object-oriented programming languages (Figure 7.5).

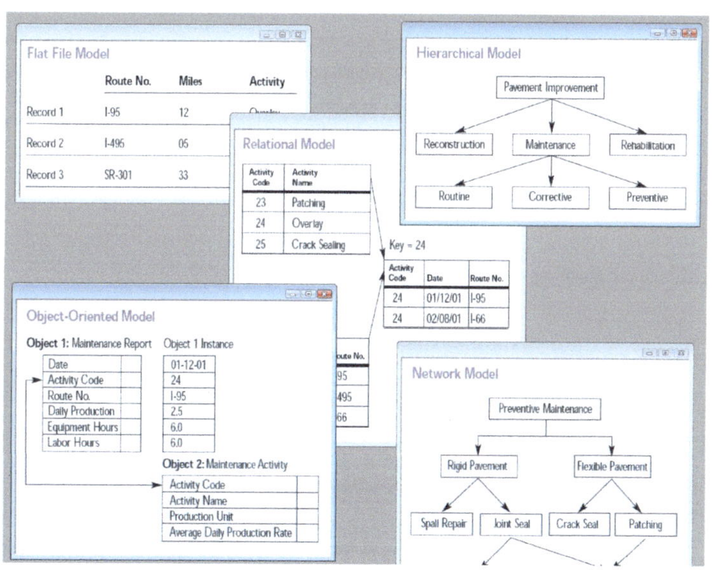

Figure 7.5. Database model.

Source: Image by Wikimedia Commons.

7.7.4. Providing Storage Structures and Search Techniques for Efficient Query Processing

Database systems must provide capabilities for efficiently executing queries and updates. Because the database is typically stored on disk, the DBMS must provide specialized data structures and search techniques to speed up disk search for the desired records. Auxiliary files called indexes are used for this purpose.

KEYWORD

Database design is a method of identifying the gaps and opportunities of designing a proper utilization method.

Indexes are typically based on tree data structures or hash data structures that are suitably modified for disk search. In order to process the database records needed by a particular query, those records must be copied from disk to main memory. Therefore, the DBMS often has a buffering or caching module that maintains parts of the database in main memory buffers.

In general, the operating system is responsible for disk-to-memory buffering. However, because data buffering is crucial to the DBMS performance, most DBMSs do their own data buffering. The query processing and optimization module of the DBMS is responsible for choosing an efficient query execution plan for each query based on the existing storage structures.

The choice of which indexes to create and maintain is part of physical database design and tuning, which is one of the responsibilities of the DBA staff. We discuss the query processing, optimization, and tuning.

7.7.5. Providing Backup and Recovery

A DBMS must provide facilities for recovering from hardware or software failures. The backup and recovery subsystem of the DBMS is responsible for recovery. For example, if the computer system fails in the middle of a complex update transaction, the recovery subsystem is responsible for making sure that the database is restored to the state it was in before the transaction started executing.

Alternatively, the recovery subsystem could ensure that the transaction is resumed from the point at which it was interrupted so that its full effect is recorded in the database. Disk backup is also necessary in case of a catastrophic disk failure.

7.7.6. Providing Multiple User Interfaces

Because many types of users with varying levels of technical knowledge use a database, a DBMS should provide a variety of user interfaces. These include query languages for casual users, programming language interfaces for application programmers, forms and command codes for parametric users, and menu-driven interfaces and natural language interfaces for standalone users.

Both forms-style interfaces and menu-driven interfaces are commonly known as graphical user interfaces (GUIs). Many specialized languages and environments exist for specifying GUIs. Capabilities for providing Web GUI interfaces to a database—or Web enabling a database—are also quite common.

KEYWORD

Menu-driven interface is an interface consisting of a series of screens which are navigated by choosing options from lists, i.e. menus.

7.7.7. Representing Complex Relationships among Data

A database may include numerous varieties of data that are interrelated in many ways. The record for 'Brown' in the STUDENT file is related to four records in the GRADE_REPORT file. Similarly, each section record is related to one course record and to a number of GRADE_REPORT records—one for each student who completed that section. A DBMS must have the capability to represent a variety of complex relationships among the data, to define new relationships as they arise, and to retrieve and update related data easily and efficiently.

7.7.8. Enforcing Integrity Constraints

Most database applications have certain integrity constraints that must hold for the data. A DBMS should provide capabilities for defining and enforcing the simplest type of integrity constraint involves specifying a data type for each data item. For example, we specified that the value of the Class data item within each STUDENT record must be a one-digit integer and that the value of Name must be a string of no more than 30 alphabetic characters.

To restrict the value of Class between 1 and 5 would be an additional constraint that is not shown in the current catalog. A more complex type of constraint that frequently occurs involves specifying that a record in one file must be related to records in other files. For example, we can specify that every section record must be related to a course record.

This is known as a referential integrity constraint. Another type of constraint specifies uniqueness on data item values, such as every course record must have a unique value for Course_number. This is known as a key or uniqueness constraint. These constraints are derived from the meaning or semantics of the data and of the mini world it represents.

> **Remember**
>
> It was particularly challenging to execute new inquiries, which needed a specific storage organization for effective handling. The database had to be laboriously reorganized whenever the prerequisites for the implementation changed. Early models also had the disadvantage of only providing computer language interactions.

It is the responsibility of the database designers to identify integrity constraints during database design. Some constraints can be specified to the DBMS and automatically enforced. Other constraints may have to be checked by update programs or at the time of data entry. For typical large applications, it is customary to call such constraints business rules.

A data item may be entered erroneously and still satisfy the specified integrity constraints. For example, if a student receives a grade of 'A' but a grade of 'C' is entered in the data base, the DBMS cannot discover this error automatically because 'C' is a valid value for the Grade data type. Such data entry errors can only be discovered manually (when the student receives the grade and complains) and corrected later by updating the database.

However, a grade of 'Z' would be rejected automatically by the DBMS because 'Z' is not a valid value for the Grade data type. When we discuss each data model in subsequent chapters, we will introduce rules that pertain to that model implicitly. For example, in the Entity-Relationship model, a relationship must involve at least two entities. Such rules are inherent rules of the data model and are automatically assumed to guarantee the validity of the model.

7.7.9. Permitting Inferencing and Actions Using Rules

Some database systems provide capabilities for defining deduction rules for inferencing new information from the stored database facts. Such systems are called deductive database systems. For example, there may be complex rules in the mini world application for determining when a student is on probation. These can be specified declaratively as rules, which when compiled and maintained by the DBMS can determine all students on probation.

In a traditional DBMS, an explicit procedural program code would have to be written to support such applications. But if the mini world rules change, it is generally more convenient to change the declared deduction rules than to recode procedural programs.

In today's relational database systems, it is possible to associate triggers with tables.

A trigger is a form of a rule activated by updates to the table, which results in performing some additional operations to some other tables, sending messages, and so on. More involved procedures to enforce rules are popularly called stored procedures; they become a part of the overall database definition and are invoked appropriately when certain conditions are met. More powerful functionality is provided by active database systems, Databases and Database Users provide active rules that can automatically initiate actions when certain events and conditions occur.

KEYWORD

File system is a process of managing how and where data on a storage disk, which is also referred to as file management or FS.

7.7.10. Additional Implications of Using the Database Approach

This section discusses a few additional implications of using the database approach that can benefit most organizations.

7.7.10.1. Potential for Enforcing Standards

The database approach permits the DBA to define and enforce standards among database users in a large organization. This facilitates communication and cooperation among various departments, projects, and users within the organization.

Standards can be defined for names and formats of data elements, display formats, report structures, terminology, and so on. The DBA can enforce standards in a centralized database environment more easily than in an environment where each user group has control of its own data files and software.

7.7.10.2. Reduced Application Development Time

A prime selling feature of the database approach is that developing a new application—such as the retrieval of certain data from the database for printing a new report—takes very little time. Designing and implementing a large multiuser database from scratch may take more time than writing a single specialized file application.

However, once a database is up and running, substantially less time is generally required to create new applications using DBMS facilities. Development time using a DBMS is estimated to be one sixth to one-fourth of that for a file system.

7.7.10.3. Flexibility

It may be necessary to change the structure of a database as requirements change. For example, a new user group may emerge that needs information not currently in the database. In response, it may be necessary to add a file to the database or to extend the data elements in an existing file.

Modern DBMSs allow certain types of evolutionary changes to the structure of the database without affecting the stored data and the existing application programs.

TIPS

Each row in a table represents a record. A tuple is a collection of attribute values that makes a record unique.

7.7.10.4. Availability of Up-to-Date Information

A DBMS makes the database available to all users. As soon as one user's update is applied to the database, all other users can immediately see this update. This availability of up-to-date information is essential for many transaction-processing applications, such as reservation systems or banking databases, and it is made possible by the concurrency control and recovery subsystems of a DBMS.

7.7.10.5. Economies of Scale

The DBMS approach permits consolidation of data and applications, thus reducing the amount of wasteful overlap between activities of data-processing personnel in different projects or departments as well as redundancies among applications. This enables the whole organization to invest in more powerful processors, storage devices, or networking gear, rather than having each department purchase its own (lower performance) equipment. This reduces overall costs of operation and management (Figure 7.6).

Figure 7.6. Web, domain, service, website, development, SEO, access, backup, and data.

Source: Image by Pxhere.

7.8. A BRIEF HISTORY OF DATABASE APPLICATIONS

We now give a brief historical overview of the applications that use DBMSs and how these applications provided the impetus for new types of database systems (Figure 7.7).

Figure 7.7. Database application.

Source: Image by Thebluediamondgallery.

7.8.1. Early Database Applications Using Hierarchical and Network Systems

Numerous initial database systems kept track of substantial institutions like businesses, institutions of higher learning, healthcare facilities, and financial institutions. Multiple records with similar patterns were present in abundance in a lot of these applications. In a college application, for instance, identical details would be held for each student, each lesson, each student's grade history, and so forth.

Furthermore, there were a number of different data types and connections between them. The blending of abstract relationships with the storage device and the placing of record keeping on the storage device were among the primary concerns with initial database systems. As a consequence, such processes lacked adequate functionality for program-data autonomy and data abstraction.

For instance, the student's record might be physically saved alongside the student's grade levels. Whereas the database was created to deal with the initial enquires and transactions, this offered extremely effective record accessibility. However, it failed to provide sufficient leeway to access records effectively once new requests and transactions were found.

Even though new programs needed to be written, evaluated, and debugged, adding new questions and transactions became time-consuming and costly. Beginning in the middle of the 1960s and persisting through the 1970s and 1980s, the majority of these database systems have been built on costly, big mainframe computers. Three assumptions formed the foundation for the primary initial system types: hierarchical systems, network model-based systems, and inverted file systems.

KEYWORD

Data Representation refers to the form in which data is stored, processed, and transmitted.

7.8.2. Making Use of Relational Databases for Data Abstraction and Software Adaptability

Relational databases were first suggested as a method to differentiate the physical storage of information from its comprehensive explanation, as well as a method for providing data representation and query processing with a mathematical foundation. High query languages, which served as a viable alternative to computer language integrations and made it so much quicker to write new queries, were also presented by the relational data model.

The example provided by the researchers is similar to the relational representation of data. Originally designed to serve the same applications as previous standards, relational systems offered adaptability to create new inquiries rapidly and rearrange the database as needs to be adjusted.

As a consequence, when compared with previous systems, data abstraction and program-data autonomy have because there were no storage device pointers or record placement to connect associated data documentation, the initial exploratory relational processes established in the late 1970s and the advertising relational database management systems (RDBMS) presented in the early 1980s were rather slow.

Their efficiency increased as a result of the creation of new memory and cataloging methods as well as good querying and enhancement. Relational databases finally took over as the standard type of database management system for conventional database implementations. These days, almost all computer categories, from small desktop PCs to large servers, endorse relational databases.

7.8.3. Object-Oriented Software and the Requirement for More Complicated Database Systems

Object-oriented databases were developed as a result of the advancement of object-oriented computer languages within the 1980s as well as the requirement to hold and share intricate, organized objects (OODBs). Due to their availability of more universal data structures, OODBs was originally seen as a rival to relational databases. They also added a number of beneficial object-oriented concepts, which include inheritance, object identity, encapsulation of operational processes, and abstract data types.

KEYWORD

E-commerce is the buying and selling of goods and services over the internet.

Even so, their restricted consumption was a result of the model's complexity and the absence of an initial benchmark. These days, their major functions are in specialized fields like engineering design, multimedia publication, and production lines.

But besides the vain hope that they will create a massive effect, their overall market infiltration for database product lines is still lesser. The latest variants of relational DBMSs also introduced a number of object-oriented ideas, resulting in object-relational database management systems, or ORDBMSs.

7.8.4. Using XML in E-Commerce for Web-based Data Exchange

The WorldWide Internet promises a substantial network of computers that have been linked together. Using only a web publishing language, such as Hyper Text Markup Language (HTML), users can create static website content, which is then stored on web applications for many other consumers (clients) to visit and view via an internet browser.

Through hyperlinks—pointers to certain other documents—documents can also be connected. Electronic commerce, also referred to as e-commerce, started to take off as a significant Web-based application in the 1990s. A huge percentage of the crucial data regarding e-commerce Data from DBMSs, including flight details, selling prices, and stock availability, is adaptively derived and used on website pages.

A variety of methods have been developed to allow the interaction of dynamically extracted information from the Internet for display on website pages. One standard for data transmission between many different sorts of databases and web-based pages is the extended Markup Language (XML). In XML, database modeling ideas are combined with those derived from the document system models.

KEYWORD

Economic data are data describing an actual economy, past or present.

7.8.5. Extending Database Capabilities for New Applications

The success of database systems in traditional applications encouraged developers of other types of applications to attempt to use them. Such applications traditionally used their own specialized software and file and data structures. Database systems now offer extensions to better support the specialized requirements for some of these applications.

The following are some examples of these applications:

- Scientific applications that store large amounts of data resulting from scientific experiments in areas such as high-energy physics, the mapping of the human genome, and the discovery of protein structures.
- Storage and retrieval of images, including scanned news or personal photographs, satellite photographic images, and images from medical procedures such as x-rays and MRI (magnetic resonance imaging) tests.
- Storage and retrieval of videos, such as movies, and video clips from news or personal digital cameras.
- Data mining applications that analyze large amounts of data to search for the occurrences of specific patterns or relationships, and for identifying unusual patterns in areas such as credit card fraud detection
- Spatial applications that store and analyze spatial locations of data, such as weather information, maps used in geographical information systems, and automobile navigational systems.
- Time series applications that store information such as economic data at regular points in time, such as daily

sales and monthly gross national product figures It was quickly apparent that basic relational systems were not very suitable for many of these applications, usually for one or more of the following reasons:

- More complex data structures were needed for modeling the application than the simple relational representation.
- New data types were needed in addition to the basic numeric and character string types.
- New operations and query language constructs were necessary to manipulate the new data types.
- New storage and indexing structures were needed for efficient searching on the new data types. This led DBMS developers to add functionality to their systems. Some functionality was general purpose, such as incorporating concepts from object-oriented databases into relational systems. Other functionality was special purpose, in the form of optional modules that could be used for specific applications. For example, users could buy a time series module to use with their relational DBMS for their time series application.

KEYWORD

Query language is a computer language used to make queries in databases and information systems.

7.8.6. Emergence of Big Data Storage Systems and NOSQL Databases

In the first decade of the 21st century, the proliferation of applications and platforms such as social media Web sites, large e-commerce companies, Web search indexes, and cloud storage/backup led to a surge in the amount of data stored on large databases and massive servers. New types of database systems were necessary to manage these huge databases—systems that would provide fast search and retrieval as well as reliable and safe storage of nontraditional types of data, such as social media posts and tweets.

Some of the requirements of these new systems were not compatible with SQL relational DBMSs (SQL is the standard data model and language for relational databases). The term NOSQL is generally interpreted as Not Only SQL, meaning that in systems than manage large amounts of data, some of the data is stored using SQL systems, whereas other data would be stored using NOSQL, depending on the application requirements.

7.9. SUMMARY

1. Fundamentals of Database

In this chapter, fundamentals of database have been explained. It also discussed about the various features of database strategy. This chapter provides highlights on the role of insulation between programs and data, and data abstraction.

2. Data and Multiuser Transaction Processing

This chapter addresses the significance of sharing of data and multiuser transaction processing such as database administrators, designers of databases, end users, and application programmers and system analysts (also known as software engineers).

3. Advantages of a DBMS

Towards the end of the chapter, it emphasizes various advantages of the using a database management system which includes, controlling redundancy, restricting unauthorized access, providing persistent storage for program objects, providing storage structures and search techniques for efficient query processing, etc.

7.10. REVIEW QUESTIONS

1. What do you understand by DBMS?
2. Give names of two commonly available DBMS software?
3. Differentiate between 'desktop database' and 'server database.'
4. What are the advantages of Access over Excel?
5. What are the ways in which data is stored and queried in an Access database?
6. What do you understand by terms 'key field,' 'primary key' and 'secondary key' in a database?
7. What are the limitations of file system that can be overcome by a relational DBMS?
8. Explain the importance of MS-Access in database.

7.11. MULTIPLE CHOICE QUESTIONS

1. What is the full form of DBMS?

a. Data of Binary Management System
b. Database Management System
c. Database Management Service
d. Data Backup Management System

2. What is DBMS?

a. DBMS is a collection of queries
b. DBMS is a high-level language
c. DBMS is a programming language
d. DBMS stores, modifies and retrieves data

3. What is a database?

a. Organized collection of information that cannot be accessed, updated, and managed
b. Collection of data or information without organizing
c. Organized collection of data or information that can be accessed, updated, and managed
d. Organized collection of data that cannot be updated

4. Which type of data can be stored in the database?

a. Image oriented data
b. Text, files containing data
c. Data in the form of audio or video
d. All of the above

5. Which of the following is not an example of DBMS?

a. MySQL
b. Microsoft Access
c. IBM DB2
d. Google

Answers to Multiple Choice Questions

1. (b) 2. (d) 3. (c) 4. (d) 5. (d)

REFERENCES

1. (n.d). *Data Communication and Network.* [e-Book] THIRUVALLUVAR UNIVERSITY. Available at: https://www.tvu.edu.in/wp-content/uploads/2020/01/DCN_Notes_Final%20(1)_compressed.pdf (accessed on 03 March 2023).
2. *Data Communication and Computer Network.* [e-Book] (2014). Tutorials Point. Available at: https://www.tutorialspoint.com/data_communication_computer_network/data_communication_computer_network_tutorial.pdf (accessed on 03 March 2023).
3. Forouzan, B., (2007). *Data Communications and Networking* (4th edn.). New York: McGraw Hill.

4. Ncert.nic.in (2022). *Data Communication*. [online] Available at: https://ncert.nic.in/textbook/pdf/lecs111.pdf (accessed on 03 March 2023).
5. Stefane, F., & Laurent, G., (n.d). *Data Communication and Computer Networks* – PDF Drive. [online] Pdfdrive.com. Available at: https://www.pdfdrive.com/data-communication-and-computer-networks-d1653022.html (accessed on 03 March 2023).
6. Yekini, N. A., Adebari, F. A., & Bello, O., (2015). *Data Communication & Networking*. [online] Available at: https://www.researchgate.net/publication/288180515_DATA_COMMUNICATION_NETWORKING (accessed on 03 March 2023).

CHAPTER 8

IOT AND COMPUTER SCIENCE

UNIT INTRODUCTION

The network of physical objects termed the Internet of Things (IoT) includes tools, hardware, automobiles, buildings, as well as other aspects that are fitted with computers, circuitry, applications, detectors, and broadband connections.

This technology enables these components to gather and share information. In order to more directly integrate the material world into computer-based processes and also to increase precision and effectiveness, the Internet of Things provides objects to also be predicted and directly controlled throughout the network's present infrastructure.

An altered Coke machine at Carnegie Mellon University functioned as the initial web appliance, stating its stock and the temperature of freshly packed beverages. The idea of a network of smart devices was first addressed in 1982. The term "the Internet of Things" was invented by British technology pioneer Kevin Ashton in 1968 to define a system in which the Web is linked to the physical realm by ubiquity detectors.

IoT can communicate without the assistance of a human. The healthcare, transportation, and automotive sectors have already created a few Software systems in their early stages. Though IoT technologies are still in their infancy, there have been numerous advancements made in the integration of physical objects with online sensor nodes.

Several more concerns, including facilities, communication services, interactions, policies and procedures, and norms, are related to the creation of the Internet of Things. This author's goal is to present a reasonable overview of the Internet of Things (IoT), as well as its architecture, levels, basic terms, and assistance.

The phrase "ubiquitous computing" was invented by Mark Weiser. The idea that processing power could be completed at any moment and anywhere is a concept that is arising in computer engineering. Such computer processing activities could be carried out on any machine, in any set – up, and with any layout.

Users are interacting with computer systems, which could also take on several various forms, which include laptops, tablet devices, and connectors embedded in common and accepted items like a refrigerator or a pair of sunglasses. In the online world, developed middleware, system software, portable code, sensor systems, microchips, innovative I/O and user interactions, connections, phone protocols, placement and positional awareness, and innovative equipment are some of the technological tools for ubiquitous computing.

It is also classified as "physical computing" or "the Internet of Things" because it involves actual physical objects. A major development in machine learning and human-computer interaction would then arise from this concept (Vermesan & Friess, 2013).

The internet, which first emerged on desktop computers and eventually spread to laptop computers, tablet devices, and cellular phones, nowadays is making progress and interconnects actual, everyday products. Presently, controlling physical objects from a remote controller is possible from every location.

It is becoming applicable in a diverse range of areas, such as business, economic systems, agricultural production, medical services, and so forth, in relation to computing science. Even so, the Internet of Things as well presents major difficulties that might limit its effectiveness. The public's attention has already been drawn to issues about surveillance, confidentiality, as well as the getting hacked of Internet-connected gadgets. For those creating IoT-based applications, technical difficulties proceed to be a top priority.

Various technological information and communication forms are employed in IoT integrations, each of which has special features. Device-to-Device, Device-to-Cloud, Device-to-Gateway, and Back-End Data-Sharing are four prevalent implementations of the concept (Vermesan & Friess, 2013).

Such cases demonstrate how IoT gadgets can communicate and benefit users in a number of different ways. Furthermore, three main elements are necessary for the Internet of Things to function: equipment, communications systems, and storage and processing equipment.

IoT platforms link the detector network and the data system, incorporating back-end implementations to intuitively provide information into massive amounts of data. An alert system could be set off automatically, for instance, in the medical industry using IoT networks whenever a wearable technology detects an issue with a user (Figure 8.1).

Figure 8.1. IoT – Internet of Things acronym with marker, concept background.

Source: Image by Flickr.

Learning Objectives

After completing this chapter, you should be able to understand the following:

- Understand the concept of Internet of Things (IoT)
- Understand the history of the Internet of Things
- Give advice about the advantages and disadvantages of IoT
- Educate about the various challenges in internet of things
- Give advice about application of IoT
- Understand the future of IoT
- Give advice about Impact of Internet of Things (IoT) on Renewable Energy

Key Terms

- Application of IoT
- Automation
- Complexity
- Computer Science
- Internet of Things
- IoT Malware
- Metaverse
- Quality of life
- Renewable Energy

8.1. INTERNET OF THINGS HISTORY (IOT)

There hasn't been enough time for the Internet of Things (IoT). The phrase "internet of things" wasn't first employed by Kevin Ashton until 1999. The term caught on even after Ashton utilized it as the subtitle of his demonstration for a new sensor venture Ashton was working on.

Even though the term "connected devices" initially showed up in 1999, the idea actually goes back to 1832. It was possible to directly communicate between two devices by sending electrical impulses when the initial electro-magnetic telegraph had been invented. But the development of the internet in the late 1960s signified the start of a real Internet of Things history.

8.1.1. The First Internet of Things Gadget

At Carnegie Mellon University, the first Internet of Things (IoT) device was developed in the early 1980s. To avoid having to make the trek if the device becomes empty, a gathering of college students created a method to get the Coca-Cola soda machine on campus to notify its components through a system. Participants added microswitches to the device to notify them of the availability and temperature of soda cans.

8.1.2. The 1990s

The first time a toaster was linked to the web was in 1990 by John Romkey. When reporting on coffee a year later, a team of University of Cambridge students used a webcam. They had the brilliant concept of employing the first web camera design to keep a close eye on the quantity of coffee left in the coffee machine in the computer room. In order to achieve this, participants configured the web camera to take images of the coffee machine three to four times every minute. The images were consequently transferred to nearby computer systems in order for everyone to see if there was coffee currently available.

Ever since the development of telephones (the first landline phones) in the 1830s and 1840s, devices have been used to conduct direct interactions. On June 3, 1900, the first wireless radio transmission—which was referred to as "wireless telegraphy"—took place, laying the foundation for the development of the Internet of Things. In the 1950s, the first computers were developed.

The internet was first developed as a core component of DARPA (Defense Advanced Research Projects Agency) in 1962. This later changed its domain name to ARPANET (Advanced Research Projects Agency Network) in 1969.

Advertising network operators started enabling the general population's usage of ARPANET in the 1980s, which helped it grow into the current Internet. The majority of the IoT, basic communication systems are provided by satellite systems and landline phones.

The Department of Defense created a reliable and extremely effective system of satellite navigation, which allowed the Global Positioning System (GPS) to become a fact at the beginning of 1993. Soon after, privately run, advertising satellites were launched into orbit, greatly enhancing the functionality of the Internet of Things.

TIPS

In the 1980s, commercial service providers began supporting public use of ARPANET, allowing it to evolve into our modern Internet. Satellites and landlines provide basic communications for much of the IoT.

8.1.3. The Early 2000s

According to Kevin Ashton, the individual who invented the term, Radio Frequency Identification (RFID) is a necessary element of the Internet of Things. RFID is mainly used as a stock monitoring system.

In retrospect, the inventory management system has surfaced to be one of IoT's quite clear benefits.

Ashton came to the conclusion that computer systems could handle, monitor, and stock all equipment if they were "tagged." Things have been partially tagged thanks to innovations like digital watermarks, barcodes, and QR codes.

The first significant businesses to implement Ashton's approach to stock management that used barcodes, RFID, and the Internet of Things were Walmart and the US Department of Defense in 2002–2003. A good illustration of the Internet of Things being utilized in households is Ring, a ringing doorbell which connects to your mobile phone. Whenever the doorbell is pushed, Ring alerts, enabling users to go see who is standing at the door and interact effectively.

Jamie Siminoff came up with the concept for the Ring doorbell in 2011 and desired to see who was knocking on the door while Simnioff was working in the garage. From the garage, Simnioff couldn't hear the doorbell and kept missing delivery orders.

In June 2012, the major online businesses and broadband providers reached a deal to facilitate IPV6 for their services and products, which also added a further critical factor to the formation of a workable IoT (Figure 8.2).

Figure 8.2. Internet of Things.

Source: Image by Wikimedia Commons.

8.1.4. The Industrial Internet of Things (IIoT)

Advancement of the Internet of Things, the Industrial Internet of Things (IIoT), creates usage sensors and smart sensors that are interconnected with a company's industry implementations. The purpose is to improve the effectiveness and dependability of industry sectors. Automation technology and software-defined manufacturing are both parts of the IIoT.

The bigger storage ability of the cloud (2002) has been needed for the advanced IoT to eventuate. Approximately 2010 had seen the beginning of the IIoT as several significant businesses formed their own processes. "Industrial Internet of Things" is credited to GE as its originator in 2012.

Remember

Any instrument that has an on/off switch which is linked to the web is considered a component of the Internet of Things. To be precise, The Internet of Things (IoT), which includes devices exchanging data via the internet, is a relatively new idea.

8.1.5. The Internet of Things Starts to Permeate Everyday Life

By 2013, the Internet of Things (IoT) had been established as a system that uses a variety of technologies, such as wireless technology, embedded devices, micro-electromechanical systems (MEMS), as well as the Online world.

These include everything from cell phones to constructing maintenance to an aero plane's jet engine, as well as remarkably much whatever else users could perhaps imagine. The Internet of Things (IoT) covers medical equipment which can transmit data through a network, like a biochip transponder in a domesticated animal or a transplanted heart rate monitor.

KEYWORD

Enthusiasm refers to intense enjoyment, interest, or approval expressed by a person.

8.1.6. The IoT Goes Mobile – 2015

Smartphone's are part of the IoT, and have become an important communications tool for many individuals. In 2015, they joined the IoT with a high degree of enthusiasm from marketers. The sensors within these devices are monitored by marketing departments, who send out certain promotions based on the customer and the product's location.

The healthcare industry has also taken advantage of this trend. Devices, such as smart watches, Smartphone's, and ingestible monitors can keep track of a patient's data regarding blood pressure, heart rate, and other concerns in real time.

Cars and trucks have become members of the IoT. A connected vehicle works with other devices over wireless networks. This technology allows various "connected networks" to access and communicate with the vehicles.

Cars and trucks are already loaded with sensors and technology, including OBD (on-board diagnostics) and GPS. By maximizing their use of these technologies, businesses can extract information from their fleets about maintenance requirements, driving conditions, and routes in real-time.

Self-driving cars use the cloud to respond to adjacent cars, traffic data, maps, weather, surface conditions, and etcetera. Use of the cloud helps the vehicles to monitor their surroundings and make better decisions.

TIPS

The first truly self-driving vehicle appeared in the 1980s. In October of 2021, May Mobility launched a pilot program to test their self-driving software.

Self-driving cars are new members of the IoT. The first truly self-driving vehicle appeared in the 1980s. In October of 2021, May Mobility launched a pilot program to test their self-driving software.

Human neighborhoods are now becoming part of the interconnected community called the Internet of Things.

8.2. ADVANTAGES OF THE INTERNET OF THINGS (IOT)

8.2.1. Data

a. **Enhanced data collection:** Once your IoT devices are connected and configured, they will collect information from the physical world and exchange such data with each other on and off the Internet, likely storing a massive amount of them on cloud storage. IoT devices produce data of all types, such as sensory and status information – from the temperature in your home to your heart rate during intense workouts. That data is updated frequently in real-time and in a classified format for easy access later on.

b. **Instant data access:** Everyone has instant access to the data their own and public IoT devices create. You can access data and information from anywhere at any time on any Internet connected smart device such as a Smartphone or a tablet, so you can stay informed about aspects of your life in real time even if you are far away from your IoT devices actual location. This makes it convenient for you to remotely interact with the physical world without being physically present resulting in life easier to manage at home, at work and on the road.

c. **Improved data-based decision making:** Having more information helps make better decisions. The more is information, the easier it is to make the right decision. Whether it is a mundane decision as needing to know the soil moisture level of your plants to water or a systemic decision as needing to alert staff of changes in processes or productivity to work out, knowledge is power, and more knowledge is better. IoT devices definitively make you know what is going on about what you care more, helping you make smarter decisions from general decisions to complex decisions.

8.2.2. Time and Money

a. **Better time management:** The IoT devices work rapidly, and data that would have taken a long time to move can now be transferred faster. Data packets are transmitted through the connected network and communicated and shared between IoT devices to make your systems efficient. By translating it into your requirements, you can automate repetitive tasks and engage yourself in some other tasks.

   For instance, you can control your thermostat from your Smartphone saving you a trip to the living room, and you can keep your cat or dog from going hungry with a smart pet feeder if you happen to forget their mealtime. You can do almost all the things from the palm of your hands. Hence accurate results can be obtained fast. Eventually, you end up saving valuable time and effort to invest in more challenging things.

KEYWORD

Data packets are units of information collected into one set for transmission through the Internet.

b. **Lower operating costs:** IoT fundamentally proves to be very helpful to people who are in charge of monitoring and maintaining systems. For example, IoT devices can issue proactive alerts about their status, allowing people to schedule maintenance before problems arise. Integrated into larger systems, IoT can significantly improve operational efficiency and reduce costs associated with bottlenecks, breakdowns and system damages. In some cases, IoT can replace humans. You can also achieve optimum utilization of energy and resources by adopting IoT. For example, you can automate switches lights off in daylight and switches them on during the onset of darkness to ensure no wasted electricity.

c. **Improved business productivity:** When it comes to success for a business, productivity plays a key role. IoT offers just-in-time training for employees, improves labor efficiency, and reduces the mismatch of skills while increasing organizational productivity. For example, in the agriculture field, if you know how to use drones then you will use its results efficiently to increase productivity.

   And because the IoT allows you to monitor your products and services 24x7, in case of a malfunctioning device, you can take immediate action to rectify the issue accordingly, even before the situation worsens further, therefore saving both money and resources. IoT also enhances the efficiency of machines by making them less prone to errors, therefore increasing the productivity of your business.

d. **Improved business profitability**: As you may be aware, information has become one of the most valuable assets of modern businesses in addition to direct income. IoT represents a new way to create value for customers and stakeholders by helping businesses, for example, to gather and access more actionable data from IoT devices and use advanced analytics to uncover business insights and opportunities.

This will help you identify areas of new work, hence new revenue streams. Therefore, the data created by IoT devices is precious to businesses to adjust business models in ways that improve business processes. As a result, perfectly competitive IoT data-driven businesses maximize profits.

KEYWORD

Direct income is the money that is received from doing tasks directly related to your business to make money.

8.2.3. Automation

a. **Efficient resource utilization:** Many IoT benefits cannot come into play without automation, which is made easier and possible thanks to the so-called machine-to-machine communication. Multiple levels of automation exist with IoT, allowing you to focus on other, more important jobs. If you understand the function of each IoT component then the resources will be utilized in an efficient manner that leads to prosperity.

Since automation is precise and repeatable, it leads to uniformity in tasks, quality of service and control of day-to-day tasks without or with minimal human intervention. Through automation, you can even carry out tasks without your input at all. The IoT devices are self-sufficient and capable to communicate with each other leading to faster and timely output while maintaining transparency in the entire process with lesser inefficiencies and greater quality, thus improving efficiency.

8.2.4. Security and Safety

a. **Increased security:** The IoT technology is based on complex advanced algorithms created by companies that are very concerned about the security of their systems. Although the huge amounts of data collected through IoT becomes very attractive to hack, these systems are almost unbreakable and hackers cannot access any personal details like credit card numbers as they only get raw data. This means that the user is strongly protected from attacks. However, nothing is perfect.

b. **Greater physical safety:** Because the IoT interconnected system senses any potential danger and warns users, it offers personal protection. For example, an IoT device that identifies a car crash or accident on the road immediately makes a call. Also, think home security cameras, smart carbon monoxide detectors, and Internet-connected fire alarms. This system will do all the dirty work for you.

ACTIVITY 8.1.

Explore and list a few IoT devices available in the market.

8.2.5. Quality of Life

a. **Improved quality of life:** All IoT applications culminate in increased comfort, convenience, and better management, thereby improving the quality of life. On a personal level, things like having connected devices that inform you are low on milk or printer ink, or that there is a malfunction with your boiler at home, will seem ubiquitous and commonplace in the near future.

Aside from helping you move through the day with ease, IoT can also improve the way your communities operate. For example, smart cities offer residents efficient ways to commute while conserving energy and reducing traffic congestion and air pollution, as well as streamlining how city workers perform their duties.

8.3. DISADVANTAGES OF THE INTERNET OF THINGS (IOT)

8.3.1. Compatibility and Integration

International standards: As of right now, there is presently no such thing as an international IoT compatibility benchmark. This creates difficulties for machines from various makers to interact with one another, making the integration of many pieces of equipment into a network challenging.

Since each business creates its own proprietary solutions, the lack of standardization makes it challenging for customers to choose between the various options available, which raises interoperability concerns among IoT application developers.

Furthermore, it can be difficult to install IoT devices effectively because each one from a variety of manufacturers might need a hardware compatibility interaction and setup. Expenses and advancement duration will thereby increase.

However, this drawback might disappear when all manufacturers comply with a set standard. There could still be technical difficulties with the connectivity of IoT equipment even once suitability has been achieved. Currently, compatibility complications could lead people to purchase equipment from a particular company, resulting in that company's monopoly over the market.

KEYWORD

Technical problem is a situation that is unsatisfactory and causes difficulties for people.

8.3.2. Complexity

System complexity: Since a big IoT system is composed of a diverse network which connects different equipment's that performs intricate processes in the background, designing, creating, maintaining, and empowering it is rather challenging.

Regardless of the fact that IoT might well appear to be handling activities efficiently, a certain solitary defect or technical problem in the hardware or the software might have severe ramifications; just a power cut could result in numerous inconveniences.

A malfunctioning or harmful IoT device that delivers important data to some other enabled device or workflow might have a significant effect on the entire system. Moreover, it might be difficult to pinpoint where the defect first popped up. IoT equipment can be implemented with minimal effort, although there is still a learning experience involved.

Establishing an IoT-equipped smart space, for example, a house, a factory, or a town, is rarely simple or straightforward. It makes perfect sense to establish a plan for when and how to implement IoT equipment prior to actually buying them to ensure they are functioning properly and that users can promote them. This is because certain consumers could require external assistance to get started and fully function.

8.3.3. Security and Safety

Despite the fact that IoT devices are linked to one another and share data via networks, any of them could become the target of malicious activities or attacks, both hardware-based and network-based. Regardless of the fact that IoT makers place top importance on cyber defense, there exists a possibility that such or even more IoT equipment could be compromised and the information available in the IoT system might be misused since nothing is full proof.

Despite the large data transfer and the usage of IoT devices in far more sensitive sectors like healthcare services and financial services, concerns and queries concerning security and confidentiality to this day exist.

Think about the data produced by all the home and office hardware, commercial machinery, medical instruments like oxygen concentrators and heart rate monitors, government programs like water distribution and transportation, as well as numerous other Internet-connected gadgets.

a. **Physical safety:** in addition to IoT devices that are employed to safeguard a place or help stop hazards, including security cameras, central locking, smart safe deposit boxes, fire warning systems, and authentication protocols, there seems to be IoT equipment like smart kitchens and water heaters, water purification devices, traffic signal control devices, hospital instruments, and automobiles that could damage or perhaps even kill other people if they malfunction.

For instance, whenever an IoT system that ensures the structural stability of a substantial bridge malfunctions, individuals will die. Businesses usually overlook a few security vulnerabilities inherent in IoT technologies as they rush to dominate the hypercompetitive IoT market.

The IoT's exponential increase in the absence of rules and regulations is the main factor responsible for these issues. It must be of greatest significance to ensure that safety-critical IoT devices cannot be brought to market except if one's cyber defense reputation is adequate given the significance of the function they perform. This is, regrettably, not really the case.

Remember

Hackers and cyber criminals will find the surroundings appealing. In the most extreme situation, population control might result from the IoT rather than its intended benefit.

8.3.4. Employment

a. **Unemployment:** Low-skilled employees, assistants, or even skilled people could lose their positions as IoT presents more coherent mechanization. The automation of mundane and dangerous everyday tasks makes it clear that there will be a sharp decline in the requirement for human labor, making employees in the community unemployable.

Robotic systems, intelligent ironing systems, intelligent washers and dryers, and other services would also replace the roles of humans who could previously perform these tasks. But technological change continues to be unpredictable and subject to revision, just like in the past. Learning new skills while receiving the best training and educational opportunities possible would then significantly raise or maintain a person's employment prospects.

8.3.5. Investment

KEYWORD

Automation system is an integration of sensors, controls, and actuators designed to perform a function with minimal or no human intervention.

a. **Time & Costs:** Establishing an IoT system regularly includes significant time and financial investment opportunities. IoT equipment needs to be purchased, set it up by employees, incorporated into the system, and ultimately arranged with service requests to the manufacturing company for additional help. Business owners could even rapidly manage that investment for a small IoT system installed in a single location.

Moreover, the expense goes through the roof once companies add a huge fleet of IoT equipment to their IoT system. Organizing the implementation spending plan and strategic plan prior to actually buying must be the primary concern of any venture that makes use of the IoT in this type of bigger situation. By accomplishing this, the IoT devices would be beneficial to the business, operate as designed, and also be sustainable for the company.

8.3.6. Reliance

Connectivity & Power: IoT is primarily a network of electronic devices that are powered and linked to the web. As a result, a constant supply of power and Web access are essential for proper operation. On the occasion that a network system fails or crashes, depending on IoT devices could cause problems.

One's home automation system can go offline due to a troublesome Wi-Fi network, which would disable one's heating systems, fire alarms, and other essential electronics. To prepare for power failures in advance, business owners should comprehend how disruptions will impact their equipment.

a. **Technology**: We are witnessing a major shift in technology and its implementation in everyday lives. Our business and private lives are becoming more and more dependent on technology. This is affecting basic human interaction social skills. IoT is not going to help that. Unlike other technologies, IoT causes people to become lethargic and inactive because they rely on smart devices instead of doing physical work.

This dependency becomes even more in daily routines. Be it young children, adults, or even old men, people are finding that they have less choice about adopting IoT and what that lifestyle means. They have to decide how much of their daily lives are they willing to mechanize and be controlled by IoT.

KEYWORD

Dependency describes the relationship among activities and specifies the particular order in which they need to be performed.

8.4. APPLICATION OF IOT

The most important characteristic of humans is that we can work with each other as team and gain knowledge from each other. What if this was true for machines as well? What if they could interact with each other and share information and data? That would lead to a truly connected world! And that is the central concept of the Internet of Things.

This concept just means a connected network of various devices that can collect data and share it with each other to obtain meaningful insights from the data. There are various applications of IoT in the modern world and these are so diverse that you cannot imagine.

There are endless possibilities for having an interconnected web of “things” that can interact with each other over the internet. IoT can be used for all types of applications ranging from connecting all the devices in your house to create a smart home or even connecting all the government and civic services in a city to create a smart city! Who knows, we may even have a smart world one day!

So, let’s see all these applications of IoT in different facets and industries of the world.

8.4.1. Smart Agriculture

Food is an integral part of life without which we cannot survive. However, it is an unfortunate fact that a lot of food is wasted in developed countries like America while people starve in poorer countries like Chad, Sudan, etc. One way to feed everyone is better agricultural practices which can be enhanced using IoT.

This can be done by first collecting data for a farm such as soil quality, sunlight levels, seed type, rainfall density from various sources like farm sensors, satellites, local weather stations, etc. and then using this data with Machine Learning and IoT to create custom recommendations for each farm that will optimize the planting procedure, irrigation levels required, fertilizer amount, etc. All this will result in better yield or crops with a focus on reducing world hunger in the future. This is done very efficiently by Subculture, which is an initiative by Microsoft AI for Earth.

KEYWORD

Thermostat is a regulating device component which senses the temperature of a physical system and performs actions so that the system's temperature is maintained near a desired setpoint.

8.4.2. Smart Vehicles

Smart vehicles or self-driving cars as they can be called are pretty dependent on IoT. These cars have a lot of features that are integrated with each other and need to communicate such as the sensors that handle navigation, various antennas, controls for speeding or slowing down, etc. Here the Internet of Things technology is critical especially in the sense that self-driving cars need to be extremely accurate and all the parts need to communicate with each other in milliseconds on the road.

Tesla Cars are quite popular and working on their self-driving cars. Tesla Motors' cars use the latest advancements in Artificial Intelligence and the Internet of Things. And they are quite popular as well!!! Tesla Model 3 was the most sold plug-in electric car in the U.S. in 2018 with a total yearly sale of around 140,000 cars.

8.4.3. Smart Home

Maybe the most famous application of IoT is in Smart Homes. After all, who hasn't heard about connecting all the home applications like lighting, air conditioners, locks, thermostat, etc. into a single system that can be controlled from your Smartphone! These IoT devices are becoming more and more popular these days because they allow you complete freedom to personalize your home as you want. In fact, these IoT devices are so popular that every second there are 127 new devices connected to the internet. Some popular ones that you might have heard have, or even have in your home, include Google Home, Amazon Echo Plus, Philips Hue Lighting System, etc. There are also all sorts of other inventions that you can install in your home including Nest Smoke Alarm and Thermostat, Foobot Air Quality Monitor, August Smart Lock, etc.

8.4.4. Smart Pollution Control

Pollution is one of the biggest problems in most of the cities in the world. Sometimes it's not clear if we are inhaling oxygen or smog! In such a situation, IoT can be a big help in controlling the pollution levels to more breathable standards. This can be done by collecting the data related to city pollution like emissions from vehicles, pollen levels, airflow direction, weather, traffic levels, etc using various sensors in combination with IoT. Using this data, Machine Learning algorithms can calculate pollution forecasts in different areas of the city that inform city officials beforehand where the problems are going to occur. Then they can try to control the pollution levels till it's much safer. An example of this is the Green Horizons project created by IBM's China Research Lab.

8.4.5. Smart Healthcare

There are many applications of IoT in the Healthcare Industry where doctors can monitor patients remotely through a web of interconnected devices and machines without needing to be in direct contact with them. This is very useful if the patients don't have any serious problems or if they have any infectious diseases like COVID-19 these days.

One of the most common uses of IoT in healthcare is using robots. These include surgical robots that can help doctors in performing surgeries more efficiently with higher precision and control. There are also disinfectant robots that can clean surfaces quickly and thoroughly using high-intensity ultraviolet light (which is pretty useful these days!) Other types of robots also include nursing robots that can handle the monotonous tasks that nurses have to perform for many patients' day in and day out where there is little risk to the patients.

8.4.6. Smart Cities

Cities can be made more efficient so that they require fewer resources and are more energy-efficient. This can be done with a combination of sensors in different capacities all over the city that can be used for various tasks ranging from managing the traffic, controlling handling waste management, creating smart buildings, optimizing streetlights, etc. There are many cities in the world that are working on incorporating IoT and becoming smarter such as Singapore, Geneva, Zurich, Oslo, etc. One example of creating smart cities is the Smart Nation Sensor Platform used by Singapore which is believed to be the smartest city in the world. This platform integrates various facets of transportation, streetlights, public safety, urban planning, etc. using sensors in conjugation with IoT.

8.4.7. Smart Retail

There is a way to make shopping even more exciting for customers and that's to use the latest tech like IoT of course! Retail stores can make use of IoT in a wide range of operations to make shopping a much smoother experience for customers and also easier for the employees. IoT can be used to handle the inventory, improve store operations, reduce shoplifting and theft, and prevent long queues at the cashiers. A prime example of this is the Amazon Go stores which provide an IoT enabled shopping experience.

These stores monitor all their products using IoT so that customers can pick up any products and just walk out of the store without stopping at the cashier's queue. The total bill amount is automatically deducted from the card associated with the customer's Amazon account after they leave the store (Figure 8.3).

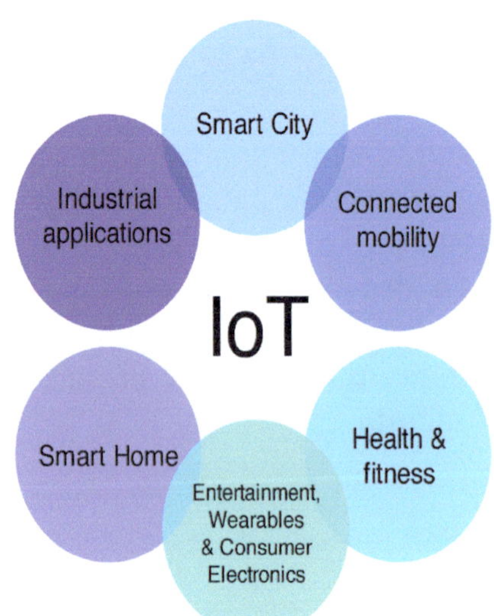

Figure 8.3. Where does the internet of things (IoT) manifest in the world?

8.5. CHALLENGES IN INTERNET OF THINGS (IOT)

The Internet of Things (IoT) has fast grown to be a large part of how human beings live, communicate and do business. All across the world, web-enabled devices are turning our global rights into a greater switched-on area to live in. There are various types of challenges in front of IoT.

> **TIPS**
>
> In 2000, the web transitioned into social networks and the internet of people. The following shift -- the mobile internet and Web 2.0 -- encompassed 3G, 4G and IoT.

8.5.1. Security Challenges in IoT

Lack of encryption: Although encryption is a great way to prevent hackers from accessing data, it is also one of the leading IoT security challenges. These drives like the storage and processing capabilities that would be found on a traditional computer. The result is an increase in attacks where hackers can easily manipulate the algorithms that were designed for protection.

Insufficient testing and updating: With the increase in the number of IoT(internet of things) devices, IoT manufacturers are more eager to produce and deliver their device as fast as they can without giving security too much of although. Most of these devices and IoT products do not get enough testing and updates and are prone to hackers and other security issues.

Brute forcing and the risk of default passwords: Weak credentials and login details leave nearly all IoT devices vulnerable to password hacking and brute force. Any company that uses factory default credentials on their devices is placing both their business and its assets and the customer and their valuable information at risk of being susceptible to a brute force attack.

IoT Malware and ransom ware: Increases with increase in devices. Ransom ware uses encryption to effectively lock out users from various devices and platforms and still use a user's valuable data and info.

Example:

A hacker can hijack a computer camera and take pictures. By using malware access points, the hackers can demand ransom to unlock the device and return the data.

IoT botnet aiming at crypto currency: IoT botnet workers can manipulate data privacy, which could be massive risks for an open

Crypto market. The exact value and creation of crypto currencies code face danger from mal-intentioned hackers. The block chain companies are trying to boost security. Block chain technology itself is not particularly vulnerable, but the app development process (Figure 8.4).

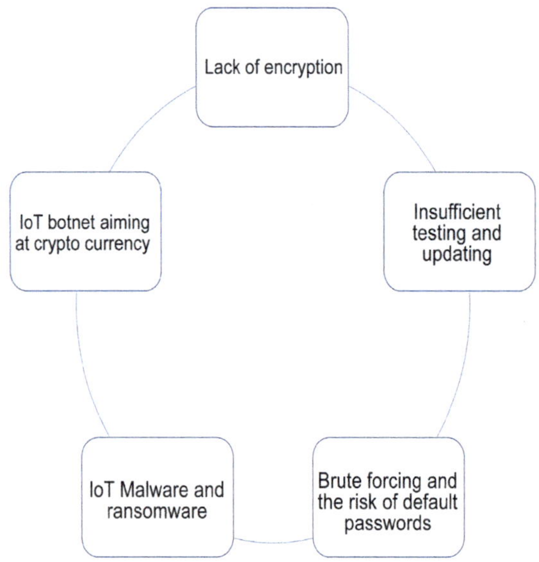

Figure 8.4. Security challenges in IoT.

8.5.2. Design Challenge in IoT

a. Battery life is a limitation: Issues in packaging and integration of small-sized chip with low weight and less power consumption. If you've been following the mobile space, you've likely seen how every yr it looks like there's no restriction in terms of display screen size. Take the upward thrust of 'phablets,' for instance, which can be telephones nearly as huge as tablets.

Although helpful, the bigger monitors aren't always only for convenience, rather, instead, display screen sizes are growing to accommodate larger batteries. Computers have getting slimmer, but battery energy stays the same.

b. **Increased cost and time to market**: Embedded systems are lightly constrained by cost. The need originates to drive better approaches when designing the IoT devices in order to handle the cost modeling or cost optimally with digital electronic components. Designers also need to solve the design time problem and bring the embedded device at the right time to the market.

c. **Security of the system:** Systems have to be designed and implemented to be robust and reliable and have to be secure with cryptographic algorithms and security procedures. It involves different approaches to secure all the components of embedded systems from prototype to deployment.

8.5.3. Deployment Challenges in IoT

a. **Connectivity**: It is the foremost concern while connecting devices, applications and cloud platforms. Connected devices that provide useful front and information are extremely valuable. But poor connectivity becomes a challenge where IoT sensors are required to monitor process data and supply information.

b. **Cross platform capability**: IoT applications must be developed, keeping in mind the technological changes of the future. Its development requires a balance of hardware and software functions. It is a challenge for IoT application developers to ensure that the device and IoT platform drivers the best performance despite heavy device rates and fixings.

c. **Data collection and processing**: In IoT development, data plays an important role. What is more critical here is the processing or usefulness of stored data. Along with security and privacy, development teams need to ensure that they plan well for the way data is collected, stored or processed within an environment.

d. **Lack of skill set**: All of the development challenges above can only be handled if there is a proper skilled resource working on the IoT application development. The right talent will always get you past the major challenges and will be an important IoT application development asset.

KEYWORD

Embedded systems are special-purpose computing systems embedded in application environments or in other computing systems and provide specialized support.

8.6. THE FUTURE OF IOT

IoT barely counts as an emerging technology these days, given that it's more than a decade old. But the technology continues to evolve. Adjacent, arguably more emergent technologies influence the future of IoT. Prominent examples include 5G and the nascent Meta verse. IoT will move into new use cases, applications and adoption scenarios as it converges with other streams of innovation.

The long-term trends are, indeed, promising. The technology's near-term prospects, however, are caught up with electronics component shortages, which put a damper on growth projections. Flexibility will be the watchword for IoT technology vendors, systems integrators and customers dealing with a changeable market.

Here are four trends to monitor in IoT.

8.6.1. IoT Meets the Metaverse

KEYWORD

Metaverse is a vision of what many in the computer industry believe is the next iteration of the internet: a single, shared, immersive, persistent, 3D virtual space where humans experience life in ways they could not in the physical world.

IoT promises to play a pivotal role in the Meta verse, linking the physical world to the virtual variety. Digital twins -- i.e., virtual representations of physical devices -- rely on IoT data and could prove particularly relevant. A variety of IoT-driven digital twins seem likely to populate the Meta verse.

Paul Daugherty, group chief executive for technology and CTO at Accenture, cited IoT, along with developments such as synthetic data and quantum computing, as technologies that will influence the Meta verse -- and reshape business in the process.

"The real world, itself, is becoming programmable," Daugherty said, speaking at Accenture's annual Technology Vision event. "This is about IoT. This is about operational technology. This is about digital twins."

In the bigger picture, IoT and other technologies are evolving into Web 3.0, according to Daugherty. The original World Wide Web was an internet of data and search, he contended. In 2000, the web transitioned into social networks and the internet of people. The following shift -- the mobile internet and Web 2.0 -- encompassed 3G, 4G and IoT, he noted.

Now, Daugherty said, the industry is moving to Web 3.0 and two fundamental capabilities: the internet of place and the internet of ownership. The former provides interoperable online venues for shared, collaborative experiences, while the latter uses block chain and distributed ledgers to create secure digital identities, he added. IoT is poised to serve as a building block within that ongoing development.

8.6.2. High Growth for Cellular IoT

Juniper Research identified cellular low-power wide-area (LPWA) offerings and 5G as the key technologies driving this growth. The

LPWA category, including narrowband IoT and LTE for Machines, will experience the fastest growth during the forecast period. The market researcher said it expects the low cost of connectivity and hardware to boost the technology's adoption for remote monitoring in verticals such as agriculture, smart cities and manufacturing.

5G trails LPWA when it comes to growth, but its day is coming.

"5G is still not as cost-effective as technologies such as 4G, so 5G will be adopted on a case-by-case basis," said Sam Barker, head of analytics and forecasting at Juniper Research. "As the number of IoT connections grows, we do expect the value of 5G to increase and adoption to rise. Next year [2023] will experience growth. However, we expect this growth rate to accelerate over the next few years."

KEYWORD

Remote Monitoring (RMON) is a standard specification that facilitates the monitoring of network operational activities through the use of remote devices known as monitors or probes.

8.6.3. Chip Shortages Continue to Complicate IoT

The technology's prospects aren't entirely rose-colored -- the expanding metaverse and cellular IoT applications notwithstanding.

Forrester Research predicted that the continuing chip shortage will impede IoT market growth by 10% to 15% in 2022. While high-end chip sets from Intel and Nvidia remain available, those that power IoT devices aren't always on offer. The lack of supply affects IoT-enabled connected devices, from appliances to industrial products.

IoT-based smart devices often use lower-end chip set configurations -- 4-bit or 8-bit microcontrollers, for example -- that are less expensive and have lower processing demands, noted Glenn O'Donnell, vice president and research director at Forrester.

"Demand for these lower-end chip sets to power IoT-enabled smart devices will continue to outpace supply through 2022," O'Donnell noted.

Market research company IoT Analytics pointed to IoT growth headwinds, including chip shortages, which the company said are expected to persist into 2024 and potentially beyond. That said, the company still forecasted the global enterprise IoT market to expand at a compound annual growth rate of 22% through 2027. IoT Analytics expects the market to reach $525 billion that year.

8.6.4. IoT Botnet to Hit Infrastructure

Security persists as a long-time concern with IoT, given the ample attack surface that myriad connected sensors and devices provide.

Further threats are in store. Forrester predicted that, in 2022, an IoT botnet will take down some critical communications infrastructure successfully through a DDoS attack. That attack will surpass 30 million requests per second, Forrester said, cutting off availability and inflicting economic pain.

KEYWORD

Botnet is a group of Internet-connected devices, each of which runs one or more bots.

"Even if we leave [out] the cyber components of the current Russia-Ukraine conflict -- where DDoS is definitely at play -- the likelihood of an IoT botnet hitting the private sector elsewhere in the world is still very high," said Merritt Maxim, vice president and research director at Forrester.

8.7. IMPACT OF INTERNET OF THINGS (IOT) ON RENEWABLE ENERGY

The emerging computing technology in this era is the Internet of Things. The network of intelligence that bridges various devices, systems located in remote locations together by means of cloud portal. IoT maybe equipped with millions or billions of devices. IoT handles large volume of data, process the huge data and performs useful control actions to make our life safe and simple.

IoT evolves Human-human communication with thing-thing communication. IoT applications are not confined to a particular sector. In the fields such as healthcare, smart homes, industries, transportation, etc., the technology which is more influential is IoT. Energy sectors are now undergoing transformation. The transformation is driven by IoT.

Green energy without IoT cannot be imagined in this energy sector. Renewable energy sources will be the major power producers among all the other sources due to the depletion of conventional energy sources. Among the renewable energy sources, Solar and Wind contributes more when compared to geothermal, biomass, etc.

Renewable energy power production depends on environmental factors such as temperature, wind speed, light intensity, etc. These factors affect the performance of energy conversion in renewable energy sources. Since our future generation will depend only on renewable energy, it becomes necessary for the researchers to integrate IoT to provide reliable and affordable energy. Renewable power generation helps in reducing the toxic level of gasses which may be produced by thermal power stations during power generation. IoT brings about changes from generation to transmission to distribution.

Consider comparing the conventional matrix to the smart grid as an example. Conventionally, electricity produced at a hydroelectric plant is transferred to the consumer in a one-way interaction network. Customers are mandated to pay for the electricity they use. However, the smart grid features two-way interaction. Only the energy required by the consumer could be charged, except if extra generated power could be fed back into the grid again.

IoT aids in planning the load to minimize the total cost and facilitates in analyzing the energy demand and waste. It is possible to remotely control and operate renewable power farms smartly with the assistance of sensors and information sciences in the Internet of Things (IoT). This increases the farms' productivity and dependability in order to achieve the consumer's expected need for electricity.

KEYWORD

Smart grid (SG) is a modern electric grid with a two-way flow of electricity and data between power utilities and consumers.

8.8. HOW THE INTERNET OF THINGS (IOT) IS CHANGING OUR LIVES

The term "Internet of Things" (IoT) basically refers to a WiFi system that links components such as machines, automobiles, or other equipment. With the assistance of detectors, applications, and other tools, such components could gather and transmit data over a WiFi router without the requirement for human involvement.

Technology is developing at an exponential rate, making it possible for people to perform complicated tasks that would ordinarily take them days to accomplish while doing so in a matter of minutes, thereby saving them both time and effort. Every industry here on earth has begun to incorporate IoT into one's everyday activities, not only because it empowers people to "assemble useful information, but it also enables them to evaluate it and frame future activities upon it.

The Internet of Things (IoT) has indeed made it to every household since it can now regulate household appliances without the requirement for human involvement. For example, an air conditioner can now adjust the room's temperature instantly, and there are also mood-sensing music devices, smart lighting fixtures, computer-controlled windows and doors, and automobiles that are able to be unlocked by pushing a button once users leave the house. With the support of the IoT, all of these things are possible.

Without a question, IoT has made life simpler for people, and that's why an increasing number of individuals are adopting it in their everyday chores. IoT is also being used in every industry, including education, transportation, financial services, agricultural production, and others, and it saves a significant amount of funds and effort.

IoT does have a drawback, though, in that humans are becoming overly reliant on technology, which reduces their productivity and strengthens machine learning, which might be dangerous in the long term. Then let's talk about both the advantages and disadvantages of IoT on our everyday routines in order to obtain a clear understanding of how it will influence humans.

Did you Know?

Cellular IoT technology, which harnesses mobile networks for device connectivity, will travel a high-growth track over the next few years. Market research firm Juniper Research pegged the global market as nearly doubling in four years, expanding from $31 billion in 2022 to $61 billion in 2026.

8.8.1. The Advantages of IoT

a. **Enhanced Connections:** Human-to-human interaction was formerly thought to be difficult due to the lack of phone lines or portable device accessibility. Presently, through the Internet of Things, people could simply interact with appliances like lights, air conditioners, TVs, audio equipment, refrigerators, and more thanks to detectors that allow these devices to link with their physical environments.

b. **Cost-Effective:** The Internet of Things (IoT) is gaining popularity as a consequence of its low cost-effectiveness, ease of access, and greatest of all, its total absence of servicing costs. Everybody could benefit from the Internet of Things (IoT) since its ultimate focus is to ease complicated tasks for individuals. As a consequence, users are not required to be incredibly precise or possess a deep knowledge of innovative computer science or machine intelligence to benefit from the IoT.

c. **Aids in Fitness, Wellbeing, and Education:** The Internet of Things (IoT) has progressed to the point where it is able to assist learners in their academic work through a variety of innovations in which students ask the equipment a question and the device replies with the relevant information. Text-to-speech is another feature that helps children who struggle to read lengthy and complex texts and will significantly improve learning.

IoT, on the contrary, supports keeping a healthy lifestyle through a variety of gadgets like smartwatches that provide users with the smallest specifics concerning their health in a short amount of time and that may also assist in setting goals for one's health.

Numerous medical equipment now has IoT, which helps in saving doctors' time since several patients have these gadgets at home that allow them to periodically assess their blood pressure, sugar level, and other vital signs. The skill of using IoT to easily regulate the majority of domestic chores has totally transformed the lives of individuals who are physically disabled or even elderly.

8.8.2. The Adverse Effect of the IoT

1. Job Automation

In the coming ten to 20 years, it's possible that millions of employment opportunities could be eliminated by technology because it's more efficient and therefore can complete complicated tasks faster than human beings. Since the majority of businesses and corporations use technology because it's productive and can accomplish complicated assignments in a timely manner. Several highly desirable experts and workers could lose their value in the near future as machine learning replaces them.

2. Threat to security

Humans have been bounded by multiple IoT gadgets which gather and transfer files, which raises a potential threat since individuals do not understand that all these gadgets could obtain confidential material. The above details may be compromised shortly as attackers discover new methods to attempt to break confidentiality since it is challenging for normal individuals to stay on top of security concerns. Individuals have frequently voiced concerns that somebody was overhearing their home conversations since Alexa and Siri are all listening systems.

3. IoT dependency has gone too far

IoT has made people's lives have been made easier because the primary goal is to increase people's dependence on advanced technologies. This causes individuals to become less efficient because it restricts one's ability to think strategically and creatively, so it ends up making them restless since they desire immediate outcomes.

8.9. SUMMARY

1. Internet of Things and its History

In this chapter, the significance of Internet of Things (IoT) has been explained. It also explains about the history of internet of things which includes, the first internet of things gadget, the industrial internet of things (IIoT), the internet of things starts to permeate everyday life, and so on.

2. Pros and Cons of IoT

This chapter also provides highlights to the various advantages as well as disadvantages of the internet of things. It also addresses different applications of internet of things such as smart agriculture, smart vehicles, smart homes, smart pollution control, etc.

3. Relation of Internet of Things in Future Technology

Towards the end of the chapter, it discussed about the various challenges in Internet of things which includes, security challenges in IoT, design challenges in IoT, and deployment challenges in IoT. It also emphasizes on the impact of IoT on renewable energy.

8.10. REVIEW QUESTIONS

1. What do you understand by the term Internet of Things (IoT)?
2. What is the history of Internet of Things (IoT)?
3. How is Internet of Things (IoT) important for the society?
4. Explain the various applications of IoT.
5. Explain the pros and cons of Internet of Things (IoT).
6. What are the different components of IoT?
7. Explain the term 'smart city' in IoT.

8.11. MULTIPLE CHOICE QUESTIONS

1. IoT stands for _____.

a. Internet object Things
b. Internet out Things
c. Internet or Things
d. Internet of Things

2. Who is group chief executive for technology and CTO at Accenture?

a. Paul Daugherty
b. Jaron Lanier

c. Oculus

d. Williams

3. **When the first Internet of Things (IoT) device was developed?**

a. 1990s

b. 1970s

c. 1980s

d. 2000

4. **Where the first Internet of Things (IoT) device was developed?**

a. Carnegie Mellon University

b. University of Cambridge

c. University of Oxford

d. Loughborough University

5. **Who discovered the first time a toaster was linked to the web?**

a. Paul Daugherty

b. Jaron Lanier

c. John Romkey

d. Williams

Answers to Multiple Choice Questions

1. (d) 2. (a) 3. (c) 4. (a) 5. (c)

REFERENCES

1. *Advantages and Disadvantages of IoT*. (n.d). [online] Available at: https://techvidvan.com/tutorials/advantages-and-disadvantages-of-iot/ (accessed on 03 March 2023).
2. GeeksforGeeks, (2020). *Top Applications of IoT in the World* – GeeksforGeeks. [online] Available at: https://www.geeksforgeeks.org/top-applications-of-iot-in-the-world/ (accessed on 03 March 2023).
3. GeeksforGeeks, (2021). *Challenges in Internet of things (IoT)* – GeeksforGeeks. [online] Available at: https://www.geeksforgeeks.org/challenges-in-internet-of-things-iot/ (accessed on 03 March 2023).
4. John, M., (2022). *Future of IoT Offers Mixed Bag of Opportunity, Shortages*. [online] IoT Agenda. Available at: https://www.techtarget.com/iotagenda/feature/Future-of-IoT-6-trends-and-predictions-to-watch (accessed on 03 March 2023).
5. Keith, D. F., (2022). *A Brief History of the Internet of Things* – Dataversity. [online] DATAVERSITY. Available at: https://www.dataversity.net/brief-history-internet-things/# (accessed on 03 March 2023).

6. Lapenna Sergio, (2022). *Advantages and Disadvantages of the Internet of Things (IoT)*. [online] RT. Available at: https://www.rtsrl.eu/blog/advantages-and-disadvantages-of-the-internet-of-things-iot/ (accessed on 03 March 2023).
7. Mohammed, R. A., (n.d). *Internet of Things (IOT) Basics – An Introduction to the New Digital World*. [online] Academia.edu. Available at: https://www.academia.edu/36860816/Internet_of_Things_IOT_Basics_An_Introduction_to_the_New_Digital_World (accessed on 03 March 2023).
8. Ponnalagarsamy, S., Geetha, V., Pushpavalli, M., & Abirami, P., (2021). Impact of IoT on Renewable Energy. *IoT Applications Computing*, [online] Available at: https://www.intechopen.com/chapters/79133 (accessed on 03 March 2023).
9. Pradyumna, G., Omkar, B., & Sagar, B., (2018). *Introduction to IoT*. [online] Available at: https://www.researchgate.net/publication/330114646_Introduction_to_IOT (accessed on 03 March 2023).
10. Scammells, J., (2020). *History of the Internet of Things (IoT)* | IT Blog | ITonlinelearning. [online] ITonlinelearning. Available at: https://www.itonlinelearning.com/blog-history-iot/ (accessed on 03 March 2023).
11. Shamama, A., (n.d). *Internet of Things (IoT): An Introduction* (pp. 1–4). [e-Book] Rai Journal of Technology Research & Innovation. Available at: https://www.jru.edu.in/wp-content/uploads/RTJ/vol-5/INTERNET%20OF%20THINGS%20(IoT)%20AN%20INTRODUCTION.pdf (accessed on 03 March 2023).

INDEX

D

N

O

P

R

V

W